D1457631

JOCKO

 By JOCKO CONLAN

and ROBERT W. CREAMER

Afterword to the Bison Books Edition
by Robert W. Creamer

University of Nebraska Press
Lincoln and London

© 1967 by Time, Inc.
Afterword to the Bison Books Edition © 1997 by the University of Nebraska
Press

⊛ The paper in this book meets the minimum requirements of American
National Standard for Information Sciences—Permanence of Paper for
Printed Library Materials, ANSI Z39.48-1984.

First Bison Books printing: 1997
Most recent printing indicated by the last digit below:
10   9   8   7   6   5   4   3   2   1

Library of Congress Cataloging-in-Publicaction Data
Conlan, Jocko, 1899–
Jocko / by Jocko Conlan and Robert Creamer; afterword to the Bison Books
edition by Robert W. Creamer.
p.   cm.
Originally published: Philadelphia: Lippincott, 1967. With new afterword
ISBN 0-8032-6381-3 (pbk., alk. paper)
1. Conlan, Jocko, 1899–   .   2. Baseball umpires—United States—
Biography.   I. Creamer, Robert W.   II. Title.
GV865.C67A3   1997
796.357'3'092—dc20
[B]
96-51860   CIP

Reprinted from the original 1967 edition by J. B. Lippincott Company,
Philadelphia and New York. Portions of this book have appeared in *Sports
Illustrated*.

In memory of BILL KLEM

The Old Arbitrator

and the greatest umpire of us all

CO-AUTHOR'S NOTE

My job in preparing this book was to listen to Jocko Conlan talk and put it down on paper, take his stories and anecdotes and commentaries and criticisms and put them into a more or less cohesive form, winnowing out whatever was repetitive or excessive and presenting, in essence, Jocko Conlan as he is.

But putting Jocko Conlan down on paper is like taking a photograph of a flower garden with black-and-white film; it is all there, but there is still an awful lot missing. For Jocko Conlan is an actor, a performer. When he tells a story it is not just a succession of words. It is a dramatic presentation. Jocko is a mimic of considerable skill, and the dialogue in his stories is not merely reported but rendered. Let him tell a Casey Stengel story, and you *hear* Casey's wandering growl. Let him do Bill Klem, and there is Klem's stentorian dignity. Let him bring in Tommy Connolly, and you learn that Connolly spoke with a prissy, fussy brogue.

Or let him tell a story about himself in an argument with, say, Leo Durocher, whom Jocko does not love. Conlan's blue eyes shift from a twinkle to a glint; the bulldog jaw juts out; the soft voice hardens into an intensity that is startling. When he cries out, in a story, to an errant player or manager, "Don't come up here! I don't need you! Get out! You're gone!" well, type such as this simply does not suffice. We need boldface Bodoni, Steamboat Gothic, End of the World Heroic.

It must be admitted that along with his many virtues—and they are many—Jocko has a few faults. He is vain about some things. He can be testy at times. He sometimes gives the impression that he feels he has never been wrong in his life.

But consider him . . . the chin, the mouth, the eyes, the umpire's regalia, the little blue hat, the bow tie, the cocky walk, the imperious gesture, the insistent voice. He is unique. He is Jocko Conlan. He is *the* umpire. Bernard Berenson used to talk about Man as a Work of Art, the idea that a man himself can create in himself something enduring, that he can become, in effect, a living work of art. What else is Jocko?

ROBERT CREAMER

CONTENTS

JOCKO

Courtesy John B. Conlan

1

FOR WANT OF A THUMB

I NEVER WANTED to be an umpire. When I was a ballplayer the thought never entered my mind. I wanted to play ball in the big leagues, and then I wanted to become a manager. I was an outfielder and I was a pretty good one, even if that sounds like blowing my own horn. But I was in the minor leagues for more than ten years, and when I got to the big leagues with the Chicago White Sox I was thirty-four years old. That's pretty late in the day.

Oh, how I remember that first game in the big leagues after all those years in the minors. I always wanted to play with the White Sox. I grew up in the neighborhood, within walking distance of the White Sox park. I was a bat boy for them, and I was a Sox fan. Baseball was a big thing in the neighborhood, and a lot of old-time ballplayers came out of it. Charlie O'Leary. He was a shortstop with Detroit and later a coach with the New York Yankees. Germany Schaefer. One of the most colorful players ever. Bobby "Braggo" Roth. He played in the American League for eight years and then jumped to the Midwest League, a fast semipro league in Chicago. Braggo was a real good hitter, and he knew it. "They leave it up to me every time," he used to say. That's where he got the name "Braggo." His brother Frank was a coach and a scout for the Yankees.

And George Moriarty. George Moriarty was a big-league ballplayer for more than ten years and then he became an American League umpire. He umpired for ten years, quit umpiring to go manage the Detroit Tigers for two years and then went back to umpiring again for another ten or twelve years. Moriarty was a very highly respected man both off and on the field. A big, handsome, rough fellow. Nobody fooled with him too much. Except one time when four White Sox players attacked him. That was in 1932, two years before I made it to the Sox. The Sox were sore at Moriarty about some decision he made that cost them a game, and the four of them fought him in the runway under the stands. They pummeled him pretty good; they had him down. But even so, Moriarty broke one guy's jaw. George was tough. There wasn't any one of those alone could have licked him, or any two.

Anyway, this was the next year and I was playing my first game for the White Sox, and I was proud. Moriarty was working the game and of course I knew him and I respected him and I liked him. He was a lot older than I was, but he knew my brothers well. He knew a lot of people I knew. So I waited for him as he came down the runway before the game to go out onto the field, and I put my hand out and I said, "Hello, George."

He went right past me like I was a piece of clay. Never said hello or even looked at me. Left me standing there with my hand out. I said to myself, "Is that the way they do it in the big league?" I couldn't figure it out. I was playing center field and he was working third base, and when I ran past him on my way to the outfield I looked at him. He didn't say a word. I think I looked at him every time I passed him for nine innings, and he never batted an eye. He saw me, but he just totally ignored me. It infuriated me. I thought what kind of a guy is this, comes from our neighborhood, and here I am in my first big-league game, and he won't even talk to me. Big league or no big league, I thought it was lousy. It made me sick. I had felt so good at seeing him and so proud that I was in the big league with him.

After the game I got dressed and I went outside to meet my brothers, Pete and Joe and Heinie (his name was Henry, but we called him Heinie). They were all older than me—I was the youngest in the family—and I had gotten to the big leagues, even though so late, and this was my first game, and they had come to see it. Well, as I came out, there was George Moriarty standing there talking with them, because, as I say, he knew them real well.

I walked over to where they were standing, but I wasn't sure if I should say hello to him. He hadn't spoken to me; maybe I shouldn't speak to him. I was still mixed up and angry to think he had passed me up. But I went up to them, and what do you think Moriarty did? He smiled and he stuck out his hand and he said, "How are you, kid? It's good to see you. I'm glad you made it."

I think my mouth was hanging open. I said, "I don't get it. I put my hand out to shake hands in the runway and you wouldn't even look at me. You passed me up every time I went out to the outfield."

"Kid," he said, "I don't mix with ballplayers. I don't waste any time talking to them. If you ever had this job of umpiring you wouldn't talk to one of them. It's the only way you can get respect."

After, when I was an umpire myself, I often thought about that. And I'd say to myself, "You know, he was right." Because there would be days when you'd come on the field and try to be congenial and you'd say hello to a ballplayer, and he wouldn't have anything to do with you or he'd get in an argument and call you the foulest names you ever heard. And you'd wonder, "Why should I ever talk to any of them?" And you'd say, "I'm *not* going to talk to them. The hell with them." But it isn't your nature to be that way. And I did have the faculty, or the reputation, of being able to talk to a fellow and still throw him out of the ball game, if he deserved to be thrown out. So that my conversation with players had nothing to do with me umpiring the way I was supposed to umpire.

When I went to umpiring in the minors after I finished playing, Moriarty gave me a chest protector. "Wear it in good health, kid," he said, "and remember what I'm telling you. Don't let any ballplayer run over you. If you do, you'll lose all your respect from everybody, from the top on down."

That was later. When I was talking to him outside the park that day, I had no idea of ever umpiring. Yet, actually I started the very next year. This is how it happened. My best friend on the Sox was Ted Lyons, the pitcher. Teddy was one of the real fine men of all time in baseball, a terrific pitcher and personally a wonderful guy.

I always admired him in everything he did. Before I came to the Sox he'd been a star with them for ten years, a 20-game winner in three different seasons, but he and I became great friends.

Teddy was the kind of guy who, if he liked you, his way of showing it was to give you a trimming. He'd punch you and wrestle you and twist your arm back until you hollered for mercy. Then he'd say, "Hey, where will we eat tonight? I'll treat you to dinner."

Teddy and I were fooling around one day in the dressing room, sparring. We played pretty rough. He hurt a finger on his pitching hand punching me, and I broke my thumb punching him. He was blocking my punches with his arms, and I caught the thumb on one of his elbows. We didn't bother to tell Jimmie Dykes, who was managing the White Sox. He didn't know anything had happened, and we thought we'd let sleeping dogs lie. Teddy wasn't due to start again for three days, and I hadn't been playing much, anyway. But the next day Dykes came to me and he said, "Jocko, you're playing center field today."

"I don't think I can, Jim," I said. "I hurt my thumb and I can't grip the bat."

"How did you do that?"

"I dove for a ball in practice," I said, "and my thumb caught in the dirt, I think it's sprained."

"All right," he said. "I'll put somebody else in."

Lyons whispered to me, "I hope he don't ask me how I got mine." I don't know what Teddy ever told Dykes, if anything. He missed a turn, and that was about all.

Now, we were in St. Louis when this happened. We were playing the Browns a doubleheader in Sportsman's Park, and it was 114°. This was the summer of 1935. They thought it was hot in St. Louis in 1966 when they played the All-Star Game there and the temperature hit 106°. This was eight degrees hotter. Boy, you could just see the heat coming up out of the ground. They had no grass on the infield in Sportsman's Park then; it was all dirt. Both the Browns and the Cardinals played their games there, you see, and when one team was on the road the other was home, so the ball park was always being used. The grass never had a chance. It was worn off by the end of April. Oh, it was terrible, just like a brickyard.

There were only two umpires working the game, Harry Geisel and Red Ormsby, and during the first game of the doubleheader the heat got to Ormsby, and he passed out. They carried him off the field into the dressing room to take care of him, but he was through for the day. They said Geisel needed somebody to umpire with him, and I spoke up, just off the cuff. I said, "I'll umpire. I can't play, anyway."

Dykes, he could be pretty sarcastic, and he said something, I forget exactly what, but it was like, "That's for sure." And I said, "Yeah? Well, never mind. I'll umpire." Rogers Hornsby, who was managing the Browns, said, "All right. That's all right with me. Jocko will call them the way he sees them. He's not afraid."

In other words, Hornsby accepted a player from the opposing team as umpire. Can you imagine Leo Durocher doing that? Or Bobby Bragan? But Hornsby was always great with umpires. Maybe nobody was better. I remember once in spring training when I was a minor-league umpire, and Minneapolis was playing St. Louis. I was behind the plate and one of the Browns tapped the ball down the first-base line, very slowly, foul by a couple of feet. The batter just stood at the plate watching it, and the first baseman let it roll. Just before it went past the base it struck a stone or a piece of uneven ground, veered over, hit first base and stopped. And, of course, that meant it was a fair ball. The first baseman picked it up and stepped on the bag and I said to the batter, "You're out." He had been standing at the plate saying, "Foul," but I hadn't said fair *or* foul. I couldn't. The ball was still rolling and it hadn't gone past the base and nobody had touched it or stopped it. But when it hit the base that made it fair and when the first baseman picked it up and stepped on the base I called the batter out. He started to yell and argue, and Hornsby came running up from the bench. He didn't say a word to me. He said to the batter, "Look, you. When you're on my ball club, you run the ball out and let the umpire make the decision. If you don't know what a fair ball is, get in the clubhouse and take your uniform off." He took him right out of the ball game.

So, this day in St. Louis, I went out and umpired a game between the White Sox and the Browns in my White Sox uniform. I worked the bases and I didn't have any trouble, though I had several close decisions. Well, they seemed close then, though looking back now I guess they weren't very hard. I remember one play especially. Luke Appling of the Sox hit a ball between the outfielders and it looked like a triple. I was inside the base lines and as Luke ran around the bases, I ran along with him, inside of him. Luke wasn't the fastest runner in the world, you know, and I kept yelling, "Come on! Let's go! Get the trunk off your back." I was his teammate, and I was rooting for him to get the triple. Luke was yelping in that old country accent of his, "I'm doin' the best I kin!" He came into third base, and the ball came in from the outfield, and they had him.

"You're out!" I said.

Dykes was coaching at third base, and he screamed.

"Out? What do you mean, out? He's safe!"

I said, "He's out."

"The man was safe," Dykes yelled.

Appling was still lying there in the dirt, and he looked up at Jimmie.

"Papa Dykes," he said. "He's right. He had me. He just touched me."

"He missed you," Dykes said.

"He didn't miss him," I said. "I called him out, and he's out."

Dykes looked at me with a hurt look, and he said, "You're a fine guy to have on a ball club." He got a kick out of it, arguing with his own ballplayer. Dykes was a wonderful fellow, very funny, and a smart baseball man. I always liked Jimmie.

I worked both games of that doubleheader and because Ormsby was still feeling weak I finished the series in St. Louis. That was all the umpiring I did that year, but it turned out to be the beginning of my career. When the season was over, Harry Grabiner, the general manager of the White Sox, called me into his office and asked me if I'd like to go umpiring. Well, as I said, that was the last thing I ever thought of, umpiring. I was a player.

Grabiner said, "You're down pretty near to the end of your career, Jock. If I were you, I'd give it a try. You know, if you make it to the majors as an umpire, you'll be eligible for a pension."

The players didn't have a pension plan then, only the umpires.

"An umpire gets a pension of $100 a year for each year he's in the majors," Harry said. "That means if you stay 18 seasons, you'd retire on $1,800 a year."

I guess I didn't look too impressed.

"Do you realize what it would cost to buy an annuity that would pay you $1,800 a year?" Grabiner said. "$50,000."

I said, "Gosh, I didn't realize that."

"Well, that's what it costs," he said.

Now, $1,800 was $150 a month, and at that time that was pretty good for a pension.

"All right," I said. "I'll try it."

Grabiner talked to Will Harridge, the president of the American League, and in a few days Harridge sent for me. The American League office was in Chicago then. After that thing in St. Louis, the newspapermen in Chicago all wrote favorable pieces about me: if the American League was looking for umpires why go any further than Jocko Conlan? He's quick. He's active. He looks as though he has real good judgment. And he can run faster than the ballplayers.

So, when Harridge called me in, I thought I was going to start right off umpiring in the big leagues.

"We had good reports on you on the job you did in St. Louis," Harridge said. "The big leagues can always use good umpires. I thought if you were interested, we'd help you along."

"I'm interested," I said, "but how would you help me along?"

"Why, we'd see to it that you would get a job."

"In the American League?" I said. "I'll take it."

19

"Oh, no," he said. "No, sir. Nobody will ever come to umpire in the American League without experience, not ever again."

That was because of Fred Marberry. That season the American League had taken on Marberry as an umpire, even though he had never umpired before. He was a great relief pitcher and his career was about over, and they gave him a chance. They worked him three weeks on the bases to break him in, and then they put him behind the plate to call balls and strikes. And a funny coincidence: I happened to see that game. It was between the White Sox and the Athletics in Philadelphia, when I was with the Sox. Tommy Connolly, the supervisor of American League umpires, was there looking at Marberry to see how he did.

I have always said that Fred Marberry was the best-looking man I ever saw in an umpire's suit. He was a big, handsome guy—the ballplayers called him Firpo because he looked like the fighter—and he had a nice build, a nice bearing, and he must have had his umpire's suit tailor-made, it fit him so well. It looked great on him. And he looked great—on the bases. But when he went behind the plate he was nothing. We had a pitcher pitching for us named Babe Phelps. There was a catcher at Brooklyn at the same time named Babe Phelps, but this was a different guy. Phelps was big and strong and he threw strike after strike that day, but all Marberry could say was ball . . . ball . . . ball . . . ball. He had been a big-league pitcher for a dozen years, but it was as if he knew nothing about balls and strikes. Everything was a ball. He got in a rut and couldn't get out. I don't know whether it was stage fright or not. It's hard to figure stage fright because Marberry was a game pitcher. But he could not call balls and strikes. Afterwards he said, "I'm not a plate umpire. I'm a base umpire. I'll just umpire on the bases." Hell, anybody can umpire on the bases. They tried him behind the plate once or twice again, but he couldn't do it, and when the season was over they let him go.

So Harridge said, "No, sir. We won't take an umpire on again unless he has experience. You'll have to go to the minor leagues for that, Jocko. You think it over and let me know."

I thought it over and then I told Harridge I'd like to try it. He got me a job in the New York-Pennsylvania League, and I went there the next year—1936—and started umpiring. I got paid $300 a month. The New York-Pennsylvania League paid me $225, and the American League added $75 to that. Three hundred dollars a month, for the season, which ran about four-and-a-half or five months. I was thirty-six years old, I was married, I had two children, and I was starting a minor-league job at $1,500 a year. And minor-league time did not count towards the pension.

2

KID GLEASON'S MITT

I DIDN'T MIND going into the minors again. I was used to the minor leagues. I had played in them long enough. The main thing was, it was baseball, and I was still in the game. I loved baseball, and I still do. It has always been the most important thing in my life, except my family. It was my hobby, my fun, my livelihood, everything.

I figure I started playing baseball about 1907 or 1908, when I was about eight or nine years old. I was born December 6, 1899. I remember there was a team called the Diamond Grays, and they had a diamond, about a half block from our house, at 25th and Butler in the near South Side of Chicago. The diamond was surrounded by the gashouse, a barrel factory and a brewery. (The barrel factory was owned by my mother's stepfather. Her father had died, and her mother married Charles Clayton, who owned the Clayton Barrel Factory. He had a 20-mule team at the factory. Remember the Borax ads and the "20-mule team"? They used his mules in the ads.)

Across the street from the barrel factory was a candle factory, and on the other side was the brewery, Gottfried's Brewery. Gashouse, candle factory, brewery—what smells. The diamond didn't have a name but we used to refer to it as the Stinkbuck. It was a prairie corner, and we cleaned it off ourselves and made the diamond. We walked off the distances between the bases and marked out the base lines with a shovel. Each kid had to work on the diamond if he wanted to play. My brother Pete was on the team, and I was the bat boy.

I was only about seven or eight, but I'd be out at seven o'clock

22

every morning, throwing a ball against the wall of the brewery. I wouldn't catch the ball on the fly. Instead, I'd be trying to learn how to catch it on the pickup, the short hop. At that age I was trying to learn how to be a good fielder. Even when I was in organized baseball I would catch only four or five balls in outfield practice. Then I used to come in and take infield practice to get used to handling grounders, and I had so much practice that I became a good outfielder on ground balls. You don't see too much of that today. I think Willie Mays does it. At least he used to come in and fool around at shortstop. Isn't that the way? The one player you would figure doesn't need it, and he's the one who takes extra practice.

When we were kids in Chicago, we used a taped ball. We almost never had a real baseball. We couldn't afford to buy one, and you didn't get foul balls at the ball park. If you ever happened to get your hands on a foul ball you threw it back on the field, or they'd throw you out of the park. So we made our own baseballs. We'd get a cork center, or we'd buy a rubber-ball center for two cents, and we'd buy a ball of string for three cents or a nickel. We'd wrap the string around the center as round and tight as we could get it, and then we'd tape it. We didn't have the money to buy good tape, so we'd wait for the telephone man to come through, working on the poles. He had that real good friction tape. He'd say to us, "If you kids don't steal anything when I'm up on the pole, I'll tape that ball of yours for you every time I come by."

And he would tape it for us, tape it real good. He'd give it a couple of layers. We could play two or three games with a good taped ball from the telephone man, so nobody ever went near that wagon of his to steal anything. Otherwise, we'd have to raise some money and buy a ten-cent roll of tape in the store, the kind with the tinfoil around it. And that wasn't much good. A couple of hard hits, and the tape was cracked.

It weighed like a rock, that taped ball, but we didn't care. It was a ball. And it went with the field. The field, it was like —— Well, I always think of that Chico Fernandez. He was a Cuban who

broke in with the Dodgers and later played with the Phils and
Detroit. You know how they rake the infield smooth halfway
through the game? Well, that's a fairly recent custom. I think Luke
Sewell put it in when he was managing Cincinnati around 1950. I
always thought it was unnecessary. The grounds keepers liked me
because they didn't want to go to the trouble of raking it in the
middle of a game, and they used to look out at me—I was the
senior umpire—and say, "What about it? Should we rake it today?"

"No," I'd say. "Not today. Forget about it."

This one particular day they asked if I wanted it raked, and I
said, "No, it's all right. They can't play any better anyway." So
Fernandez booted two balls at shortstop and he said to me, "You
no rake the ground. I make two errors."

I said, "Look, Chico, where you learned to play ball the infield
was a rock pile. Whether it's raked or not won't make any difference to you." Because I grew up on rock-pile ballfields, too, and
I knew what I was talking about. The fields today are like pool
tables. They're beautiful. It's nothing to see a first baseman, for
instance, reach down backhand and come up with a low throw in
the dirt. Thirty years ago that was a great play. Now it's automatic
because the ball bounces true. No pebbles, no stones, no bumps,
no holes. Nowadays you see fielding plays every day that you might
have seen once a year then. It's because of pool-table fields and
big gloves, those peach baskets they use now. I still have the glove
I used when I played center field for the White Sox in 1934 and
1935. It doesn't look any bigger than a toy mitt for a six-year-old.
It looks like a motorman's glove.

That reminds me of something. When I was about, oh, thirteen
years old—twelve or thirteen—I used to pick up bats for the White
Sox. I wasn't the regular bat boy. I worked in the morning. They
had morning practice in the big leagues in those days, and I used
to come over and pick up bats and stack them and chase balls and,
you know, just help out. Just to be around the big-leaguers. My
eye was set on being an outfielder someday with the Sox.

I was out in the outfield one morning shagging flies. All I had on was a pair of overalls. I was barefoot. Practice ended and the ball-players ran in, and I walked in after them. They were all off the field by the time I got in by the infield, and then I spotted a glove lying in the grass near third base. Oh, it was nice and shiny and oily. I had never had a big-league glove on my hand or even seen one up close. I picked it up. I'm left-handed, but I never looked to see whether it was left-handed or right-handed or what. I shoved the glove under my overalls and walked out of the park.

There were grounds keepers and sweepers working, and as I walked out I thought they were all looking at me. They looked to me as if they were the president of the ball club, because I knew I was doing wrong, taking that glove. But I just walked all the way through and out one of the turnstiles, and I had no more than got outside, at the corner of 35th and Shields, than I turned right and started to run. I ran barefoot all the way home from 35th and Shields to 25th and Wallace, which is close to two miles. I never looked around once. I just ran.

I got home and I took the glove out and looked at it. I put it on, and I felt it and I smacked it and I punched a hole in the pocket. It was so nice and oiled up and soft, just like kangaroo leather or kid. I held that glove and punched it and, oh boy, I had a big-league glove.

Kid Gleason was a coach with the Sox at the time, about 1911 or 1912, and his name was printed on it in indelible ink. There was the proof: I had a big-league glove. I was proud of it. I wasn't worrying about my conscience. I was proud. A day or so later I went and played a game and, boy, I could catch the ball one-handed. It was a right-handed glove and I was left-handed, but that didn't make any difference. I wore it on the wrong hand. I didn't care. It was a big-league glove, and I could catch the ball easy with it. I remember I said to myself, "Oh, gosh. This is the greatest thing that ever happened to me."

I had the glove for about a week. There was a streetcar conductor we knew named Amber Nolan. His real name was Andy, but everybody called him Amber. I don't know why. He was a pretty good ballplayer—he played in the Streetcar League—and he knew that I had that glove. Heck, every kid in the neighborhood knew that Johnny Conlan had Kid Gleason's glove.

Right away I became a businessman. Amber Nolan wanted the glove, so I sold it to him for two dollars and a left-handed glove for me. That left-handed glove was nothing like Kid Gleason's mitt, but it was real nice and it fit me good. I had a regular glove that fit, and I was two dollars ahead. Amber Nolan paid me eight quarters right out of the changemaker that he wore on his belt. Eight quarters. It looked like a mint to me. I ran home and gave the money to my mother. I told her I had a baseball glove and sold it. "Oh, you're a good boy, Johnny," she said.

My mother was a wonderful woman. She raised nine children and lived to the age of eighty-eight. My father died when he was forty-nine. He was a policeman. I don't remember him at all, except from pictures of him in his policeman's uniform. I was only three when he died. My mother did all our washing and sewing and baking, and she kept us all together. She really was wonderful. But I didn't tell her I stole that mitt.

The left-handed glove I got for it helped me a lot fielding, and I went on to become a pretty good ballplayer. About fifteen years later, in 1927, I was playing for the Newark ball club in the International League. We had an exhibition game in Miami, Florida, against the Philadelphia Athletics, and Kid Gleason was a coach on the Athletics under Connie Mack. He was hitting fungos to the outfielders before the game, and as soon as I saw him my conscience began to bother me. I watched him for a while, and finally I went over to him.

"Mr. Gleason?" I said.

"Yes?" he said. "What can I do for you?"

"Mr. Gleason," I said. "My name is Jocko Conlan. I'm an outfielder with the Newark club."

"Yes," he said. "Yes. I've heard of you, kid. How are you?"

He was a grand old guy. He really loved baseball.

"Well," he said. "You're a good ballplayer, kid. How's everything going for you?"

"Fine," I said.

"It's a great game, isn't it?"

"Yes, sir," I said. "Mr. Gleason, I have a little confession to make to you."

"To me?" he said.

"Yes, sir."

"What's on your mind, son?"

I said, "You remember when you were coaching with the White Sox?"

"Sure," he said.

"Well," I said. "I was a kid in Chicago then, and I used to pick up bats and shag flies in the outfield during morning practice."

"Oh?"

"One day I was shagging flies and I was the last one in from the outfield. Everybody was off the field except me. You had been hitting fungos and when I came in there was a glove lying near third base. I never had the price to buy a glove when I was a kid, so I picked that glove up and put it in my overalls and I ran two miles home with it without ever turning around. And when I got it home and looked at it, it said 'Kid Gleason' on it."

He was studying me, and he said, "Yes. I remember that glove. That was the greatest glove I ever had. So you were the one that swiped it?"

"Yes, sir," I said. "I was."

He looked at me.

"Well," he said. "Let me tell you something, kid. If that glove helped make a ballplayer out of you, I'm glad you swiped it. Now go on out there and get yourself in the big leagues."

And he reached out and he swatted me right across the shins with that fungo bat. Oh, boy, did that hurt! But he was grinning, and he waved the bat at me as I hobbled away, and I felt a lot better.

We played a lot of baseball in Chicago when I was a kid. I

went to All Saints Parochial School, and we were in a league with four Catholic parochial schools and four grammar schools. Four public schools, but they called them grammar schools then. We won the championship, but I nearly lost it. I was pitching, and I told the umpire off. How do you like that? Me telling an umpire what I thought of him. But I didn't like his judgment on a pitch he called a ball, and I told him so. He said, "Just pitch and let me umpire, or I'll put you out of the ball game."

I said something else and he said, "Well, for answering me back, I'm going to take some points off." He was the playground director and he umpired all the league games, and he took points off for deportment. We were tied for first place with P. D. Armour Grammar School, which was mostly Polish kids, and the way the league worked, in case of a tie the team with the best deportment won the championship. I had been named manager of our team by a great nun, Sister Mary Alexander, but there was a priest there named Father McClellan, and he sort of kept an eye on the team. He came running out and he pushed me to one side and quieted me down and talked to the umpire, and I went back in and pitched. When the final standings for the league came out both All Saints and P. D. Armour had seven wins and one loss, but we won the championship because it turned out that our deportment was two points better than theirs. I figured they must have told the playground director even more than I did, and in Polish, too.

Freddy Lindstrom, who starred with the Giants in the 1920s, played on our team. He went to one of the public schools, but one day we had only eight players, so I drafted him to play third base for All Saints. His school had a team in the league, but they didn't even know he went there. He was much younger than the rest of us, but a good ballplayer. If anyone wants to know who discovered Lindstrom, it was me, when he was about nine.

I was pretty good then, too. I pitched and played first base. Later on I played the outfield with the semipro teams around Chicago. They had that semipro Midwest League there, and it was a great league. It really was. They had ballplayers who had been in the majors and the high minors. Some of them got good money in the Midwest League, better than they would have in organized baseball. Jim "Hippo" Vaughn of the Cubs, who had been in that famous double no-hitter with Fred Toney, pitched there. And Dickie Kerr, the honest pitcher who won two games for the Black Sox when his teammates were throwing the 1919 World Series. He was getting about $3,500 from the White Sox even though he had won 40 games in two seasons and had beaten the Reds twice in that Series. So he jumped from the Sox to the Midwest League and got $10,000 on a two-year contract.

My brother Joe pitched in the Midwest League. He was good. He had a trial with Brooklyn in 1920 when Wilbert Robinson was managing the Dodgers. Joe went to spring training with them, and in Florida he pitched against the Yankees and Babe Ruth. It came out in the paper later that Babe Ruth said the longest ball he ever hit in his life was in Florida off a young left-hander the Dodgers had, whose name he couldn't remember. Joe told me when he came home that he was the pitcher. He said he struck out Babe the first time he faced him, but the second time—there it went. Joe said there was a racetrack beyond the outfield with a lot of open space and that the ball was hit so hard and kept on rolling so far that they lost track of it. Nobody even went after it. I don't think they've found it yet.

But Joe was a good pitcher. Wilbert Robinson liked him well enough to send him to Reading in the Eastern League. He won four ball games there and lost one, and in the one he lost he pitched a four-hitter. But he had just gotten married, and he and his wife were lonesome for home. He had never been away from Chicago before. So the two of them went home and that was that. He never played in organized ball again. He became a policeman.

Joe loved baseball. In later years he would come out to the White Sox park when I was playing and to the Cub park when I was umpiring. I'd give him a ball for his kids, and he'd sort of finger the ball and look at it. It was too bad he couldn't have stayed in the game. I think he would have been a fine major-league pitcher. I know that he did pretty well around Chicago, and they played crack baseball there in the Midwest League. They had teams from Beloit and Kenosha and Racine in Wisconsin, and in Chicago there were the Pyotts from the West Side, the Logan Squares from the northwest, the Marquette Manors from out on the South Side, and the Famous Chicagos, who were sponsored by politicians and were a roaming team that didn't have a home ground.

Those teams used to draw crowds of 8,000 to 10,000 people for semipro baseball. People have forgotten how popular the semipros used to be, and how good they were. In the fall they would be even stronger, because they would bring in pitchers from organized baseball who had finished their season. In 1906 after the Cubs and the White Sox met in the World Series, they each played an exhibition game with the Logan Squares, who were owned by John J. Callahan, the king of semipro baseball in Chicago in those days. The Logan Squares played the Cubs on Saturday and the White Sox on Sunday, and they beat both of them. Charlie Comiskey, who owned the Sox, wouldn't let his teams play the semipros any more after that. They're showing us up, he said. It was good baseball, excellent baseball.

There were the Negro teams, too, like the American Giants of Chicago, and the Kansas City Monarchs, and the Homestead Grays out of Pittsburgh. They weren't in the league, but they came and played special dates before big crowds. They had marvelous players, those colored teams. Oscar Charleston was *the* great Negro ballplayer then. He would pitch and he'd play first base and center field. He was a beautiful center fielder. They always compared him with Tris Speaker because he was just like Speaker—left-handed and a great hitter. Josh Gibson played. And a Cuban named Torriente. He was the Cuban that John McGraw tried to get in the league back then when they still had the color bar. They wouldn't let him come in. What a hitter he was!

Rube Foster managed the American Giants. He was a big fat guy, and he gave signals with his pipe. He'd hold the pipe a certain way in his hand, pointed down or up or sideways, or he'd hold it by the bowl or in the middle. Each position meant something: a bunt, hit-and-run, sacrifice, steal, squeeze play. Rube Foster had a nephew, and they called him Rube, too. He was a left-handed pitcher, and he reminded you of Herb Pennock, who is in the Hall of Fame. But Foster was faster than Pennock. He had beautiful control, a good fast ball, a great curve ball. He was really something to watch.

They had Bullet Joe Rogan. And Heavy Johnson, with Kansas City. He was fat, must have weighed 260, and he could hit a ball out of any park. Oh, they had great ballplayers. DeMoss, the second baseman. They used to drive us crazy. They'd bunt with three men on. DeMoss could drop a bunt on a dime. And Francis, a little third baseman. And Beckwith, a terrific hitter with the American Giants.

All these colored ballplayers I mention would have been stars in the big leagues today. They would have been stars then if they had been given the chance. But they wouldn't let the colored into baseball then. They let them into football. Duke Slater was All-American tackle at Iowa and later he was All-League with the Chicago Cardinals. He became a famous judge in Chicago, a Superior Court judge.

I played in the Midwest League, and a fellow named Matty Fitzpatrick, who umpired in it and scouted players, recommended me to Tulsa. That was in 1920, and I went down there and played ball, except that just after the season began I was traded from Tulsa to Wichita in the Union Station in Kansas City. The two clubs were passing through. Wichita was a man short on the roster and Tulsa a man over, so they made a trade and threw me in.

I didn't finish the year. I was playing good enough, but ten days before the end of the season my brother came up from Oklahoma and joined me. He had been down there working in the oil fields, and he was going home to Chicago to get married. I was kind of lonesome, so I went home with him. I was just a kid, and I didn't even think about the contract I had. I just went home. And I was suspended.

The suspension meant that I could not play anywhere in organized baseball for a year. I wasn't supposed to play semipro ball either because I'd be playing against baseball "outlaws," fellows who had jumped their contracts. But I couldn't afford not to play baseball. I had to make a living. So I joined the Pyotts in the Midwest League, and when I went back to Wichita for the 1922 season after my suspension was up, the club got a notice from minor-league headquarters saying now that I was under suspension for playing against outlaws. And I couldn't play any more that year.

The following November or December I went to Louisville to the minor-league winter meetings in order to get reinstated. I had to go up before Judge Bramham, later the head of the minor leagues, and John Conway Toole, the president of the International League, and old Dan O'Neill of the Eastern League. Frank Isbell, the owner of the Wichita club, pleaded for me. He said I was just a boy and hadn't known I was doing wrong. Bramham and Toole and O'Neill listened and then they said, all right, give the boy a chance.

I went back to Wichita in 1923, and after that season I was sold to the Rochester club in the International League. That's where I played for George Stallings, the smartest, the most intelligent, the greatest baseball man I ever met in my life.

3

GEORGE STALLINGS

I THOUGHT THE WORLD of George Stallings. He was the man who managed the miracle Braves of 1914 to the National League pennant after they were in last place in July, and then went on to sweep four straight games in the World Series from the Philadelphia Athletics, the greatest team in baseball at that time. Ten years later, when I met him, he was running the Rochester club in the International League. The minor leagues, especially the big minor leagues like the International League and the American Association and the Pacific Coast League, were a lot more important then than they are now. Today, they're just incubators for major-league players, but then they were important in themselves; you could spend a career in the minors, ten or twelve years. The men who ran the ball clubs, like Stallings, would develop a player and sell him to the majors. If they couldn't get the price they wanted they could hold on to the player and keep him year after year.

I played three years for Stallings, 1924, 1925, 1926. I played twelve years of minor-league ball in all, and the last nine were in Triple A (called Double A then). I was a good ballplayer. I hit over .300 six times in my nine years in Triple A—my lowest batting average was .283. I could go and get them in the outfield, and I had a good arm; I averaged about 20 assists a year for several years.

You didn't make an awful lot of money in the minors. Money was scarce. They called the Twenties "boom times," but everybody wasn't booming. I was paid only $2,500 my first year with Stallings. But I had a great season and I wanted more money the next year.

I led the International League in hits, runs, triples and stolen bases, and even though I was a lead-off man I was second in total bases; and I had the most putouts and assists by an outfielder. Merwin Jacobson of the Baltimore Orioles (Baltimore was in the International then) was the star center fielder of the league, and he had taken a liking to me. He told me, "Top salary in this league is $5,500. Get it next year."

I asked Stallings for $5,500. He growled and said no ballplayer was worth that much. I held out. I was ten days late reporting in 1925, but after dickering back and forth I got $5,200, which was pretty good. But that's where it stayed for the rest of my career in the minors. It just stayed the same every year; it never got any higher. When I went with the White Sox in 1934, I was paid around $6,000. Harry Grabiner said he'd give me an extra thousand in 1935 if the Sox drew 450,000 for the season. Major-league clubs didn't draw the crowds then that they do now, except for one or two teams. I remember Harry telling me once that if it hadn't been for the money they made from the concessions in the ball park the White Sox would have been flat. Concessions have saved many a ball club.

That year of 1935, Luke Appling and myself and someone else had that clause in our contracts, and we watched the attendance. I remember one day in July or August the Yankees came in for a doubleheader and we had 51,000 people in the park, the biggest crowd they'd had in Chicago for years and years. We got about three innings played in the first game and it started to rain. It rained and rained, and it washed out the doubleheader, washed out the crowd and the money they would have spent at the concessions during a doubleheader. It was heartbreaking—and funny, too. I can still remember a bug who ran out from the stands in a white linen suit while it was raining—I guess the games had just been called off. The field was a sea of mud and he ran around the bases, one after another, sliding into each one in that white linen suit. There wasn't a white spot left when he slid across home plate. Later that year the Yankees came back and played four doubleheaders in a row; we drew 91,000 people to the four dates and just did get over 450,000 in attendance.

After my first year with Rochester, after that good season I had, Stallings could have sold me to a major-league club, but he was waiting for a bigger price. I stayed at Rochester for three straight seasons. I didn't get sore at Stallings because of it. That's the way it was then. I've always been sort of a fatalist anyway, taking things as they come. Besides, I loved playing for Stallings. He ate, drank and slept baseball. He had a meeting with his players every morning, whether he was on the road or at home. You learned things in those meetings. You especially learned the dumb things you had done. Stallings would excuse mechanical errors, because he said they were part of the game. But you couldn't make a mental error and get away with it.

Stallings managed in a business suit; he didn't wear a uniform. He was always fidgety on the bench. He'd sit on his hands and rock back and forth, or he'd slide back and forth. He used to wear beautiful, expensive clothes—he was a handsome man, a great-looking man—but he would wear out maybe three or four pairs of pants a season. He was very intelligent, but he was as superstitious as any ballplayer who ever lived. If he saw a certain cloud in the sky and the man at bat at the time got a base hit, Stallings would never take his eye off that cloud until somebody made an out. If the next two or three men happened to get on base, Stallings would keep looking at the cloud the whole time. He had a rough way of saying things. If he didn't like the way you were playing, he'd call you a piece of junk. If you were big, he'd call you a big piece of junk; if you were little he'd call you a little piece of junk. He didn't bother to praise you when you did something right. He expected that.

I don't think ballplayers today could play for a man like Stallings. They can't stand to be told things directly today when they do something wrong, and when they do something right you have to praise them. You have to baby them, pat them on the back, almost apologize when you criticize them. You have to be just so

35

careful with them and not mishandle them, or their feelings will be hurt, and they'll say you don't like them, or that you're holding something against them. If some of the players today, and this goes for umpires today, too, had to listen to some of the things I've been called, they'd have a fit.

But it wasn't really rough in those days. It was just that men like Stallings were interested in the players, interested in how we played and how we could improve ourselves. They were interested enough to tell us what we were doing wrong and how we could correct it and improve ourselves. Of course, they told us directly and sometimes pretty bluntly. When they didn't talk to a player, it meant they weren't worried about him. It meant he was doing fine. You didn't expect to get compliments. When you did get one it was a rare occasion.

I remember once when we were playing Baltimore. Baltimore was the best team in the league, and probably the best minor-league team that ever existed, except maybe that Newark team in 1937. They won seven straight International League pennants. They had Lefty Grove and George Earnshaw and Tommy Thomas and Jack Ogden. These were great pitchers. They had a pitcher named Harry Franks who was considered just another guy on the ball club, and he won 18 games. One year they had an old guy named Rube Parnham who won 35 games for them. They had Jack Bentley, Max Bishop, Joe Boley, Fritzie Maisel, Merwin Jacobson, Otis Lowrey, Dick Porter, a fellow named Egan catching and another catcher named Joe Cobb, a good hitter. Most of these names don't mean much today, but they were ballplayers, good ones. I think most of them went up to the major leagues, and several were outstanding stars.

Well, this season we were second—we finished second three straight years to Baltimore—and I guess we still had a shot at catching them. In this particular game we were winning by three runs, and the Orioles got three men on base. We had a catcher named Harry Lake—a wonderful guy and we all liked him—but he couldn't catch a pop fly. Merwin Jacobson came up, bases loaded, the Orioles three runs behind. Jacobson was a good hitter, but he hit a foul pop-up behind the plate. Harry Lake had a habit of circling around under a pop-up instead of waiting and then moving toward it. He'd keep circling and he'd get dizzy and he'd lose the ball, which is what he did this day. The foul came down and hit him right in the head, right over the eye, and bounced away. Well, it was funny, because we knew how weak Harry was on pop-ups, and everybody burst out laughing, except Stallings. Jacobson got up to the plate again, and this time he hit a sharp single to center, right to me. I ran in quick to field it, and the ball went between my legs. It went all the way to the scoreboard. I chased it, but the man on third scored, the man on second scored, the man on first scored and Merwin Jacobson scored, and we were beaten.

I felt terrible. I was considered a good outfielder and to make an error like that was awful. Of course, it was a pretty rough field, that old Oriole park. You'd find rocks and everything else out there, and you had to be careful or you'd pick up a rock instead of the ball. But I still felt terrible and I was wondering what Stallings would think about me.

That night I was getting in the elevator at the Kernan Hotel, where we stayed in Baltimore. It was next door to a big theater, where a stock company used to play all the time. The orchestra used to practice every morning, and Stallings would say to us, "You see what practice means? That orchestra plays every night, but they practice every morning."

I got on the elevator, and Stallings was on the elevator, too. He didn't say a word to me. Then a salesman got on, carrying a little valise with him. He didn't know me, but he recognized Stallings. He said, "Mr. Stallings?"

"Yes?" Stallings said.

The salesman got to talking about the game and finally he said, "Boy, if I were you, I'd get rid of that center fielder of yours. There is one lousy ballplayer. He lost that game for you today."

Stallings said, cold as ice, "I want to tell you something, you smart punk. Go peddle your papers. He's the best man I have on the ball club."

That's the kind of man he was. He would not criticize me for making a mechanical error, any more than he would praise me for making a good play. But he would stick up for me. He would not let anybody else criticize his ballplayers. *He* could say what he wanted, but no one else could.

I remember another game against Baltimore, this one in our own park in Rochester. There was a terrace in left-center field that ran up from the regular part of the outfield and then flattened out. On top of the terrace there were boards that slanted up toward the wall, like a slanted fence. Joe Cobb of the Orioles hit a long one, deep to left center. I was playing center field, and I went back for it. I have seen some spectacular catches in baseball, but I really don't believe there has ever been another catch quite like this one. I ran back across the outfield, up on the terrace, across the flat space, and then I kept right on going up the side of the slanted fence. I turned, grabbed the ball one-handed and then slid down the fence on my back. I ran into the bench, and what do you think Stallings said? "Showing off, hey?"

Stallings would never let you talk to an opposition player. If you happened to exchange a word or two with a friend of yours on another team, you'd never hear the end of it. He'd say, "You're here to beat them, not talk to them. If you have any business with any of them, about hunting or fishing or anything, talk about it during the winter. Not here. Not during the season. Never in my presence. I want ballplayers who are here to play to win, not to hold conversations with the visiting club."

Stallings would never say anything good about an opposing club or an opposing player. Fred Merkle played first base with us at the time. He had had a long career in the majors, and he was on his way down. Merkle was a very quiet fellow and very studious about baseball. Charlie Gehringer, who became maybe the best second baseman who ever played the game, broke in that year with Toronto, and Merkle watched him play a couple of times. I re-member this well because Fred very seldom spoke on the bench. One day he was watching Gehringer and all of a sudden he said, "There's a fellow who'll be a star in the big leagues for twenty years." Of course, he was right; Gehringer is in the Hall of Fame now. But Stallings exploded. "Like hell he will," he said. "He'll be gone by the first of June."

Stallings knew as well as Merkle did that Gehringer was outstanding, but he would never let anybody on his own team admit that anybody on any other team was good. In other words, you weren't handed any games by Stallings' teams. You had to beat them.

He was in his fifties when I played for him, but he was still a tremendous competitor. He could be very tough on umpires. There was a close play one day and the umpire called it against us. He was an old white-haired guy named Lou Fyfe, a nice old fellow. But Stallings got into an argument with him, and it ended up that they agreed to meet afterwards and fight it out, to see which one could lick the other. They were old men, the both of them. Stallings asked me to go with him. I was a cocky kid, and I'd had a few fights. I knew something about fighting. I had refereed and in Rochester I was a licensed New York State judge at fights they had there. I guess Stallings wanted me to be a sort of combination second and bodyguard.

I went with him, and they squared off. "All right," one of them said, "let's go." Each of them threw a great big roundhouse punch, and they both missed, and they both fell down. And that was the end of the fight.

We walked away and Stallings said, "By God. If I'da landed that one, I'da had him." Lord, the punch he threw wasn't hard enough to break an egg. I was trying not to laugh, but I was a fresh kid and I said, "George ——" No, not George—Mr. Stallings. I said, "Mr. Stallings, you better stay to managing and leave the gloves alone." I started to laugh. He said, "I guess you're right. I'm in the wrong game. I'm not a fighter."

In 1925, my second year with Rochester, Stallings sold me to the Cincinnati Reds. Or, at any rate, the deal was all set. I was to go up to the Reds and they were to send Tom Sheehan, Elmer Smith and Chet Fowler to Rochester, plus $17,500 in cash. Sheehan, who

39

later became chief scout for the Giants and their manager for awhile, was a pretty good pitcher, and Smith was the guy who hit the first grandslam homer ever in a World Series. Fowler had played major-league ball, too. And $17,500 was a lot of money in those days. It was a big deal, and I was pretty excited about it. I was getting my chance in the big league. It was a Saturday, and I was supposed to play for Rochester against Syracuse on Saturday and Sunday and then go to New York and report to the Cincinnati ball club there. In the Saturday game, I was leading off second base. At that time we used to play hit-and-run with a runner on second, though you had to have a hitter who really had control of the bat. The batter this day happened to be Eddie Murphy, a former White Sox player who had come back down to the minors. I could run pretty good, so Stallings called for the hit-and-run. There was one out. Murphy hit a ground ball to the shortstop, Tommy Thevenow, and Thevenow threw to first to a fellow named Swansborough. I never stopped running once I saw Tommy let the ball go toward first, and I turned third and was digging for the plate. Swansborough threw the ball home, but I had it beat. It was close, but I knew I had it beat, so I got careful. I was kind of a tough slider. I was taught that way by Stallings. Always slide. Always slide hard. Don't think you *might* slide. *Slide*.

But I had Cincinnati in my mind and my chance in the big leagues, and I didn't want to risk hurting myself sliding. I thought I'd run past the catcher and just touch the corner of the plate with my cleats as I went by. The Syracuse catcher was a fellow named Nig Niebergall, a New Yorker who lived on Long Island. He was a strong catcher. He blocked the plate as the throw came in, and my knee hit his shin guard, and I flopped. I haven't touched home plate yet. He tagged me out, and they carried me into the clubhouse. My knee was swollen up so much they could hardly get my pants off to see what was wrong with it. I had torn all the ligaments in it.

When they heard about it, Cincinnati called the deal off, and I didn't get to the major leagues until nine years later. In those days, if you cracked an ankle or hurt a knee, the big leagues simply did not want you. They were afraid your leg would go, and they'd be stuck with you after paying a price for you and paying your salary. I mean it. Once you had a bad leg, it was nearly impossible to get a major-league club to take a chance on you. The only one I can remember back then who did get a chance was Joe DiMaggio in 1936. He had a bad knee and no one would touch him, even though he was a star in the Pacific Coast League for three or four straight seasons—he hit in 61 straight games for San Francisco in 1933, eight years before he hit in those 56 straight for the Yankees. But Joe Devine, the Yankee scout in California, had watched Joe play. He insisted that the Yankees buy DiMaggio and take care of his knee. They paid $25,000 for him, fixed his knee, and he was great. After that, big-league clubs began to take a chance on players who were hurt, and now they're operating on them all the time. But DiMaggio was the first one I ever heard of.

They didn't operate on me. They told me to wrap the knee in hot towels and put liniment on it and take it easy, which I did. And it came around. The next year it was fine. That winter Stallings sold me to Newark, which was in the International League then. I played three years with Newark, hit over .300 and scored more than 100 runs in each of those three seasons. But all that the big-league clubs could remember about me was the knee.

Those are the breaks. After I hurt my knee, Cincinnati bought a guy from St. Paul by the name of Coo-Coo Christensen. He went up to the Reds and he had a hot year. He and Bubbles Hargrave, the Cincinnati catcher, were one-two in the league in hitting. Hargrave hit .353 and Christensen hit .350. The Reds gave Coo-Coo a two-year contract at $10,000 a year, but he never was any good after that one season. His average fell off to .254 the next year and the season after that he was out of the major leagues for good. It's strange.

Those were tough years for me. In the 1926 season I got in a fight with an umpire, a fellow named Augur. I suppose after all my years of umpiring I shouldn't admit that. But he called a strike on me one day in Jersey City on a pitch that was a foot over my head. I know I'm doing now what I say ballplayers shouldn't do: criticize an umpire's judgment. But I'm telling you I know where this ball was. I turned around and said, "Pretty high, wasn't it?"

"Get in there and hit," he said.

The next pitch was a foot outside, and he said, "Strike three. You're out."

I turned around, pretty mad, and I yelled, "You ought to be out, too!"

He reached back and pulled off his mask to yell back at me, and when he brought the mask down in front of him he hit me right in the nose with it. I don't think he meant to hit me, but he did, and right on my nose, so I hit him. In fact, I hit him twice. I took two shots at him, and they broke it up. I had to go up before John Conway Toole, the president of the league. The circumstances were explained, but Toole still fined me $100 for hitting an umpire. Maybe it was for the second shot. I was still with Rochester then, but I was traded to Newark in the off-season. On the opening day of the season in Newark, Paul Block, publisher of the Newark *Star-Eagle* and owner of the Newark Bears was sitting in a box with John Conway Toole and Jimmy Walker, the mayor of New York. I had met Walker before, a great guy, a colorful fellow. I had been named captain of the Newark team, and Paul Block called me over to the box.

"Jocko," he said. "I'd like you to meet Mayor Walker."

"Oh, we've met before," I said. "How are you, Mayor?"

"Hello, Jock," he said. "How are you?"

Then Paul Block said, "And this is Mr. Toole, the president of the league."

I laughed.

"I've met him before, too," I said. "And I think he knows me. How are you, Mr. Toole?"

I stood talking with them for a while, and then I said, "Say, Mr. Toole. How about giving me back that hundred dollars?"

He laughed, but he said, "I'll tell you what. I'll make a deal with you. If you don't get thrown out of a game by the first of June, I'll return the hundred."

I had a reputation for being a little quick in those days, and I had been put out of a few games. But that spring I was good as gold. A hundred dollars meant something. On June 1, I hadn't been thrown out once. We happened to be home that day, in Newark, and that's where Toole's office was. I was there waiting at nine in the morning. And I got the hundred back.

4

CASEY, WHERE ARE YOUR PANTS?

THOSE MINOR-LEAGUE YEARS were an important time in my life. I made a lot of friends then. I fell in love and got married. I even got my nickname then.

I had always been called Johnny Conlan. My full name is John Bertrand Conlan. That "Bertrand" never got around the big leagues, thank the Lord. There's nothing I could have done about it, but I was waiting to be kidded because of it. Imagine a mick like me with a name like Bertrand. There was a nun in Chicago named Sister Mary Bertrand who was a great friend of my mother's. When my mother was carrying me, Sister Bertrand said, "If it's a boy, call him after me." They named me after my Uncle John instead, and put Bertrand in as my middle name, which is just as well. I don't think Bertrand as a first name would have fitted the kind of guy I was.

When I was playing ball in Rochester there was a sportswriter on the *Democrat and Chronicle* named Corri. We called him "Geechy." I don't remember why. He was from someplace in Maine, I think. He was the fellow who hung the name "Jocko" on me. I've heard several people say that I got the name because I was a bench jockey. I never liked that, because I wasn't a bench jockey. I fought like the devil to win, but I didn't ride people. I had a few words with somebody now and then, but I wasn't one of those pop-offs.

Just about the time I was with Rochester there was a fellow named Conlon who played second base for a while with the Braves. He spelled it with two *o*'s. I spell it with an *o* and an *a*. This fellow Conlon on the Braves was called "Jocko," and Corri started calling me Jocko, too. It stuck. It seemed to fit. I wouldn't know what to do now if I didn't have Jocko as part of my name.

This other Jocko Conlon was a Harvard man, a pretty intelligent fellow. I've never met him, but I was told he became a stockbroker around Boston. We must have been about the same size and more or less the same appearance because over the years I have had at least twenty-five people come up to me and say, "Do you remember me? We were together in the class of nineteen-something-or-other." I'd say, "I'm afraid you've got the wrong fellow." They'd say, "No. Don't you remember? We went to Harvard together." I'd try to explain and then I'd say, "Is there really that close a resemblance?" A couple of them thought I was kidding them.

When I was with Rochester we went to Georgia one year for spring training. Eddie Murphy, the outfielder who had played for the White Sox, had just joined the club that winter and he was holding out. Everybody was wondering when he was going to sign, especially the newspapermen. We were staying in a place called Jones's Hotel. You walked up big wide stairs that squeaked. That was really the hot-stove league. They had one of those big iron stoves in the lobby, and we'd sit around it talking. There wasn't much else to do.

Spring training can be pretty dull, and Eddie Murphy got to be the big topic of conversation. He was about two weeks overdue. I don't think anybody else with the Rochester club knew what he looked like, but I did because I had seen him play in Chicago. He had a peculiar walk: little, short steps. One day when we were sitting around that stove, Geechy Corri and a couple of us ball-players, a cab pulled up in front of the hotel and a guy came walking in. He was wearing a cap—ballplayers used to wear caps in those days—and he had the same funny little walk that Murphy had. For no reason at all, I said, "Well, Eddie Murphy has finally arrived."

Geechy Corri jumped up and ran out of the lobby. He wrote a beautiful story about Eddie Murphy coming into camp, sent it to his paper and had a real exclusive, a scoop. Except that Murphy didn't arrive for another ten days. The guy who had come in the lobby was the cabdriver, bringing his fare's suitcase in to the desk. I hadn't meant anything when I said it was Murphy, but it made Corri look bad, and it got him down on me. From that time on, I could win a ball game with a base hit or a fine catch, and there'd never be a mention of it. If I made an error or struck out, I got headlines. But, anyway, that was the fellow who named me Jocko.

Another spring training I was in St. Augustine, Florida, with the Newark club. The New York Giants were there, too. I think it was the spring of 1927. I remember this so well. It was a Sunday evening and we had no place to go, so we sat around on the steps of the Alcazar Hotel, talking. And four of us—Bill Terry, Jack Bentley, Al Mamaux and me—started to sing. I don't know how we got started, but it was just like that quartet in *Music Man,* four guys whose voices worked together. Mamaux had sung on the stage and he had a marvelous voice. He was the lead. Bill Terry was the baritone. Jack Bentley sang bass and I sang tenor. When we began, there was hardly anybody there, but we sang for two or three hours, and by the time we finished there must have been a couple of hundred people standing and sitting around, listening. They applauded after each song and made requests. We sang *Dear Old Girl* and all those old-time songs that have some harmony. And we just kept going. It was an amazing thing. Kenny Smith, the sportswriter from New York who became curator of the Hall of Fame in Cooperstown, liked to sing—he was practically a professional and always a great success in those baseball writers' shows—and he used to say to me, years later, "I have never heard another quartet in my life like that one." Just a year or so ago, Max Kase, who was sports editor of the New York *Journal-American* right up to the time of that big newspaper merger in New York, wrote a column of reminiscences of spring training and in it he had, ". . . the melodious singing of Bill Terry, Al Mamaux, Jack Bentley and Jocko Conlan, a never-to-be-forgotten quartet, on the steps of a St. Augustine hotel. . . ." It was one of those rare things that can happen, and it's a warm memory to have.

Casey Stengel—there's another memory. Newark traded me to Toledo in 1930, and Casey was the manager at Toledo. I played for him just that one year, and then I was traded to Montreal, but he and I became good friends, real close friends. What a year! Casey used to call meetings at ten-thirty every morning. Games started at three in the afternoon. He'd call the meetings at ten-thirty, and they were the only meetings I can ever recall in baseball where the players got there early. Not just early, but an hour early, because Casey wouldn't wait until ten-thirty to start talking. He started in the minute he got to the clubhouse and nobody wanted to miss anything.

They talk about Casey and his conversations when he was managing the Yankees and the Mets. You should have heard him then. He'd walk through the clubhouse in his underwear and he'd look around and he'd say sweetly, "Are all my boys here?" We'd have lost the ball game the day before, and he'd start in on what we had done wrong. He'd give an exhibition of fielding and pitching and hitting and base-running and everything; he would go on and on and on. It was great.

He'd get dressed as he talked. One day he finally had everything on except his pants. He had his shoes on and his socks rolled at the knee, and he had on his uniform shirt and his cap, and there were his bow legs sticking out of his underwear. It was a Sunday and we had a doubleheader, which started at two-thirty instead of three, and, I swear, Casey talked steadily, without stopping, from before ten until a couple of minutes after two.

That day he was particularly getting on a fellow we had named Max Rosenfeld. Max couldn't hit a curve ball too good, and Casey was telling him what he was doing wrong and what he should do right. We were going up against Rosy Ryan of Minneapolis, and Rosy had a beautiful curve ball. He had been with the Giants under McGraw, and you had to have a curve ball if you played for McGraw. That's why the National League got the reputation for being a low-ball league, because McGraw and the Giants dominated the league, and all of McGraw's pitchers were trained to throw that curve ball low, right at the knee, so that the batter would hit the ball into the ground and you could turn it into a double play. The American League was a fast-ball league—Walter Johnson and Rube Waddell and Lefty Grove and Lefty Gomez. They over-powered the hitters. But when the hitters connected, they hit the fast ball out of the park, and that's why for so many years the American League was the home-run league. It's all changed now; the National League has had the power hitters the last fifteen years or so. But for a long time, the American had the home-run hitters, and the National the curve-ball pitchers.

Rosy Ryan's curve was one of the best, and Casey was explaining to Max Rosenfeld how to hit it. Casey had a bat in his hand, and he'd cock it and swing it, and he'd talk about how he hit .368 in the National League—which he did, and don't forget that Casey was some ballplayer, a great clutch hitter. He'd say, "Now, this is the way I did it in the National League. You stand there and you watch that pitcher and you cock the bat, and you lay for that curve ball." Max Rosenfeld was nodding his head and saying, "Yes. Okay. All right."

Max had on a light Palm Beach suit—he hadn't had a chance to dress yet with Casey talking—and he was sitting right in front of Casey. There was a box filled with sawdust between them, a low box filled with chew tobacco and all the slop that guys who had been playing cards in the clubhouse had tossed into it. It was a mess, that sawdust box. But Casey was using it as an imaginary home plate as he explained to Max how Max should wait on the pitch, and lay for the curve ball, and how to hit Ryan, and how Casey did it when he was playing ball. Casey said, "McGraw always told us to lean over." And he leaned over that sawdust box. "And lay for it." He cocked the bat and waited. "And then *hit* it!" Wham! He swung the bat and he smacked the box. The sawdust and chew tobacco and slop flew up in the air and it all hit Max, right in the Palm Beach suit, right down the front of it. Max jumped up and he was almost crying. He said, "You can show me how to hit, but you don't have to cover me with all that slop!"

Casey gave him a look, tossed the bat away and said, "Well. That's the way I hit 'em."

By then it was two o'clock and somebody said, "Time to warm up the pitchers," so we had to go out on the field. It was a good-sized crowd that day, and there were a lot of women in the park. From the dressing room we had to walk underneath the stands a little way before we got to the runway that led down to the dugout. Everybody filed out and Casey came over to me and he sort of growled out of the side of his mouth, "How did you like that exhibition of hitting?"

"Oh, it was great," I said. "You really hit that curve ball. You nearly killed poor Max. He's got to have his suit cleaned and everything now."

Casey said, "Yeah, yeah. Well, if he hit those curve balls like that he wouldn't be having trouble with his suit."

He started to go out of the dressing room and he said to me, "Take a couple of things out with you, will you? Take the ball bag."

I picked up the ball bag and followed him. He was carrying a couple of towels, I think, and a fungo bat to hit flies with to the outfielders. He still didn't have his pants on, but I didn't say a word. I walked right along with him. We went out past the concession stands and along the grandstands, and the women in the crowd were staring at Casey and saying, "Oh! Oh, my!" A couple of them called, "Casey! Casey!"

Stengel was walking along, swinging the fungo bat like a cane. He said, "They got some crazy women here in Toledo."

I said, "Yes, I guess they do."

We kept walking, and the people watching us were making more and more noise. Casey looked around and frowned and he said, "What are they hollering about? The game doesn't even start for half an hour yet."

And then he stopped. And he looked down. And he said, "Why, I haven't got my pants on."

I just smiled at him.

49

He hit me right across the shins with that fungo bat and he said, "Why didn't you tell me I didn't have any pants on?"

"Why, Casey," I said. "I didn't even notice."

He hurried back inside and put his pants on, but when he went out on the field they were all yelling, "Casey! Casey! Where are your pants?"

The women loved to yell at Casey, and he was great with them. One day in Milwaukee before a game we were crossing the field to the visitors' dugout. They really liked him in Milwaukee because it's a German town, and Casey is a Dutchman, you know. His nickname was "Dutch" before it was "Casey." He had some telegrams in his hand, wires about players and notifications from the league office and things like that, and he was glancing at them as we crossed toward the dugout. The women in the stands were shouting to him and yelling his name, and one woman called out in a fake German dialect, "Casey! Der telegram. Vot did it said?" We were right in front of our dugout by then. He looked up and said, "Just another widow died and left old Case $10,000 more." He ducked down into the dugout and said, "That'll take care of those old gals up there."

I didn't have much of a season for Casey because I broke my ankle. He used to tell about that later on, and the story got better and better. We were in the ninth inning of a tie game and Casey said, "I'll buy a suit of clothes for the man who wins this game for me." I got hold of one and I stretched it into a triple. I slid hard into third and when I did I hit my ankle. Oh, it hurt. Casey was coaching at third, and he bent over me.

"Are you hurt?" he said. "I'll put in a runner."

I said, "It's all right. I don't need a runner."

The next batter hit a long fly and I tagged up and went in and scored the winning run. And, boy, that ankle hurt then. I barely made it to home plate, and then I fell flat on my face. They carried me into the clubhouse, and then they found out that the ankle was broken.

"Jocko," Casey said. "You're tough."

"Never mind that," I said. "Where's the suit?"

Every time Casey saw me, in a World Series or an All-Star Game or in spring training, he'd tell that story. He'd be giving that double-talk to the newspapermen and I'd come out on the field and he'd say, "There's my boy. There's one of my boys. Now look at that. There's a boy scored from third for me on a broken leg." It was a chipped bone in my ankle. It hurt like the devil, I admit, and I had to hobble home, but with Casey it went from a chipped bone in the ankle to a broken leg, and I think some days he had a piece of broken bone sticking through my stocking. But that was all right with me, because I never did get that suit from him. When I reminded him, he said, "Ah, that's the way you're supposed to play for me." He was a little of the old Stallings type, too. Broken leg or not, score the run.

There was one very serious incident I was involved in with Casey at Toledo. They had a very tricky fence along the left-field line where the field boxes sort of jogged in and out. A batted ball could go out of sight temporarily down there, and if it went out of sight the ground rule was it should be a two-base hit. We were in a terrific ball game with Minneapolis, and we went into the last half of the ninth inning two runs behind. But we got men on first and second base with two out, and I was up. Rosy Ryan was pitching. I was a left-handed batter, and I sliced a ball to the opposite field, down the left-field line. The man on second scored and so did the fellow on first, tieing the score, and I ended up on third. But when I had hit the ball it had bounced into that area along the field boxes. It was very quick in and out, and I'm not even sure it did go in.

But the plate umpire, Joe Rue, who later umpired in the American League, said it did. He ruled that my hit was a ground-rule double, and I had to go back to second. More important, the man who scored from first was entitled to advance only two bases, so he had to go back to third. Which meant that the score wasn't tied after all. We were still a run behind. There was a terrific rhubarb and Casey really had it out with Rue. He said the ball never went out of sight, that Rue called it too quick, that he should have waited to see where the ball went. Casey got on him pretty good, and the crowd was howling mad. Stengel finally went back to the dugout, but the fans were still yelling. Max Rosenfeld was up next and, while he didn't strike out on Ryan's curve this time, he hit it on two bounces to the shortstop and was thrown out at first base for the final out. On that out I had rounded third and headed for the plate, trying to score in case the throw went wild or the first baseman booted it. I was going pretty fast, but even so the crowd was out of the stands and up to home plate after that umpire almost before I got there. We had to hustle Rue off the field to keep him from being killed. It was rough. I got hit pretty good three or four times, and they weren't even after me. Toledo was a rough town.

Tom Hickey was the president of the American Association, and apparently he did not like Stengel. They had had a couple of run-ins before, and now Hickey made it very hard for Casey. He accused him of behaving in such a way as to incite the crowd and cause a riot, and he wanted him thrown out of baseball. He was serious about it, and Casey was brought up before Judge Landis, the Commissioner. The owners of the Toledo club were a couple of lawyers named McMahon and Smith, criminal lawyers in Toledo, and they went with Stengel to the hearing. So did I, because Landis wanted statements from everyone who was involved in the incident. At the hearing Landis asked Joe Rue, the umpire, to draw an outline of the field so that he could understand what happened. I was just sitting there, but I spoke up. I said to Landis, "Why don't you let me draw the field?"

Landis said, "I didn't ask *you.*"

"Judge Landis," I said, "I've been playing left field in that ball park every day for the past two weeks. I think I have a better conception of how that fence runs than an umpire who only comes in the park once a month and then stands at home plate. If I do draw it wrong, he can tell you."

Landis rubbed his chin. "That makes sense," he said. "All right. Go ahead."

52

I drew the thing and I showed where the ball could have hit and where it could have come out, because, after all, I had hit the ball and naturally I had watched it. You couldn't tell from where it hit whether the umpire was right or wrong. I said to Judge Landis, "I'm not blaming the umpire. It was a very difficult play to call, and he called it the way he saw it. But I don't see how you can blame Casey, either. It cost us the tieing run and the ball game. It's the confusing ground rule that caused all the trouble, not the umpire *or* the manager."

Hickey still wanted Casey suspended, but Landis said, "I'll give my decision in a couple of days." One of the lawyers said to Casey, "If you don't get the ax, that's the guy who saved you: Jocko." And two or three days later, Landis decided in Casey's favor: no suspension.

53

5

RHUBARBS: JOCKO IN THE MIDDLE

I SEEM TO HAVE HAD A KNACK all through my career both as a player and as an umpire to be right in the middle when something wild happened. After I finally got out of the minor leagues and up to the White Sox, there was an incident one day that Bill Dickey, the Yankee catcher, always said was the longest argument he ever saw on a ball field. Who hit the ball? Me.

It happened in that series when the Yankees came into Chicago and played to 91,000 fans in four days. Joe McCarthy was managing the Yankees then, and he was one of the real top managers of all time. McCarthy never missed a thing that happened on the field. He was all business. He wasn't one of these mouths that keep running all the time over nothing. When he came out on the field, there was always a reason. He was fair. But if he saw an umpire make a mistake, an incorrect ruling, he was out there like a shot. He wasn't abusive, but you had better know what you were talking about when you dealt with McCarthy.

This day I was batting for the White Sox. Charley Donnelly was the plate umpire, Bill Summers was at first base and Bill Dinneen, a grand old guy who had won three games in the first World Series ever played, back in 1903, was at third base. Just three umpires then.

We had men on first and second and I hit a line drive off Red Ruffing that went over Lou Gehrig's head at first and down the right-field line. Gehrig was playing close to the bag and the ball hit just fair. I took off down the first-base line. Behind me I could hear Dickey, who was catching, yell, "Foul! Foul ball!" the way catchers will. Then I heard Donnelly, the plate umpire, yell,

"Foul." But I could see it was fair, and our base runners could, too. They kept running, and both of them crossed home plate, and I buzzed around and went into third base with a triple. George Selkirk, who took over for Babe Ruth in right field that year after the Babe went to the Boston Braves in the National League, hadn't gone after the ball too hard because it had been called foul.

We raised a big argument, really raised the roof, and got Donnelly to confer with Summers, the first-base umpire. Donnelly's view down the line had been partially blocked. But Summers, who had been standing about halfway between first and second had seen the play clearly. Donnelly said, "I lost sight of it. I thought it went foul." Summers said, "No. It was a fair ball."

Which meant, of course, that I was on third base and we had two runs in.

But now McCarthy came out. The Yankees' bench was on the first-base side of the field, and they all could see it was a fair ball. McCarthy didn't even dispute that decision. What he did argue was that Selkirk saw Donnelly wave the ball foul, and when that happened Selkirk naturally eased up chasing it. McCarthy claimed that if the plate umpire had not waved the ball foul, Selkirk would have fielded it and thrown me out at third; or he would have held me to a double. He said it wasn't fair for me to be given a triple. I should be sent back to second.

It was a good argument. McCarthy was smart. There was no question that I would not have had a triple if Selkirk had hustled on the ball. Summers finally nodded his head and said, "Okay. Two bases." He waved me back to second. That meant that the base runner who had been on first could advance only two bases, and he was sent back to third, which took away one of our runs.

Now it was our turn again. Jimmie Dykes and I were yelling our heads off. Dykes tried to push me away, because he was afraid I'd get tossed out of the game; a manager would rather get thrown out himself than have one of his players chased. I stayed right there. By this time old Bill Dinneen, who was the senior umpire of that team and probably the senior umpire in the league, was there listening, too.

I said to Summers, "Look. You cannot call it a two-base hit. It's either nothing at all, or it's a three-base hit. If it was foul, it's nothing. If it was fair, it's a three-base hit."

McCarthy started to say, "But the plate umpire called it foul. If Selkirk knew it was fair . . ."

I yelled, "Selkirk should have fielded the ball anyway. You learn that in the sandlots. Why didn't he field the ball first and then find out what the umpire called it?"

Summers and Donnelly talked to each other and then they said, "We'll leave it up to Dinneen." They turned to the old man.

It looked as though I was born to be an umpire right then, because Dinneen said, "Conlan is right. Let him field the ball first, and I'll make the decision after. It's a three-base hit."

It was right after that that we went to Sportsman's Park in St. Louis, where I umpired for the first time.

McCarthy had a pitcher with the Yankees a few years later named Atley Donald. Donald was a big fellow from down in the bayous in Mississippi or Louisiana. They called him Swampy. He was pretty good. He won 19 and lost 2 with the great Newark team of 1937, and in 1939 when he was with the Yankees he started off the season with twelve straight victories. In 1936, my first year of umpiring, he and I were both in the New York-Pennsylvania League. He was the star pitcher on the Yankee farm club at Binghamton, which was managed by Bill Skiff, an old pal of mine. Skiff and I had been roommates at Newark, and we were great friends. Skiff was a sound baseball man, very sensible, very solid. He managed in the Yankee system and scouted for them. They were glad to have him all those years because he was a good judge of players. He was a smart manager, too. I always thought he would end up managing in the majors.

That year he was running the Binghamton club, and Donald was his ace. I had only been umpiring a couple of months. I had never umpired anything except those games in St. Louis until opening day in 1936. Umpires didn't go to spring training in that league. On the second day of the season I umpired behind the plate for the first time in my life, calling balls and strikes. I learned what a tough job umpiring is.

I remember there was a big kid who played for Hazleton, six feet, 200 pounds, and he could run, he could throw, he could hit a ball out of any ball park. I studied him. I was still thinking like a player instead of an umpire. Heck, in my first week of umpiring I didn't even know how to put a face mask on. I had been an outfielder—I had never worn one of the things. I was really green. And I liked this kid—he looked like a real prospect to me—so I spoke to him one day.

"Bill," I said. I can't remember what his last name was. "Bill, you know I used to be a ballplayer, and I had a couple of years in the majors. I know a little bit about the game, and I think you've got a terrific chance for a great career. But do you mind me telling you something?"

"No," he said. "Go ahead. Please."

I said, "I'm down here in the minor leagues to learn how to be an umpire so I can get back up to the majors. You're down here to learn how to be a ballplayer so that you can break into the majors. We're both learning. You can run and you can throw and you can hit hard, but you have a weakness. I hope you don't mind me telling you this, but you take too many pitches. Good hitters are swingers. You stand up there with your bat on your shoulder. You keep taking good pitches on the corners of the plate. Don't take them. Swing at them. Don't let the pitcher get you in a hole. Swing at those pitches, and put the pitcher in the hole. That's the way to get to the big leagues, Bill, and the big leagues are the only place to be. I know. That's why I'm down here learning, too."

"Gee," he said. "Thanks, Jock. I appreciate that."

Two days later I was working behind the plate and the kid was up. First pitch, nice strike right at the knees, perfect. He didn't swing. I said, "Strike one." He glanced back and I looked at him. Next pitch came in just under the letters. He kept the bat on his shoulder, and I said, "Strike two." Now he turned around and I said, "Don't look back here. Get in there and swing the bat." There were a couple of waste pitches, bad balls, but then here it came right down the gut. He watched it, and I said, "Strike three! You're out."

He turned around to me and he said, "You know something, Jock?"

"What?" I said.

"You keep calling them like that, and neither one of us is going to get to the big leagues."

It was about a month or two later that I was in Binghamton, working the plate again. It was an important game because Binghamton was fighting for the league lead. George Weiss, who was farm director of the Yankees then, was there to see it. It was an exciting back-and-forth game, and at the end of the eighth inning the score was tied. Skiff sent Atley Donald in to pitch the ninth. He was using his best man in relief, but he wanted to win this game bad, what with Weiss being there. There was a big crowd, too. If you win before a big home crowd, they come back again.

Donald came in from the bullpen at the start of the ninth. He had a sort of cocky strut on him. I shouldn't criticize that because they always said I had a cocky walk, too. I didn't know I did; it was just the way I walked. Donald came strutting in and as he was walking to the mound he cursed at me and said, "You better call them right, you."

I said, *"Get out!"*

He said, "What did you say?" He was on the mound now, beginning to throw his warm-up pitches, or he thought he was going to throw them.

"You are out of the game," I said. "Get out of here."

He started toward me, and Skiff came running out.

"What did you do?" he yelled.

"I threw him out of the game."

"Jock," Skiff said. "What have you done to me? I don't have another pitcher. What am I going to do? Why did you put him out for?"

I told him what Donald called me.

He said, "Oh, my God. And you threw him out."

"I threw him out."

"What did you have to hear it for? Did you have to be listening?"

I said, "I could hear that without trying."

Skiff started to get on me a little then, and I said, "Don't you get any ideas, or you'll be gone, too."

He mumbled something and then he told Donald, "Go on. Go in the clubhouse. You're out of the game. I put my best pitcher in, and he gets himself thrown out of the game. Go on, go on."

Donald was trying to get at me, and a couple of players were holding him. They walked him off the field, and as he went he said, "I'll get you for this. I'll knock your head off. I'll be waiting for you after the game."

"Be sure you wait," I said, "because I'll be there."

Skiff was up a tree. "Look what I have to do," he said. "All my pitchers are used, and all I have left is this kid. I have to put this kid in, and he just came in from California. He just reported. I don't know whether he can pitch or not."

"All I want is his name," I said, "if he's your pitcher."

"Gay," Skiff said. "Freddie Gay."

The boy came in to warm up, and I turned around and made the announcement to the press box. You couldn't hear it. That crowd was roaring. They didn't care very much for me at the moment. Fortunately, there was a screen, a high protective screen, all around the front of the stands. If it hadn't been there, I would have been hit by everything in the park. They couldn't throw things through the screen, though some of them tried.

The first batter to face Gay was a big left-hander and *wham!* he hit a triple. I said to myself, "I'll never get out of here alive." They were yelling from the bench, "That's the way to go, Conlan. You put him on." I put him on, see? Donald is in the clubhouse, Gay threw the pitch, the batter hit it, but I'm the one who put him on.

I was worrying, too, about George Weiss being in the stands, because he was an official with a big-league club, and when a league was interested in an umpire in the minors it was always asking for reports. Here I'd thrown one of George's prize prospects out before he had thrown a pitch.

But the next batter popped up, and Gay struck the next man out. He struck him out swinging, I should add. I didn't have to call the third strike. But the next man, oh Lord, he swung and hit a line drive deep to center field that looked for all the world like it was going right out of the park.

The Binghamton center fielder was a fellow named Eddie Long-acre, a big rangy blond kid who couldn't hit too well but who could go and catch the ball with anybody. He was very fast. He turned and went back for the ball and I was saying under my breath, "Catch it. Catch it. Catch it!" Longacre went back to the fence, leaped up and took the ball one-handed, very much like the way Willie Davis caught that ball against Baltimore in the 1966 World Series. Oh, it was a beautiful catch! I never appreciated one more in all my life. If ever I felt like doing something for somebody, I wanted to do it for Eddie Longacre. I wanted to buy him a suit of clothes, anything.

Binghamton came in, scored in their half of the ninth and won the ball game. The crowd was still screaming at me, but winning had cooled them off a little, and in Binghamton you could go directly off the field to the umpires' dressing room.

That was some dressing room, by the way. You cannot imagine what it looked like. I wish I had pictures of it. It was like a place where they would put a prisoner to hold him temporarily. It was under the stands, and it had chicken-wire fencing around it, and a 15-watt bulb with a pull chain hanging from a wire. There was an old busted rocking chair that you sat on to change your shoes. We didn't actually dress there, just put on our shoes and our equipment. We dressed back at the hotel. When you came off the field you had to light a match to find the way to that cell. I was working with an umpire named Mike Murphy, and we found our way in and I started changing my shoes. Now, when Donald told me he'd be waiting for me and I said I'd be there, I did something that I never should have done, that no umpire should ever do. Leave your fights on the ball field. When a ball game is over, it's over. You start fresh the next day. Later, when I was umpiring in the National League, as soon as I made a tough decision or chased a guy, it was over right then as far as I was concerned. I didn't even wait for the next day. But in 1936 I was new at the trade. I had told Donald I would meet him, and I was going to meet him. That's all there was to that.

Murphy and I were changing our shoes, and I said, "I'm going into the clubhouse. That guy Donald said he was going to lick me. We'll see."

"Don't go in there, whatever you do," Murphy said. "You'll get killed. All those ballplayers are in there."

"Look," I said. "If you're scared, I'm not."

So I went to the clubhouse, and Murphy left for the hotel. He was a pleasant enough fellow, with a brogue. He came from Binghamton, but he sounded as though he just got off the boat from Ireland. He looked like Jack Dempsey, and you would have thought he'd have the league scared of him.

I walked into the clubhouse, and there was Donald sitting over in a corner.

I said, "I'm here, Donald. You said you were going to knock my head off. Let's go."

Donald started to get up, but Bill Skiff came running over. He told Donald to stay where he was, and he took me by the arm and started to talk to me. He had a great line, Skiff did. I had nicknamed him "Smoothie" a long time before.

He said, "Jock, the game is over. Now listen to me. I've known you a long time, and we're good friends. I want to tell you something. You know, when you started umpiring this year, you were really a pretty bad umpire. I hate to tell you that, but it's true. But now, well. You have improved so much that I think you have a definite chance to go up to the big leagues. You are really an improved umpire." He kept it up, and I had to grin.

"Old Smoothie at work again," I said.

"Now Jock," he said. "Never mind that. Here's what you do. You go back to the hotel and get dressed, and I'll be there in about fifteen or twenty minutes. We'll go get a sandwich and a cup of coffee. Okay, pal?"

I said, "Okay, Smoothie." And I left.

I never should have gone in that clubhouse in the first place. That Donald was big enough to give me a good trimming.

Several years later, after he had finished pitching, Donald became a scout for the Yankees, and I met him in Joe McCarthy's room at one of the baseball winter meetings. People always get together at those meetings and sit around and talk. Joe had invited me up and when I came through the door, Donald said, "Well, look who's here. It's Cocky."

I said, "I don't think anybody is as cocky looking as you are." I thought it was going to start all over again. But Donald just laughed and he told the story about what happened in Binghamton. When he started, I said, "Be sure to tell the truth." He said, "I will," but as he told the story all he said was that he had cussed me out, and that I had thrown him out of the game. Joe McCarthy said, "Before you had thrown one pitch?"

"Yes," Donald said.

"What did you call him?" McCarthy said.

Donald told him, and Joe said, "He was right. He should have thrown you out."

"You didn't tell him about challenging me," I said.

"What?" McCarthy said.

"Yeah," Donald said. "I told him I'd give him a trimming after the game. And the funny part was, he came into the clubhouse looking for me."

McCarthy said, "I admire that. I wouldn't respect him if he hadn't taken you up on it. What happened?"

Bill Skiff was in McCarthy's room, too, and he said, "Oh, I just gave them a nice talking to, and nothing happened."

"Yes," I said. "Old Smoothie. He smoothed things over."

I think that must still be a record, throwing a man out of a game before even one pitch was made. The closest I came to it again was when I put Del Crandall out when he was a rookie. Del broke in with the Braves in 1949 when they were still in Boston, and he was nineteen, a big, fine-looking young catcher. He was from the West Coast and when he came to the Braves the Boston papers wrote him up as another Gabby Hartnett, a good thrower, a great receiver, a strong hitter—though he never could hit like Hartnett. The papers kept saying this guy is terrific, and they had the fans all excited before Crandall ever played in Boston. He had joined the club on the road.

They came into Boston, and Crandall's folks came all the way from the Coast to see him play. And, of course, I was the umpire behind the plate. I liked Boston. All those Irishmen up there used to holler at me. I missed going there after the Braves switched to Milwaukee. It's a real city, and I had a lot of good friends there.

When they gave the lineups and announced Crandall's name, he got a tremendous ovation. The crowd loved to watch Del because he was a young fellow and so full of pep. He used to run down and back up the throw to first base more than any other catcher I ever saw. He was full of life, and he had a great deal to do with Milwaukee winning two pennants later on.

This day, though, he was too full of pep. The first pitch was a ball. Called by me. The second pitch was a ball. Called by me. After that second pitch, Crandall turned around and said, "Call them right," and he swore at me.

"Get out of here," I said.

He said, *"Get out?"*

I said, "Yes. Get out. You're gone."

He stared at me. He couldn't believe it.

Billy Southworth was managing the Braves then. I think Southworth and Eddie Sawyer, who managed the Phils to a pennant in 1950, were probably the two most considerate managers for understanding an umpire's decision. Everybody could be kicking and raging, but Southworth or Sawyer would say, "Well, now, what did you base that decision on?" You would explain it—he overslid the bag, or there was obstruction, or he tipped the bat, or whatever—and they would say, "I see. I understand. Well, that sounds reasonable. Let's go."

Southworth was a soft-spoken man anyway. He had the mildest vocabulary of any manager or player I ever knew. When I was having this little discussion with Crandall, he was in the dugout leaning over the water cooler and taking a drink before sitting down to watch the game. Some of the older players on the bench saw what was happening and one of them said, "Skipper, I think you need a new catcher."

Southworth said, "What? Oh, my." He ran up to the plate and said, "Oh, goodness gracious. Jocko, for goodness sake, what happened? Oh, gee whiz. Gosh ding it."

"Well, I'll tell you, Bill," I said. And then I said, "No, I'll let Crandall tell you. We'll see if he tells the truth."

Crandall had a high screechy voice when he got excited, and he said, "That second pitch was a strike, and I told him to call them right."

"Tell him what you called me," I said.

"Oh," Crandall said. "Well." And he told Billy.

"Oh, gracious," Southworth said. "Oh, for goodness sake. Oh, gee whiz, Del. Gosh ding it, Del. You're just a young boy, breaking into the big leagues, and you can't talk like that to an umpire in the big leagues. Oh, my. Oh, dear."

I said to Southworth, "He told you the truth, Bill."

"Yes," Billy said. "Yes, yes. Well, go on, Del. Go on. You're out of the game. Get out of here."

Crandall said, "I'm thrown out of the game in the first inning, and to think my folks came all the way east to see me catch."

I looked him right in the eye and said, "They didn't get a very good look at you, did they?"

Later, after he became captain of the Braves, whenever I worked one of their games for the first time in a season, Crandall always mentioned that incident. He'd come up to the plate with the lineup and shake his head and say, "There's the guy who made a Christian out of me. He straightened me out fast."

But he never held the incident against me. He was always real good afterward, and a good ballplayer.

6

SHOWDOWN WITH BRANCH RICKEY

CATCHERS ARE ALWAYS getting involved with umpires. It's only natural, because they are both right there with balls and strikes at the plate, and with any play at the plate. They're close to each other physically, and there is always a lot of back-and-forth between umpires and catchers.

There was a time when a catcher did me a great favor by being honest. That was Mickey Owen, when he was with the Dodgers. It was in 1943, I think, when Branch Rickey had just taken over at Brooklyn. Owen was the first-string catcher, and Leo Durocher was the manager. Johnny Allen, a hot-tempered competitor but a decent guy, I always thought, was pitching one day for Brooklyn. I was the plate umpire, and George Barr was umpiring at third base. Barr called a balk on Allen. A base umpire often does that, because frequently he can see what the pitcher is doing in his windup much more clearly than the plate umpire can. Barr called the balk, and Allen blew his top. He ran over to Barr yelling at him and he grabbed at him, and Barr fell to his knees. I can still see George losing his balance and falling and reaching up to grab his hat, which was coming off. George was bald and he liked his head covered. He wanted to put that cap back on quick.

All the Dodgers came running out and there was a big squabble. Some of them were holding Allen back, and others were yelling at Barr. I liked Johnny Allen—I had played against him in the International League—but I yelled to Barr, "Hit him. He's got no right to put his hands on you."

One of the Dodgers—I think it was Billy Herman—said, "What are you talking about?"

I said, "There isn't anybody going to put anybody down on the ground here."

"It didn't happen to you," he said.

"No," I said. "But if it does, somebody is going to get hit."

Allen was out of the game, of course. I think we all threw him out at the same time. The Dodgers were still yammering, Durocher and the rest, and I finally said, "All right, that's enough. You've been out here too long. Get back to the bench." None of them moved. They were still arguing. So I put two fingers in my watch pocket, that little pocket in the belt of the pants, and I said, "You've got two minutes to clear the field. Two minutes or I'll forfeit this ball game. If you don't think I will, just stay here."

Durocher said, "He will, too. All right, let's go." He and the rest of the benchwarmers went back to the dugout. The other Dodgers started to go to their positions, but Dolf Camilli, the first baseman, one of the nicest guys ever, came over to me. He said, "Jock?"

"What do *you* want?" I was still sore about the whole thing.

"Now, don't get excited," Camilli said. "I just wanted to ask you something."

"What?" I said.

"What time is it?"

"None of your business," I said.

He grinned and said, "I thought so," and went back to his position.

I didn't have a watch. I was bluffing.

Later, Ford Frick suspended Allen for thirty days. Frick asked me how long I thought the suspension should be. He was thinking of suspending him for a year, or for ninety days, which would have meant the rest of the season. I went to bat for Johnny. I told Frick, "Allen's not a bad guy. He just lost his temper." So Frick gave him thirty.

Something else happened because of that balk, and that's where the honest catcher comes in. It may have been the only time anyone ever had the nerve to make Branch Rickey apologize. After that game was over Rickey sent Arch Murray, a New York sportswriter, into the umpires' room to talk to me. Arch was a nice little fellow—he's dead now—but he was kind of a pigeon for the ball club. They couldn't do anything wrong. Rickey sent him in and he had Murray ask me, "On that play, why did you shake your head and tell Owen it wasn't a balk?"

I said, "What are you talking about?"

Murray said, "When Barr called the balk, you shook your head."

"Get out of here, Arch," I said. I opened the door and ushered him through it.

He said, "Jocko, we're still friends, aren't we?"

"Yes," I said. "Sure. But don't give me that baloney." And I closed the door.

I got dressed and when I left the dressing room Rickey was there waiting for me. He was angry.

"Young man," he said in that big voice of his, with his eyebrows hanging down over his face. "Young man. When Barr called that balk, Owen asked you if *you* thought it was a balk, and you shook your head No."

I said, "I did not."

He said again, "Owen asked you if you saw Allen balk, and you said No."

"I did *not*," I said.

Now, I did shake my head at Owen, but Rickey meant that I had been looking at the pitcher and had not seen him balk and therefore I thought Barr had made a mistake. What I meant when I shook my head was that I hadn't *seen* a balk—not that there hadn't been one. A plate umpire adjusts his mask and crouches to get ready for the pitch, and he looks down at the plate to get his bearings. He takes his eye off the pitcher for an instant. That's why we have three umpires—three then, four now. If Barr called a balk, Allen balked.

"You are a liar," Rickey said.

"Don't you tell *me* I'm lying," I said. "*You* are making up the lie."

67

He glared at me and snapped, "Good night," and he left.

That thing stayed with me. I couldn't sleep. I said to myself, I don't belong in this game if I'm lying. But I wasn't lying. Rickey was a big man in the league, and I'd only been an umpire in it for two or three seasons. But, I thought, I can't umpire if a man calls me a liar.

The next day, early, I went to Owen and I said, "Mickey, did I tell you that Allen didn't balk?"

He said, "No."

"What did we say to each other?"

"I asked you if you saw the balk, and you said No."

"But did I say he hadn't balked?"

"No."

I said, "Mickey, would you vouch for that with Branch Rickey? It's kind of a hard thing to ask you to do."

He said, "Jock, I believe in telling the truth."

"That's all I want," I said. "Tell Rickey the truth."

Barr and some others knew what I was planning and they said, "Don't do that. You're only going to make trouble for yourself. You could lose your job."

"I don't need the job that bad," I said.

Before the game began Rickey came down and sat in his box, and I walked over to him. I was still in my street clothes and I said, "Do you know me, Mr. Rickey?" Sometimes people don't recognize umpires in street clothes.

"Yes," he said. "I know you."

"You owe me an apology," I said.

"I do?" And the eyebrows went up.

"Yes, you do," I said. "You interpreted that balk thing yesterday entirely differently from the way it happened. I'm honest and on the square, and you owe me an apology for the remarks you made to me. If you don't apologize, I'm not going to umpire."

He gave me a long look, and then he said, "Young man, you are 100 per cent right. I found out this morning. I spoke to Owen. I was wrong. I apologize. And I admire your courage."

"Thank you," I said. "That's all I want."

I walked back and I saw Owen.

"Thanks, Mickey," I said.

"What did he do?" Mickey asked.

"He apologized."

"Son of a gun. That's all right." He went over and told Durocher and Camilli and all those guys and they said, "Hey, what do you think of that? The old man apologized to him."

Rickey was always a booster of mine after that. Just because I stood up for my rights, and because Mickey Owen told the truth.

Johnny Allen had a pretty bad temper, but he wasn't the angriest man I ever saw on a ball field. The worst—for one day, anyway—was a fellow who had a reputation for being a nice, even-tempered guy: Robin Roberts, when he was with the Phillies. Roberts was a great pitcher. He was an umpire's delight to work the plate with because he had uncanny control. The ball was always in or near the strike zone, and he had the players swinging at the ball all the time. They weren't waiting for bases on balls because Roberts didn't give up bases on balls, or very few of them. You'd get a fast ball game when he pitched, two hours or less, and a very well-pitched game, too. And no trouble. Roberts never complained, and the hitters didn't complain when he was pitching. They just couldn't hit him.

But when Roberts' arm went bad, he seemed to go bad with it. I remember this one day especially, the Phils against the Braves in Philadelphia. A play occurred in that game that happens surprisingly often in the big leagues, and yet I have never seen an infielder execute it properly. The Phils were at bat. Granny Hamner was on second base and Ed Bouchee was on first. Johnny Logan was playing shortstop for the Braves and Red Schoendienst was playing second. Only one out.

The batter hit a soft line drive to Logan at shortstop, a dying liner that was hit too slow for Logan to take it and catch either Hamner or Bouchee off base for a double play. Logan saw Hamner ducking back into second, so instead of catching the liner he backed

up and trapped it on the short hop and threw the ball to Schoendienst. Red was standing on the bag at second when he caught the
ball, which meant that the runner from first, Bouchee, was out on
the force. Then Red touched Hamner. He and Logan thought they
had a double play and that the inning was over. All the Braves did.
Eddie Mathews, the third baseman, jogged across the infield toward
the Braves' dugout.

But it wasn't a double play at all. It would have been if Red had
touched Hamner *first* and then touched second base. But when he
touched the base first, that took the force off Hamner and Granny
was entitled to stay on the base. Red could touch him all day and
he wouldn't have been out.

Vinnie Smith was umpiring at second, and he didn't see what
had happened. I was umpiring at third and I could see Vinnie was
confused, so I ran over and yelled, "Bouchee is out, Hamner is
safe."

Just about then Hamner noticed that Mathews was running in
toward the dugout, and that nobody was covering, so he took off for
third. But Schoendienst—oh, he was quick; what a ballplayer—
realized what had happened; he heard me holler, and when Hamner
broke for third Red reached out, tagged him right on the behind
and yelled, "I got him now, Jock!"

"You sure have," I said, and I called Hamner out. Mayo Smith
was managing the Phils, and he came out to me. Mayo is a very
fair, decent guy, a reasonable fellow. "What's the ruling?" he said.
I explained to him what had happened, and what I had called, and
why. He listened and he nodded his head.

"That sounds right," he said. "You mean, they just goofed up
the play in the beginning?"

"That's right," I said.

"But why did *you* make the decision?" he said. "You weren't at
second."

"Somebody had to make it," I said. "Vinnie didn't call it. I did.
That's why we have four men out here. And I got it right."

Everybody seemed satisfied, and things settled down. This was the bottom of the first inning, and we started to go to the top of the second. But now the press wanted to know exactly what had happened. They didn't know. I told Augie Donatelli, the plate umpire, and he went and gave it to Pete, the public address announcer, who was sitting right by the dugout. He was supposed to phone it up to the press box. But instead of just giving it to the newspapermen Pete announced it over the public address system.

When he heard that announcement Granny Hamner came running at me yelling that Schoendienst had never touched him. Granny thought he was out from when he had gone back to second, that it had been a double play then. He didn't understand the ruling at all. Robin Roberts, who was warming up for the second inning, came running over to me, raging mad. I never saw a wilder looking man in my life. He was shrieking at me, and his eyes were bulging out. It wasn't Roberts, the great pitcher, I was looking at. I saw a fellow who had lost his stuff. And lost his head, too. They had three or four players holding him back—the pictures in the newspapers the next day showed it.

I chased him out of the game for the language he used, and when he went into the clubhouse—I didn't see this—they claim he tore the place apart. After the game he was still furious. He wouldn't talk to the newspapermen. He wouldn't listen to anybody.

There was an old guy who had written sports in Philadelphia for years, and he had come back to report on just a few games. His name was something like Donegan, Ed Donegan, I think; he was an old-time writer. There was a big contingent of Boy Scouts at this game that day. When the newspapermen came in to see me after the game to ask me my version of what had happened, Donegan said very courteously, "Mr. Conlan, I've been writing sports for a long time, but I really don't understand what happened out there. Could you explain your decision?"

He was so nice. The other reporters were saying, "Where was he?" . . . "What happened next?" . . . "What did you do then?" . . . "Why were you standing there?" You felt as though you were on a witness stand, fighting for your life. That's the way they all do it, the reporters. They're district attorneys. But this nice old fellow asked in a pleasant way if I would explain it. So I did. When I finished, he asked, "Was it as simple as that?"

"As simple as that," I said.

Another guy with a great reputation for being nice but who wasn't always so nice was Mel Ott. I had a run-in with him once that raised such a fuss that the Giants were after my job. This was in 1941, my first year of umpiring in the National League —and the Giants were playing a doubleheader with Cincinnati in the Polo Grounds on a Sunday. The Reds had one of the best teams in the league then, and they were a big attraction with guys like Bucky Walters and Paul Derringer and Elmer Riddle and Frank McCormick and Ernie Lombardi. It was a beautiful summer day, and the ball park was packed. It was like a picnic. The fans brought their lunch. There were whole families there. They were there for a nice long afternoon of baseball.

Ott was their favorite, Ott and Carl Hubbell. They were so popular, those two, that the fans didn't even boo them in Brooklyn. I think people have forgotten what a big man Ott was in New York in those days. He had been a star with the Giants for fifteen seasons. He was the National League home-run champion, the nice guy. Everybody loved him.

Ott came up to bat in the first inning of the first game of the doubleheader, and I called him out on strikes. He banged his bat on the plate after the third strike, and he turned and yelled, "Where was that pitch?"

"It was a good pitch," I said.

"You're a liar," he said, except that he put an adjective before the word liar. A pretty interesting adjective, not one that a nice guy is supposed to use.

"Not for anybody in baseball," I said. "From Judge Landis on down to you. Get out of here. You're through." And I threw him out of the game.

Now, this was the first time in his career that Ott had ever been thrown out of a ball game. And in those days when you were thrown out during the first game of a doubleheader you were gone all day. You couldn't come back for the second game. That rule was changed later, and it was changed mostly because of me chasing Ott on this particular day. I chased him in the *first* inning of the *first* game, and here were over 50,000 people with picnic baskets who had come to watch Ott play eighteen innings.

They threw everything at me. They emptied the picnic baskets. Honestly, there was lettuce all over the field. In the second inning, when the Giants came up again—this was a full inning after Ott got chased—Babe Young, the first baseman, came to bat. He leaned over to get some dirt on his hands and—well, it had to be the biggest tomato I have ever seen in my life. It must have come from the upper deck because it came down right past my ear and *wham!* it split open on Babe Young's hands.

"I'm shot!" he yelled.

He looked at his hands and then he realized what it was, and he started shaking it off.

"I guess this was meant for you," he said.

"I don't know about that," I said. "It got you."

The crowd was on me all day. The Giants lost both games of the doubleheader and, of course, I was the guy that lost them. Baloney. What was Ott going to do? Win both games singlehanded? There wasn't anybody going to hit Riddle and Derringer that day.

But the Giants—the whole ball club, including Horace Stoneham, the owner—complained about me, and the next day, Monday, I had to appear before Ford Frick in the National League office in New York. Frick got Ott on the phone, and he put me on with him, and we gave each other a pretty good going-over.

"You had no business putting me out," he said.

"You can't call me what you did," I said. "I need this job, but I don't need it that bad. I don't take that from anybody, you included. You got such a great reputation for being a nice guy. The newspapermen all think you're a goody-goody. You didn't show it to me out on the field."

We went at it for a while, and I admit I was worried. When you antagonize an owner, you're in trouble. The owners run baseball, and if you get an owner down on you, it can be tough. There was a time the following spring, when I was out in Arizona working with the Giants, that I was worried again about my job. Umpires are assigned to a specific club in spring training, and you generally stay with that club for a certain stretch of time and work all their games. We had been in Bisbee, Arizona, for an exhibition between the Giants and Cleveland, and Horace Stoneham was sitting way out in right field in these portable bleachers. I had a double play and I called it against the Giants. It was close, but there wasn't any question about it—both men were out.

After the game we were flying back to Phoenix. We had three planes, little DC3's. I was on a plane with some of the Giants, including Stoneham. We had to wait for him at the airport; he was late, but you know we weren't going to leave without him. This was my first time umpiring in Arizona. I had been in Florida for the first part of spring training, and then I had been switched out West. We did that, switch assignments, about halfway through training.

I felt a little funny about being with the Giants because after that incident with Ott I had been rapped pretty steadily by the New York writers. But, anyway, there I was, sitting on the plane. And I had called that double play against the Giants in the game that day.

Stoneham arrived at the airport eventually, and he got on the plane. He was walking through the aisle to his seat when he saw me and stopped. He said, "That was a lousy decision you made today on that double play." He kept it up and he gave me a pretty good going-over. He could give it to you pretty good.

I was still fairly new in the league, and I didn't want to answer an owner back, but finally I couldn't stand it any longer. I said, "Where were you sitting?"

He said, "In the bleachers, down there in right field."

I said, "I thought so. Right field. That's too far away to make a decision for me. I was in close, right on top of the play."

He didn't say anything.

"Besides," I said, "I'm an umpire and you're not. You don't know anything about umpiring. You're an owner and you know how to run a ball club. But you're not umpiring for me."

He looked at me and laughed, and he went on down the aisle to his seat.

We got back to Phoenix and landed, and as we were getting off the plane Ott spoke to me. I should mention that after that time in the Polo Grounds, he and I always got along well. He really was a nice guy. This night in Phoenix he said, "Gee, Jocko, I hope you don't take anything out on us because of that thing on the plane there."

I said, "What are you talking about?"

"Stoneham getting on you like that," he said. "I hope you don't hold it against us on the field."

I said, "I'm an umpire! I don't care what people tell me, or what they say to me. That has nothing to do with my decisions on the field. Because I put you out of that game last year, do you think for a minute that I hold any grievance against you? I don't. I couldn't. If I did, I couldn't umpire."

Ott said, "Okay, Jock. That's good enough for me. I've forgotten last year."

"So have I," I said. "I forgot it when I left the ball park. Even though you guys tried to get my job."

But I was worried. No use kidding about it. Stoneham was important, one of the old owners. He had influence. If he was down on me—which is the way it sounded on the plane—I was in trouble.

I was staying at the Adams Hotel in Phoenix, right in the middle of town, where the ball clubs all used to stay. The day after that thing in Bisbee I was walking down the street, near the Adams, and here came Stoneham. I sort of stiffened. I knew he had seen me.

He came right over to me, with his hand out, and he shook hands and said, "Jocko, how are you? It's good to see you. Where

75

are you staying, the Adams? Fine. If there's anything you need, speak up and let us know. Good to see you, Jock."

I thought he was going to bawl me out again, and here he was being as nice as he could be—going out of his way to be nice. I understand it now. Stoneham likes to ride people. Every time I saw him over the years he kidded me, ribbed me. They say the only people he does that to are people he likes. I've found Stoneham to be a great guy. He has always treated me wonderfully, both in New York, when the Giants were still there, and in San Francisco.

But I didn't know this then. And that day in New York, the day after I threw Ott out of the doubleheader, I know Stoneham didn't feel too favorably toward me then. The Giants were mad, and they would just as soon have had me thrown right out of the league. It was serious enough for Ford Frick to call a hearing. I was a rookie umpire, and you have to be around a while as an umpire before you count for very much. All the New York newspapers had criticized me. Ott was sore, and the Giants were sore. There was nobody there to speak up for me.

Except one man.

Bill Klem was over in Brooklyn that Sunday, watching a game the Dodgers were playing in Ebbets Field. Klem had retired as an active umpire after thirty-six years, and he was now the National League's supervisor of umpires. He had broken me in during spring training that year. When he read in the papers about the dispute at the Polo Grounds, he came right into Frick's office.

He was there at nine-thirty in the morning. It was awfully hot. Klem had on a light blue silk shirt, and he was perspiring so much that even that early in the day the shirt was black, it was so damp. He was supposed to have gone for a preoperative examination that day; he had a hernia, and it was to be corrected. But he skipped the examination to come in to the hearing. They all were surprised to see him there. No one had told him about it.

Klem listened to all the talk, and all the accusations, and he could see that Frick was concerned. I guess I can't blame Frick.

Here was a rookie umpire and here was one of the big teams in the league all out against him. But Klem stood up, and he walked up and down in front of Frick's desk. Finally, he spoke. He was a great actor, you know. He had a marvelous voice.

"Ford," he said in that voice, walking up and down. "I was to go into the hospital this morning, but I canceled my appointment. I could not go into the hospital and leave this young man here alone to be abused or hurt. I read about the play in the Polo Grounds yesterday. I was surprised to see that Mel Ott was in the middle of it. But I know this young man. I have umpired with him. I have never seen an umpire better at handling a situation than this fellow. He's a standup umpire. Now, I want to tell you something. Many years ago, when I was his age umpiring in this league I had a situation in the Polo Grounds. I recall it as well as I'm standing here. I made a difficult call against a favorite Giant player. And John McGraw, the great manager, came out on the field, and he chewed me out. He abused me, and I threw the great McGraw out of the game. I would not take his abuse. That was the making of me as an umpire, the stand I took that day. Now, I want to tell you, Ford, that this fellow here is the best young umpire to come into the National League in years. We're lucky to have him."

He leaned over Frick's desk, and he said, "That's all I have to say." And he turned and walked out.

Well, Frick ended the hearing and he said to me, "Go on. Go ahead."

I went outside and caught up with Klem. I said, "I'll never forget you for that."

He said, "I didn't see it, you know. I was over in Brooklyn. But I read it in the paper, and I knew they'd be up here to crucify you. Like they always do."

7

BILL KLEM IN CUBA

BILL KLEM WAS the best umpire who ever lived. He made it a profession. Before Klem, umpires were treated like dirt. In the days of Jack Sheridan and Silk O'Loughlin and Hank O'Day and the other pioneer umpires, conditions were terrible. But Klem demanded respect, on the field and off, and he raised standards all around. Those other men were great umpires, too, but Klem was more of a leader than they were. He got more things established.

Klem told me that when he first started umpiring in the major leagues, he'd go into the ball park and ask where the umpires were to dress, and he'd be told, "In the toilet." And that's what he had to use. Then the umpires were promoted to the grounds keeper's shed, where the lime and the sand for the field were kept, and the rakes and shovels and wheelbarrows. This wasn't minor-league baseball. This was major-league baseball. It was so bad that the umpires would change their clothes in the hotel and ride out to the park in their umpire's suit. Klem was against that because if an umpire had a tough game—and sometimes even if he didn't—and he went out in his umpire's clothes looking for a streetcar or a taxi, the fans would jump him. Even if he was simply riding out to the park in a streetcar, the fans would get on him. He'd have to listen to all their jeering and name-calling all the way to the park.

You often hear people say that umpiring is a lonely life. It isn't that at all. It's not lonely. You meet lots of fine people. I made friends all over the country that I never would have met if I hadn't been umpiring. But it's an uncomfortable life. In any other business, if you meet somebody and they find out what you do for a living, it's accepted. Nobody thinks much about it one way or the other. But when people find out you're an umpire, they automatically feel they have to criticize you, kiddingly or seriously. You go out and work as hard and as honestly as you can on a ball field, and you're on your way home, or back to your hotel (because you never are home; you're always on the road going from one town to the next), and you find yourself being abused by strangers for doing your job the way you're supposed to do it, criticized by people who don't know the first thing about it.

It's still bad that way today, though it's a lot milder than it was when Klem was first umpiring. It got so difficult in those days that Klem said, "Why dress in the hotel and take all that ridicule? There has to be a place for us at the park." But the place was the toilet, the grounds keeper's hut, any old junky corner.

One day Governor John Tener, president of the National League and former governor of the state of Pennsylvania, said to Klem before a game, "I'd like you to have dinner with me tonight. I'll meet you up right after the last out and we'll drive back to the hotel. You'll be ready right after the game, won't you?"

"No, not right after," Klem said. "But it won't take me long. Just ten or fifteen minutes to change my clothes."

"Why don't you dress back at the hotel?" Tener said.

"Oh, no," Klem said, and he told about the ridicule and the abuse in the streetcars. He explained that they had to change at the park because of that, but then he saw his opportunity and he described the places where the umpires were forced to dress in the ball parks. "We need decent dressing rooms," he told Tener.

Tener was startled, and he did something about it. After that the umpires had their own quarters in each park. Of course some of the places were still pretty bad. The worst thing was where they were situated; in most parks you had to walk through the crowds or right along with the players on your way to or from the field. Some of the new stadiums they've built in recent years have corrected that.

But that was the sort of thing that Klem did. He fought for the umpire's rights. He insisted on the umpire's authority over the game. He argued for higher pay and better conditions.

When I went into the National League as an umpire in 1941, Klem was sixty-nine years old and had just retired, following the 1940 season. He had started in the league in 1905. I went to Havana with him for spring training. Larry MacPhail had the Dodgers training in Cuba that year, and Klem took me down there to break me in. The first game we had I worked behind the plate, and everything went fine. I never felt so good. After the game Klem came over to me and he said, "My boy, you'll do."

That night—it was a Saturday—MacPhail gave a party for all the newspapermen with the club and he invited Klem. Larry was a hothead, and he used to yell at the umpires about decisions. He screamed at Klem once, and Bill said to him, "You are an apple-head. You know as much about umpiring as my Aunt Kate, which is nothing." But MacPhail liked Klem, and he respected him. In Havana he said, "Bill, we're having a little party for the newspapermen tonight, and I'd like you to join us."

"I'd be very happy to," Klem said, "under one consideration." He had that stentorian voice and a sort of profound way of saying everything.

"What's that?" MacPhail said.

"I will come," Klem said, "if my boy comes with me."

"Who's your boy? I didn't know you had anybody down here with you."

"Jocko Conlan," Klem said.

"Oh, I'm sorry," MacPhail said. "Certainly. By all means, bring Jocko along."

I didn't even know MacPhail then. But that's the way he was. MacPhail always made you feel as if you were a good friend of his. I always liked him.

Well, we went out, Klem and I and MacPhail and the newspapermen. Saturday night in Havana, Cuba. Before Castro. Way before Castro. What a party. MacPhail took us all over Havana, to shows and to dinner and to this night club and to that one. We had a great time, and no one had a better time than Klem. I only drank

Coca-Cola, but I must have had twenty of them, because we were out all night. Klem didn't drink Coca-Colas. He drank martinis, he drank champagne, he drank scotch-and-sodas. He kept saying, "Roll out the barrel."

We ended up in Sloppy Joe's, that famous old place in Havana, and Klem had one of those big, thick, long-bun ham sandwiches and three huge steins of beer. It looked like a quart of beer in each one. It was five in the morning, and I was exhausted. Here I was young—I was about forty—and here he was old—he was pushing seventy—and he had had all those drinks. But he ran everybody into the ground. He had a cast-iron stomach. "Roll out the barrel," he kept saying.

I finally got him back to the hotel and into his room. I slept a few hours and then I got up and went to mass at eleven o'clock. I came back to the hotel and I went up to get him. The game started at two o'clock, and it was getting late.

I knocked on the door, and I heard him call, "Just a minute." Then he came to the door, opened it and looked out. His face was a brilliant red, like a ripe tomato.

"My God, Bill," I said. "What happened?"

"Come in, my boy," he said. "Come in."

I went in and steam was pouring out of the bathroom. He'd been sitting in a hot tub filled with Epsom salts, sweating it out.

"Young man," he said. He sounded like a professor. "Young man, any time while you're an umpire that you have occasion to go out the way we did last night, always be sure to have a five-pound bag of Epsom salts with you. And in the morning, take a hot bath with the Epsom salts, and sweat all that stuff out of you. *If* you ever get to the point that I did."

He got dressed, and we went out to get a cab. I was a little worried about him, Epsom salts or no Epsom salts, because he was supposed to work the plate that day. Calling balls and strikes, even in an exhibition game, is hard work. I knew what he had been through; I was kind of pooped myself.

"Mr. Klem," I said in the cab.

"Bill," he said. "You call me Bill from now on. You are my

partner. And when you are my partner, you call me Bill. Of course, I do make some of those ballplayers call me mister. But I want you to know this, my boy. You are my friend. And whatever you do, don't ever be jealous of another umpire. There's too much jealousy attached to this game. It's terrible. If one man can umpire a little better than another, if the papers give him more publicity than the other, the jealousy comes out. Never do they give him credit for how he has protected that other umpire. Never do they realize that because he has control of the game and the respect of the players, he can carry the weaker umpire, the one who may have good judgment and good mechanical ability but who does not know how to control the game."

I knew later on what he meant, not about jealous umpires, but about controlling a game. One of the nicest compliments I got from younger umpires was when they'd say, "Just having Jocko out on the field is a big help. The game moves along." I remember the compliments I've received, because umpires don't get many. The greatest I ever got was when Klem wrote me a letter after I'd been in the league five years. He wrote, "My good friend, Jocko. I will always regard you as that. . . . And I want to tell you that you are the one umpire in baseball today who could have umpired single-handed in the old days." To me that is the greatest compliment I have ever received, coming as it did from the master of them all.

But that Sunday in Havana, the master of them all was still feeling the effects of the night before. I said, "Mr. Klem," and he said, "Call me Bill," and I said, "All right, Bill."

I said, "Bill, don't you think after a rough night like you had ———"

"I had a great time," he said.

"Yes, I know," I said. "But it was a long night. Why don't you take it easy today, and let me umpire the plate?"

"No," he said. "No, no. My boy, when you have had a night like that, always have the Epsom salts handy, and *always umpire the plate*. Put the mask on. Then nobody will be able to tell whether you had a bad night or a good night."

He went behind the plate and he umpired, and it was a master-piece. There wasn't one player who questioned a ball or a strike. He was terrific. He was always dramatic, you know, a great show-man. He wasn't a *showoff;* he was just a first-class actor. All his moves meant something.

He was really marvelous that day, and none of the players real-ized how he felt. But the newspapermen did. They had been out with him. Garry Schumacher, who later became publicity man for the Giants, was a baseball writer with the New York *Journal-American* then, and his story of the game was all about Klem. It was a funny piece—I saw it later—and the headline said: KLEM UMPIRES FROM MEMORY.

He could have. Back in the early days he umpired behind the plate every day for thirteen consecutive years. He was good. John McGraw hated him, but also respected him. McGraw ran the National League in those days. There was no question about that. Different league presidents came and went, but McGraw ran things. He'd have a tough series coming up and he'd tell the league presi-dent, "Send that Dutchman over to work those games." Klem's father was German. His mother was Irish.

Klem came from Rochester, N. Y. I asked him once how he got started umpiring, and he said, "Silk O'Loughlin." Silk O'Loughlin was one of the early umpires, and he was from Rochester, too. Klem saw him umpire a ball game one day and it didn't look too difficult. He asked O'Loughlin, "Is it easy?" O'Loughlin said, "No, it's not easy. But if you think you can do it, you ought to try it."

Klem went and umpired a semipro game with O'Loughlin one day, and he enjoyed it. But that was all the umpiring he did at that time. Later, he had been out of work and he got a job tending bar in Boston. He was always a great storyteller, and I suppose he told somebody the story of umpiring a game once with Silk O'Loughlin. One day a friend came to him and said, "Can you umpire, Bill? Didn't you umpire once?"

"Yes, I did," Klem said.

"Well, there's a doubleheader in Providence, Rhode Island,"

the friend said. "And they need a couple of neutral umpires. We can have the job, and we'll get ten bucks for the doubleheader."

Klem said, "How do we get there?"

"I've got a tandem bike," the friend said. "We'll ride it."

Klem said the two of them got on the tandem bike, pedaled the fifty miles from Boston to Providence, worked the first game, worked the second game, and then pedaled the fifty miles back from Providence to Boston.

"I got back just in time to keep my bartending job," Klem told me. "And I had earned ten bucks. I said to myself, 'Why, this is easy.'"

Ride a bike 100 miles, work a doubleheader, earn ten bucks, and call it easy. He had to be a born umpire.

But he was. He was always umpiring, on the field and off. He lived and talked the game the way George Stallings did, and Casey Stengel, and John McGraw, all the old-timers. Except that Klem talked the game of umpiring.

I was in the league office one day in New York, and Klem was there. Whenever we came into New York we were supposed to stop by the league office. This was when Frick was president; when Warren Giles succeeded Frick they moved the National League office to Cincinnati. Klem was sitting there, talking about umpiring as usual.

"The whole secret of umpiring," he said, "is keeping your eye on the ball. Never take your eye off the ball, Jocko. That is the whole ball game, that little round thing. I preach that to every umpire. I preach it to the fans, too, whenever I'm talking someplace. Watch the ball, I tell them. Watch it all the time. If you do, you'll make much better decisions in the stands than you ever did before. You'll never become great umpires up there in the stands, but you'll be better than you have been. Watch the ball. Let's say there's a man on third and the pitcher is winding up and his hand hits his leg and the ball drops out of it. But you don't see it because you're watching the batter, and suddenly the umpire is waving the batter in from third base. You get all upset because you don't know

84

what's going on. But if you had kept your eye on the ball you would have seen the pitcher drop it, and you would have said, 'A balk! The run scores.' Watch the ball. If a batter hits the ball to short, follow the ball to the shortstop, keep your eye on it as he picks it up and throws it, follow it to first base and into the first-baseman's mitt. Follow it all the way, and you'll know what's happening all the time. An umpire must watch the ball; his eye will pick up the bag and the first-baseman's foot and the base runner coming down the line. He'll see it all. He lines himself up with the base and the man catching the ball and the runner. He can do it."

He got to talking about the hand signals an umpire uses. I had been telling him about Brick Owens, who was an American League umpire when I was playing. One day I topped a ground ball to the infield and I dug down to first base as fast as I could, trying to beat it out. I gave it everything I had. I really pushed, but the ball beat me to the bag by a fraction of a second. I didn't know whether I was safe or out and I looked at Owens, who was umpiring at first base. He was standing past the base down the line. He was standing there with his hands in the side pockets of his jacket, with just the thumbs sticking out. I went across that base, running as hard as I could, and I looked at Brick Owens, and I saw his right thumb move. Nothing else. He didn't say a word. His expression didn't change. He didn't move a muscle, except that his thumb moved about an inch. I blew my stack.

"Was it that easy?" I said. "Was it that easy? Wasn't it any closer than that?"

"Go on," he said. "Go on back to the bench or I'll throw you out of the game."

Klem said, "Never stand with your hands in your pockets. Put your hands on your lapels. And when you call the play, raise your arm. Spread your hands wide. Let them see it, especially on those close plays."

We left Frick's office, and we walked down Broadway. There were people all around, of course. Klem was telling a story about signals, and he stopped right there in the middle of the sidewalk.

He crouched down and he yelled, "Here comes the guy, and he's sliding into second, and I give it to him!" He gave a big wave of his arm in the out sign, and he missed hitting a man walking past by this much—he didn't miss hitting him in the back of the head by an inch.

Klem shut his mouth, stood up, straightened his coat and continued walking down Broadway as calm as you'd please. But he whispered, "I pretty near gave it to that guy, too."

He had a lot of ideas about umpiring, a lot of practical theories. He taught them to the umpires who followed him. But, and this is a strange thing, he wasn't great on rules. His strength was, he could handle situations. He could see things. He had great common sense. He didn't need the rule book. He used to say, "There's many a spot where common sense will help you more than a rule book." Like the rule that says a man must touch every base on the way round. Umpires always used to be asked at dinners and functions, "Suppose a man hits a ball out of the park for a home run, but on the way around the bases he doesn't touch second base. Can the team in the field take the next baseball that's put in play, touch second and claim that the man is out?" Klem would say, "He hit the ball over the fence? Out of the park? For me, he touched second."

There was a famous play he called once on the infield fly rule. The infield fly rule is the most technical thing in baseball, I suppose. It says, in effect, that with men on first and second, or with the bases loaded, and nobody out or one out, any fly ball that an infielder can normally be expected to handle is an automatic out. In other words, you cannot drop it on purpose and force the runners to get a cheap double play. But the runners can try to advance at their own risk.

Klem had an infield-fly call back in the '20s in Chicago. The bases were loaded with one out, and the batter hit a high foul ball. It was thirty feet foul. But it lifted above the stands, and there was a terrific wind blowing. The wind took that foul and blew it back into fair territory. The third baseman and the shortstop and the catcher were circling under it as though they were drunk; first they were way over in foul territory and then they came skittering back into fair territory. And the ball dropped between them. None of them even touched it. It fell right in the middle, between home plate and the pitcher's mound and third base.

When it fell, the fielders looked so confused that the man on third broke for the plate and tried to score. When he did, the other runners moved up, too, and the fellow who had hit the ball ran to first. But the third baseman picked up the ball in time, threw it home to the first baseman, who had come in to cover, and they got the man out.

The team in the field claimed that that made it a double play, arguing that the batter was out automatically because of the infield fly rule and that the base runner on third had advanced at his own risk. Klem ruled against them. He said that the base runner who tried to score from third was out, but that the batter was safe at first because it was *not* an infield fly. He said an infield fly was a ball an infielder could normally be expected to handle, and this fly ball wasn't. He wouldn't change his mind. The ball club protested, and they won the protest. Klem said, "Well, I'm overruled, but I'm still right. An infield fly is a ball that an infielder can handle, and there wasn't anyone in the whole damn ballpark who could have handled that one."

Common sense.

8

YOU'VE GOT TO WEAVE, JOCK

THERE WAS ONLY ONE THING that Bill Klem and I disagreed about. That was the chest protector. Klem always favored the inside protector, a chest protector that was designed to be worn under the jacket of the home-plate umpire. Klem insisted that National League umpires use the inside protector, and they did. They still do. American League umpires use the outside protector, a big thing that's worn outside the coat.

I eventually wore an outside protector, too, despite Klem, though I used an inside protector for the first ten years I was in the league. The first protector I had when I broke in, back in the New York-Pennsylvania League, was an outside protector that George Moriarty gave me, and I still had one when I got to the majors. But Klem made me use that inside job. It had been invented by the man Klem always said was the greatest umpire who ever lived, Jack Sheridan. Klem told me, "Jock, he was just about your size. He may have been ten pounds heavier, one seventy-five, maybe. But your height, five seven, five eight. He was the one who taught me how to weave."

Umpires didn't wear chest protectors when Sheridan was first umpiring. I think catchers had them then, but they were probably nothing but cotton batting sewed up. That was all right for a catcher who had a glove to protect him, but not much for an umpire. And it was a terrible-looking thing, especially strapped around an umpire. It had no dignity. It would be like wearing shin guards outside your trousers. That looks sloppy, so we wear them underneath.

"Sheridan wore a mask," Klem said, "and he umpired with his

arms folded across his chest, and that was all. He was rugged; he could take it. He had the art of weaving, of going with the pitch, like a fighter with a punch. Yet he was hit by foul balls all the time, anyway. You can't dodge them all. In one series he was hit by so many foul balls that he was in real pain. His collarbone was sprained, his elbows were cracked, his wrists hurt, everything.

"He came into the hotel at the next town he was umpiring in, and he went to the desk to register. They had this old-time tablet register, a big book with the four corners bound in red leather. It would lie open on the desk for the guests to sign, and then after a night's work the clerk could fold it up and put it away. It was about twenty inches high and twenty inches wide when it was open, twenty by ten when it was closed. Sheridan was signing this register, thinking about his aches and pains, and he felt the heavy cardboard and the leather corners. The clerk turned away to get the room key, and Sheridan picked the ledger up, closed it and held it in front of him. He opened his coat and fit the ledger against his chest. Then he called the manager, and he said, 'Do you have another one of these?' The manager said Yes, and Jack said, 'Can I buy it from you?' The manager said, 'What would you want that for, Jack?' Sheridan said, 'I've been hit too many times. I've been riding the pitches, but lately I think they've taken to shooting at me. If I had this under my coat, I'd never get hurt.' The manager said, 'Take it. It's yours.'

"Jack took it out to the park the next day, and he put it under his coat and buttoned the coat. He held the corners of the ledger with just the tips of his fingers, but his arms were folded back so they were out of the way. A foul tip came back and hit the thing, and it didn't hurt. He said, 'This is it!' And that's how it started."

Klem said Sheridan worked the rest of that season with the ledger and then in the off-season they developed a regular protector from it with straps. Klem's own protector was a little thing. It was just a piece of fiber with sponge rubber underneath, and it had no straps—just two hooks that went over his shoulder. He put that thing on in no more time than it takes to say it, and he'd call, "Let's go, boys."

But he'd still get hit. His arms would get hit. He'd hold the protector the way Sheridan did, with his fingers, but sooner or later his arms would be exposed. He got hit in the shoulders. He had his wrist broken. He had his collarbone broken. He had a hole in his chest under his collarbone that you could put your finger in.

I said, "It's a wonder you didn't get killed wearing that thing."

He said, "You've got to weave."

I broke my collarbone wearing that inside protector one day. Klem was there.

"Where did you get hit, boy?" he said.

"Right in the collarbone," I said.

"You didn't weave! You have to *weave*."

I reached out with my good arm and I poked him in his chest. I knew where that hole was. I had roomed with him. I poked it with my finger.

I said, "How did you get that?"

He lowered his voice and he said, "I didn't weave, either, that day."

I got black-and-blue weaving, though I admit it makes sense. It puts you in a better position and it did save me from getting killed half the time. But I got my collarbone broken twice, I was hit in the larynx, and in the 1950 World Series I had my elbow smashed by a foul tip. That was the end of the inside protector for me. I had worn the thing for ten years, too. I was behind the plate in the first game of the 1950 Series umpiring that big pitcher with the Yankees, Vic Raschi—boy, he was a good pitcher, and he could throw hard. He threw a fast ball, and a foul tip came back and cracked me in the right elbow. I stayed behind the plate the whole game, but in the dressing room afterwards Happy Chandler came in—he was still the Commissioner then, and he was the only Commissioner I ever saw who came into the umpires' dressing room. He said, "Let me see that arm."

They could hardly get my coat off, the elbow was swollen so. It was terrible looking; the ligaments were torn and blood vessels were broken. It was all black-and-blue. Chandler took me to the hospital himself, in his limousine, and waited for me and took me back to my hotel. I didn't sleep at all that night, and the next day I had a sling under my coat. I had my right hand sticking inside my coat resting in the sling, and nobody realized that my arm was hurt. Luckily, that Series went only four games. I was scheduled to go behind the plate again in the fifth game, and I wouldn't have been able to. I couldn't use my right arm. It didn't bother me on the bases, because I'm left-handed and I always used my left arm to signal "out." But I would have had to use my right arm for strikes.

I went home to Chicago for the winter, and I decided to do something. I took a big piece of brown wrapping paper and held it up in front of me and my wife, Ruth, pinned it on me. Then we marked an outline of a protector that would cover my shoulders and my arms, a protector I could get behind. I cut it out and took the pattern over to the Wilson sporting-goods people and I said, "I want a chest protector made like this, and I don't care what it costs." They made it. It's a balloon. You blow it up before a ball game just like you'd blow up a little beach toy. There are two straps that loop over your shoulders. I worked with my hands behind my back, and when I put my hands back there my shoulders would tighten the straps so that the protector lifted up close to my neck under the mask. I used a special mask, too, the biggest mask in the major leagues. After I got hit in the larynx that time, a fellow in New Jersey called me and asked me if I'd try a mask he'd made. It had an extra-long chin piece. Of course, it was sort of homemade, and I got hit in the chin by a foul ball one day and my chin split open as though I had been cut by a razor. I took the mask apart, opened it up and took the padding out, and where the extra piece had been added there was a ridge that stuck out about a half inch. I took the mask to a metalworking shop and had the ridge ground down smooth and put sponge rubber in and closed it up, and after that it was wonderful. I put rubber in the shin guards, too. The knee cap was nothing but fiber, and when you got hit there with a foul your knee took an awful wallop. I went over to

91

the five-and-ten one day and bought a square of that rubber that a woman uses to kneel on when she has a floor to scrub. I cut out a couple of doughnuts of rubber and put them in the part of the shin guard that fits over the knee, and that worked fine, too.

But the outside protector was my favorite. It became sort of a trademark with me because I was the only umpire in the league who used an outside protector. I had fun with it, too. One day Durocher was being very smart in the Polo Grounds when he was managing the Giants. He always did everything he could to cross up everybody. This time he was trying to have his catchers beat the umpires. He had Wes Westrum squat about a foot to the outside of the plate. The pitcher would throw a pitch that would be a strike for height and it would go straight into Westrum's mitt. It looked like a perfect strike, but it was five or six inches or a foot outside the plate. Durocher was trying to get the umpires to call the pitch a strike. If you called it a ball he'd yell, "Where was that pitch?"

This day I yelled back, "If he catches like he's supposed to and he catches pitches like that, then they'd be strikes."

"Those were strikes," Durocher yelled.

"Not with me," I said. "The ball has got to be over the plate."

I told Westrum to get behind the plate, but he said, "I got orders to stay outside it. What am I supposed to do?"

"Durocher is only hurting himself," I said. "He's not bothering me. You still have to get the ball over the plate to have it called a strike."

I was wearing the outside protector and a batter hit a foul tip that came straight back, bounced off that big balloon and hit Westrum in the back of the head. The ball could really bounce off that protector. I've seen it bounce all the way back to the pitcher. It made a big boom sound when the ball hit the protector. The crowd used to love it. I guess they thought I was killed, or at least hurt.

But the ball had never hit a catcher before. This time, probably because he was off to one side, Westrum got it right in the head. He said, "Oh, my gosh, Jock. What happened? My head is splitting."

I said, "If you stand behind the plate that wouldn't happen." And then I said, "You know, I can do that any time I want."

I don't know whether he believed me or not, but I had no more got the words out of my mouth when here comes the next pitch, and it was another foul. It hit the protector, bounced off and hit Westrum in the back of the head again. He had such a headache they had to take him out of the game. I still don't know whether he thinks I did it on purpose.

That inside chest protector was the only weakness Bill Klem had, as far as I was concerned. Otherwise, he was perfect. He did some amazing things. I don't believe it's widely known, but Klem umpired his last year or two without the sight of one eye. He was so good that no one noticed.

Though he was retired when I broke in, he would help out now and then. I worked with Larry Goetz and Beans Reardon when I was first in the league, and Beans was sick one day, so Klem filled in at third base. I was at first base. With three umpires, the two base umpires ordinarily swing back and forth to cover the three bases, depending on where the base runners are and where the ball is hit. But I told Bill that he didn't have to come over to second on a base hit, that I'd take the base runners around.

"Would you do that?" he said. "The legs are a little bad. I'll just stand here at third."

Sid Gordon was playing left field, and there was a low fly ball hit down the line—a tough ball to catch and tough to call, because you have to be sure the outfielder doesn't trap the ball. Klem started out a couple of steps into the outfield, and I went that way, too. I wanted to get a peek at the play, because I knew about Bill's eye. I was one of the few who did know, and he had told me in confidence.

Gordon trapped the ball and I saw that he did, so I called, "No! No, Bill!" The crowd was making so much noise that I couldn't be sure he heard me. I didn't see him signal that it was either an out or a hit. I turned back toward first to make sure the batter touched the base, and watched as he turned and headed for second, trying to stretch it into a double. Gordon threw the ball into second and the runner was safe. And there was Bill, over near the left-field line, spreading his hands wide in the signal that meant, "Base hit. No catch." It was all neat and simple. No trouble.

After the inning, I walked over to him and said, "Did you hear me calling 'No' on that play?"

"No, I didn't."

I said, "I didn't think you'd be able to see whether he trapped it or not."

"I didn't," he said.

"Well, how did you make the decision?"

"I didn't make the decision," he said. "Gordon made it for me. He told me."

"He *told* you?" I said.

"Not with words. With his actions. He didn't hesitate on that play. He was up and throwing that ball toward second right away. He knew he didn't catch it. And then I knew, too."

That's experience, and poise, and control. Klem didn't panic. He waited an extra moment. He had seen that play a hundred times. He knew what to look for. And he made the correct call. That's what Garry Schumacher meant when he said Klem umpired from memory.

Klem used to tell me, "Always have the answers, boy. If you've got the answers, you've got them beat." He beat Frank Frisch and Casey Stengel one day, and they were pretty quick with the answers themselves. Klem, Frisch and Stengel, three Dutchmen. This was when Klem's eyes were beginning to go bad, and Frisch and Stengel sensed it. I don't believe they knew how really bad his eyes were. I think they felt his sight was getting a little uncertain with age, and they jumped at the chance to show an umpire up, especially the kingpin. Frisch and Stengel could give an umpire a going-over, though they were never mean about it. There was nothing malicious.

Klem was umpiring a series between Boston and Pittsburgh when Casey was managing the Braves and Frisch the Pirates. He was behind the plate, and Frisch started in on him about his strike and ball calls.

"Come on, Bill," Frank kept yelling. "Get that ball up. That was a strike. Get the ball up, Bill. You must be having trouble with your eyesight, Bill."

He gave it to Klem a few times, and then Klem said, "Frank. I've listened to you long enough." He had a great way of doing this. He said, "You can leave now."

Frisch yelled a couple of other things, and Klem pointed.

"There is the exit," he said. "Go ahead. I've had enough of you for the day." And Frisch left.

About two innings later, Stengel called out from his dugout.

"I think Frisch is right," he said. "Those balls you're calling aren't strikes. You can see from here that they're high."

Klem had been getting beefs on low pitches from Frisch, and now he was getting beefs on high ones from Stengel. Casey kept it up, and finally Klem turned toward the Boston dugout.

"Charlie," he said. Stengel's first name is Charles. "Charlie, you can follow Frisch. Get out of here."

Stengel growled, "Ah, Frank's right. Lousy strike calls. Your eyesight is going."

"Go on," Klem said. "Go on. You're through."

That night Frisch and Stengel met in the Schenley Hotel in Pittsburgh, where the visiting clubs used to stay. They were great friends. They had played together on those pennant winners McGraw had had in New York in the early '20s. They sat down together and had a couple of beers.

Casey said, "You know something, Frank? There is no question that Klem was a great umpire. But he's getting old."

Frisch said, "I think so, too. I agree with you."

They drank their beer.

"I think his eyesight is going," Frisch said. Stengel said he felt that way, too. They had another beer.

"I'll tell you what we'll do tomorrow," Stengel said. "You write out your lineup in big letters, great big letters. I'll write mine out in little tiny letters, so small it'll be hard for him to read it. Then we'll see how good his eyesight is."

Frisch said, "That's a great idea. Great. We'll test him."

The next day they went up to the plate with the lineups, and Klem said, "How are you, boys?" They just scowled and muttered and didn't say anything, as if they were both still mad at being chased. They handed Klem their lineups and he held them out, the way you do when you're farsighted. He had Frank's lineup on top, the one with the big letters, and he read off the names, whatever they were that day: "Waner, Handley, Van Robays, Elliott, and so on. . . ." Right down the list. He finished it and then he slapped the Boston lineup on top. And he didn't say anything. He looked at it. He held it out there, looking at it, for about ten seconds, as though he were reading it. He nodded his head, smacked the lineups together, stuck them in his pocket and said, "Well, that's fine. Let's go, boys." And he walked away to start the game. Frisch and Stengel looked at each other as if to say, "What the hell can you do?"

"Always have the answers, my boy," Klem said when he told me that story. "They tried to stump me. I couldn't see that lineup no more than the man in the moon. But I could still umpire." And he could.

9

THE MINORS
AND THE MAJORS

WHEN I BEGAN UMPIRING in the New York-Pennsylvania League in 1936, I had no idea that someday I'd be working with Klem. In fact, I probably never thought of him at all, because he was a National League umpire and I considered myself an American leaguer all the way. I had played in the American League, and the American League had arranged for me to go to the minors to umpire, and the American League was paying part of my salary. I was sure I was going to be an American League umpire.

After that 1936 season I went back home to Chicago, and Pants Rowland came to me. Clarence "Pants" Rowland. He had managed the White Sox to a pennant and a world championship during World War I, and now he was an executive with the Cubs. He asked me to quit umpiring and take a job managing the Cubs' minor-league farm in Birmingham, in the Southern Association. Pants said, "I'll leave you there one year and then I'll bring you up to manage Los Angeles in the Coast league." Los Angeles was the Cubs' Number One farm team then. Pants said, "You're a very popular guy in Chicago, Jock, and I think you'll become a good manager. You know baseball and you like it, and I don't think it will be too long before we have you back up here with the Cubs as manager."

It seemed funny. I had always been such a rabid White Sox fan when I was a kid, and here I was being offered a job with the Cubs. When we were kids, if you got caught going over to the Cubs' park you could get killed, and vice versa. It was a tremendous rivalry.

Rowland had been an umpire for a while. He wasn't much of an umpire. Pants and I were close friends, and he was always very good to me, but it's the truth: he couldn't umpire. He was hired without experience, like Marberry. They tell a story that he was umpiring at third base one day, and Babe Ruth slid in. Rowland called him out and praised him at the same time. "Great slide, Babe," he said, "but he just had you." He helped Ruth up and brushed him off. The Yankee players were yelling about the decision and wondering why the Babe didn't put up a beef. Babe came into the dugout and said, "What could I do? I thought I was safe, but the guy was dusting my clothes off and telling me what a great slide I made. What could I say to him?"

Pants offered me that job managing and I had always wanted to be a manager. But I told him No. I said, "Pants, I tried umpiring this one year, and I kind of like it. I improved a little, and I've got to give myself another year at it. But if I don't go to a higher league after next season, I'd be interested in the offer."

"The job may not be here next year," he said.

"That's my hard luck then," I said. "But I've got to give myself another year."

And after that year I did advance. I went up to the American Association, and I worked there for three seasons. Tommy Connolly, the supervisor of umpires for the American League, scouted me several times. I was a little discouraged because other umpires who had started at about the same time I had—Bill Grieve and George Pipgras and Ed Rommel—had gone up to the big leagues already. Then, in the summer of 1940, Connolly came down to Columbus, Ohio, to watch us work, and when he was leaving he said, "Come and walk to the depot with me."

We walked along and we stopped on a bridge to talk. He said, "I won't see you again this season, Jocko, but I want to tell you that you are a finished performer." Later on I got to thinking about what he said and I wondered how he meant that "finished."

He said, "You are going to be all right for the American League." Then he asked me about my partner, Ernie Stewart, who was umpiring with me in the Association.

"I want to ask you something," Connolly said. He was a short, sort of fussy man, and he had a little brogue. "I want to ask you about Stewart. They tell me that Ernie is a bit of a rounder. That he drinks and steps out."

Connolly was there scouting both of us, and if I was a rat I could have said something that would have knifed Ernie. But what he said was an absolute untruth.

"I want to tell you something, Tommy," I said. "Ernie Stewart is a fine upstanding man, a college graduate. He's a good umpire and he's a good man. He has one child and his wife is in the family way expecting another. Anybody who told you that Stewart is a rounder is a liar, and if I were you I think you ought to go check that person out and find what *he* is."

"Fine, Jocko," he said. "Fine. I'm glad to hear you tell me that."

I figured that one out later, too. No one had ever told him anything about Stewart. He just wanted to find out *if* there was anything.

But the result was, he took Stewart up to the American League that winter. And he also took Art Passarella, who had been umpiring in the Texas League. I didn't mind about Ernie; at least, he was in the same classification as me. But when they took a guy out of a lower league and passed me by, that hurt. That hurt a lot. I was disheartened.

They hired Stewart and Passarella about the beginning of December during the winter meetings. A few days later—I remember it was the night of December 5, because the next day was my birthday—I got a phone call at midnight from Pants Rowland. I had been sound asleep and the call woke me up. I said hello, but I was too sleepy to know who it was. He said, "Meet Ford Frick at the Palmer House at one o'clock tomorrow."

I said, *"Who* is this? Quit being such a wise guy, calling someone up at twelve o'clock at night." I hung up. I thought it was somebody ribbing me because they knew how badly I wanted to go up to the majors.

Pants called me right back. I said hello again, and he said, "Now listen to me, John. I know it's twelve o'clock and that you're asleep, but I want you to listen to me. This is Pants. Do you hear me?"

I said, "Oh, Pants. Yes. I'm awake now. What is it?"

He said, "Ford Frick wants to see you in the Palmer House at one o'clock tomorrow. Call him from the lobby and then go up to his room."

Frick was the president of the National League, and I suddenly felt a lot better, knowing that the National League was interested in me.

"Does it look like I have a chance?" I asked Rowland.

"All I can tell you is, he wants to see you." And he hung up.

I got there early, and I waited three hours for one o'clock to come around. It seemed like thirty hours. I called Frick's room exactly at one. I knew Ford because when I was with Newark we had played exhibitions against the Yankees when Ford was a New York newspaperman. He was Babe Ruth's ghostwriter.

Frick said, "Yes, Jock. Come on up to my room right away. I'm in a hurry because I'm leaving for New York in a little while."

I went up and he said, "Ernie Quigley scouted you in the Association and he tells me you'll make a good umpire for the National League. I don't have time now to give you a contract, but I'll send you one when I get back to New York."

I felt great.

He said, "I don't want you to tell anyone about this for a few days. I don't want any newspapermen to know, because all of our news comes out of our office in New York. We'll announce it there."

"Can I tell my wife?" I said.

He laughed and said, "Sure, but keep it in the family for a few days."

I was happy as a bird.

Next day I came downtown again to the baseball meetings, and I ran into Tommy Connolly in the hotel. I hadn't seen him since that day in Columbus, Ohio. He didn't know that I had been hired by the National. And I didn't tell him.

"Tommy," I said. "Why didn't you take me up to the American League?"

"Now, Jocko," he said in that fussy voice. "You're a great young prospect."

"I've had five years in the minors," I said. "Three of those in the Association. And you passed over me. You took two fellows, and one of them was from the Texas League. That's a lower league."

"I'm sorry, Jocko," he said. "The American League thinks you're just a bit too short for an umpire."

"I'm too short?" I said.

"I'm afraid you are."

"Tommy," I said. "Will you do me a favor?"

"Yes, Jocko," he said. "Anything."

"Take your hat off a minute, will you?"

"Well, all right. But why? Why?"

"I want to see something," I said. He took his hat off and I turned him around so that we were both facing this big mirror that ran all the way down to the floor there in the lobby of the hotel. We were standing side by side.

I said, "How many years did you umpire in the American League, Tommy?"

"Thirty-one," he said, very proud.

"Look in the mirror," I said. "Who's taller, you or me?"

"Ah, you've got more hair on your head than I have," he said.

We were exactly the same size, except he was right: with the hair I had then, I did look a little taller.

I said, "You say I'm too small, but I'm the same size you are. You say I'm a great young prospect, but you bring up two other umpires. So long, Tommy." And I walked away.

The next day it came out in the newspapers that the National League had purchased Jocko Conlan's contract from the American Association. I was walking through the lobby and Connolly saw me.

"Hey!" he said. "Jocko! I want to speak to you."

He came over to me and he said, "Did you know yesterday

101

when you told me to take off my hat that you were going to the National League?"

"Yes, I knew it," I said.

"Why didn't you tell me?"

"Because you told me in Columbus that I was going to be all right for the American League, and then you didn't take me. So I didn't think this was any of your business."

"Hah," he said, and he walked away.

Then I ran into George Moriarty and Billy Evans, both of whom had been great American League umpires for years and neither of whom liked Connolly. The two of them grabbed me, and they were both strong men. They hustled me along between them. I was still feeling a little strange at going up to the National instead of the American, but Evans said, "Let me tell you something. You should be the happiest guy in baseball because you're going to umpire in the National League instead of the American."

"Why do you say that?"

"Because," Evans said, "you're going to be working for a man over there instead of an old woman. You're going to be working for Bill Klem. He's all umpire, and he's all man. Besides, you wouldn't last in the American League."

"Why wouldn't I?" I said.

"Because you have to make reports all the time," Moriarty said. "You have to tell Connolly what the other umpires are doing on and off the field. He watches things like a schoolteacher. You couldn't last doing that. But in the National League, you'll be under Klem. He's the best. He's the greatest of all time."

Which made me feel a lot better.

After I had been in the National League for a few years, Klem saw Connolly one day. There was a great rivalry between them. They didn't care for each other too much.

"Tommy," Klem said, "you missed the prize when you missed Conlan."

"Jocko is a good umpire," Connolly said. "He's a good umpire."

"Good?" Klem roared. "Good? Tommy, he's the best young

umpire to come into baseball in forty years. And you missed him."

I'm not making this up. Those were Klem's words. He told me, and I'll never forget them.

When I think about Connolly and "short" umpires, it makes me mad. Because the trend is still towards big men. I sometimes think that all you have to do to get into the American League is play a couple of years of pro football and then write a letter to Cal Hubbard, the supervisor of umpires over there.

I'm not prejudiced against big guys, but I'm against the prejudice against short guys. Go back in the history of umpiring and you can't show me one big man who was *better* than the smaller man. First of all, who could come up to Klem? Nobody. And he was the same size as me, exactly. Five feet seven and a half. Connolly was the American League's best for more than thirty years. He was the same size. Jack Sheridan, the one Klem said was the greatest, was the same size. Bill McGowan in the American League. Bill Stewart. Charlie Moran. Bill Grieve. Babe Pinelli. Name any big umpire who was better than them. Beans Reardon. He was about five ten. Augie Donatelli; five nine. Lots of others.

I don't say the tall men aren't good umpires, but I do say that the shorter umpire has an advantage on balls and strikes, particularly on the low pitch at the knees, the toughest call in baseball. The big guy has to bend. The short guy is down there. It's easier for the shorter fellow becouse he has the better perspective. I'll be criticized by taller umpires for saying this, but I don't care. That's the way I feel.

10

DERE AIN'T NO IN-BETWEEN

NOBODY KNOWS THE TROUBLES umpires have. For instance, when I was in the minors there was a fellow in Hazleton, Pa., who drove us crazy. He was a foreman in the mines. Hazleton was a coal-mining town. You could hear the blasts under the ground sometimes, and feel the ground shake. The mines let out at four o'clock, and the ball games started at ten after four so that the miners could get to the game. They'd come up from the pits and go right to the ball game with their faces still dirty and wearing those caps with the headlights on.

We'd come on the field down the left-field line and walk past the bleachers on our way in. It was 410 feet to the left-field fence in Hazelton, and we'd get insulted every foot of the way. Not malicious, but insults, anyway. Every day, all the way. This foreman didn't sit there. He sat in a box directly behind home plate. He wore a sun visor because the park was laid out wrong, and the sun used to shine in toward the plate. With the games starting after four o'clock and the sun getting lower in the sky, it was tough umpiring there in the first place. Then you had the foreman on top of it.

We'd come in past the bleachers, getting insulted, and when we about reached third base he'd start in. He'd cup his hands like a megaphone and talk through them in a big loud voice.

"Hello, Jocko," he'd say. "Hello, Bill. It's nice to see you. How are you feeling today? I hope you have a good game today."

When the game started, he would call every pitch, in that same loud voice. He was right behind us. The grandstand was only about fifteen feet from home plate. If you fouled out in that park you felt terrible.

"Uh-oh," he'd say. "Oh-oh. A little bit low, Jocko. You can do better than that. That one was inside. Watch that inside pitch, Jocko. Uh-oh. A little bit high." He'd call the entire ball game, pitch by pitch, both sides, nine innings, all the way. "Oh, that was a good one. That *was* a strike. That was real good. Uh-oh. That one was outside."

With the sun and that voice, it was a terrible strain. We hated to go to Hazelton. We used to talk about what we would do to him if we ever met him outside the ball park, but then we'd have to admit that he never said anything nasty, never called us names. Maybe it would have been better if he had; you'd almost feel relieved.

It got to be July, and one night in Hazleton I was hurrying for a train. Oh, those trains. Windows open, cinders flying in, everything coming in. When you got off you were filthy dirty. The players complain today how tough it is, with all the flying and night games. Listen, I was in baseball in both eras, and there is no comparison. You can have the good old days. Sure, night games and day games mixed up are tough, and flying out of airports at two in the morning is tough. But these players never rode a sleeper from Boston to St. Louis, with the cinders and the filth and no air conditiong and trying to sleep with the train rocking. Sometimes you'd be on a train for twenty-four hours. Now the longest trip they have, coast to coast, is four and one-half or five hours, and you get to sleep in a nice bed in an air-conditioned room. If they complain now, what would they have done thirty years ago?

Anyway, I was walking towards the railroad station in Hazelton, carrying my two bags, and, lo and behold, there was the foreman.

"Hey!" I said.

He turned and saw me and, as nice as you'd want, he said, "Jocko Conlan. How are you?"

"Listen," I said. "I want to ask you something."

"What?"

105

"What kind of work do you do?"

"Why, I'm a foreman in the mines," he said.

"You're in charge of guys with picks and sledges and all that stuff?"

"Yes," he said.

I said, "Every time one of your men picks up a hammer and a spike to knock a piece of coal loose, do you tell him, 'Uh-oh. That's a little too low. Oh-oh. That one's high'?"

"No," he said. "I don't do that."

"Why do you do it to us then? How do you think it feels to hear that all the time? Too high, too low. Outside, inside." I was yelling at him. I was getting ready to pop him.

"Now wait a minute," he said. "Don't get so excited. Keep your hands down. You have improved."

"What?" I said.

"You have improved so much," he said, "that I have made the prediction that you will go up to the big leagues." He was taking the sting out of me. "Don't you like me to call all those pitches?"

"No!" I said. "No. I don't like it. It's very distracting. It distracts us from our work. How can we work when on every pitch we hear you calling it behind us?"

"I'm sorry," he said. "If that's the case, I won't do it again. I want you to know that I followed your career when you were in the minor leagues and when you were with the White Sox. And I think you're going to be a big-league umpire."

So I didn't take a crack at him, and when I left to get on the train everything was peaceful and friendly.

We came back to Hazleton again about three weeks later. I was working with Bill Grieve, who went up to the American League later. We started in from the outfield and went past all those bleachers and took all those insults and we got to third base, and what do we hear?

"Hello, Jocko. Hello, Bill. Nice to see you, boys. How are you feeling?"

It was a doubleheader and Grieve worked the plate in the first

106

game. He called the first pitch a ball. "Oh-oh. That was a strike, Bill. *That* one was low. Oh, that was a good one, Bill. Calm down, Bill, you're doing good today. Oops, that was a little bit high." He called every pitch again, all the way through.

Grieve came in between games and he had his hands up to his temples and he said, "That lousy so-and-so. Nine innings. Every pitch." I had the plate for the second game and just thinking about it made me feel as bad as Grieve did. "Oh, Lord," I thought. "Now *I've* got to go out and listen to that."

I wanted to go into the stands and hit him.

We went out to start the second game, and he called out, "Jocko, nice to see you back of the plate this game. Bill, you take it easy out there on the bases." I said to Grieve, "The dirty bum. Oh, if I meet him again."

I got behind the plate, the game started, and he never said a word. He didn't call one pitch. I couldn't believe it. I finally figured out that he meant what he had said; he wouldn't call the pitches any more—for me.

I walked into the dressing room afterward and Grieve came in, all excited. "What is this?" he said. "For nine innings the guy called every pitch on me. Three hundred pitches! And he never said one word to you. How do you explain that?"

I tossed my mask into the corner and said, "Bill, class will tell." He wanted to strangle me.

Whenever Grieve and I got together later on, we'd talk about the days when we were umpiring in the minors and the fun we had down there. But there was quite a bit of action in the major leagues, too. I broke in with Beans Reardon and Larry Goetz, two of the great umpires in National League history. They were fine men, good friends of mine and good friends to each other, but they used to argue more than any other two people I ever knew. They'd argue about anything—what happened on a certain play, the taxi they took to the ball park, anything. They would get into terrible arguments. I was new in the league and new with them, and I thought they were going to end up in a fight. Goetz would get so mad the veins would stick out in his neck, like he was going to explode. Reardon would be calling him a Dutch so-and-so, and Goetz would call him an Irish this-and-that. I said, "Look, if you're going to fight, go ahead and fight and get it over with. I'll referee it." But they'd finish an argument and one would say to the other, "Where will we eat?" and the two of them would go off together like the best of friends. I thought it was an act, but it wasn't. It was a sort of continuing conversation between the two of them. I got so upset one day I told them if they didn't stop it I was going to ask to be transferred to a different team of umpires. They said, "Ah, shut up, you." I said, "Don't you tell me to shut up. Neither one of you is going to bulldoze me."

But I liked both of them very much, and they were excellent umpires, though as different as day and night. Beans was quick and lively; he loved to talk. He'd get in arguments with players. He'd swear at a player, and the player would swear back at him. I'd throw a player out if he cursed me, but Beans couldn't because he'd already cursed the player. Beans had a great sense of humor, but Goetz was more serious. Larry was a very solid, dedicated umpire. He didn't take any nonsense from anybody. He took charge. Babe Pinelli was an excellent umpire. He had good judgment. But he never wanted anybody to get mad at him, it seemed. Leo Durocher said to me once, "One thing about Pinelli—if he misses a play, he'll tell you he missed it. You wouldn't do that, would you?"

"I don't miss them!" I told him. But I wouldn't tell *him* if I did miss one. He'd run and tell the newspapermen. Besides, I wasn't out there to miss them. Pinelli was only conning Durocher when he told him that, and Durocher would fall for it. Babe would take the wind out of Leo's argument.

When I broke in with Reardon and Goetz in 1941, we opened the season in Chicago. I worked the bases for two games there. Then we went to Pittsburgh for the Pirates' home opener, and it was my turn to umpire behind the plate. The Pirates were playing the Cincinnati Reds, and the Reds were the world champions then. They'd won the National League pennant two years in a row, and they had beaten the Detroit Tigers in the World Series in 1940.

They were an important team, and they were managed by Bill McKechnie, one of the best managers of all time. He won pennants with three different teams.

This was my first game behind the plate in the majors, but it helped to establish my reputation as a strong umpire. McKechnie was a tough man with umpires. He wore spectacles and looked like a teacher and they called him Deacon Bill and Uncle Will, but he knew all the words. He could be rough on an umpire. A lot of the managers back then liked to break an umpire, shake his courage, rattle him. They thought, I guess, that if they could make an umpire a little scared of them he might make a mistake in their favor.

In that game one of the Pirates hit a ball right down into the dirt. It came back up, hit him in the leg and rolled out in front of the plate in fair territory. The Cincinnati catcher went out for it and threw it to first base and the umpire down there signaled "Out."

But I had called, "Foul ball." Which it was. It's a common play, happens every day. McKechnie wouldn't have questioned the call if Reardon or Goetz had made it, but I was a green umpire, brand-new. He came charging out of the dugout, and I spotted him out of the corner of my eye.

I pulled my mask off, spun around and held my hand straight out in front of me, like a cop stopping traffic. I shouted, "Don't you come up here! I don't need you. That was a foul ball."

He stopped cold in his tracks. He looked at me for a second and then took his cap off, bowed to me and went back into the dugout. After the game as I was going through to the dressing room McKechnie came over.

"You run a ball game like that all the time?" he said.

"Like what, Bill?" All innocence.

He smiled at me. "That's the kind of umpire I like," he said, "the one who can run a ball game." I never had trouble with McKechnie after that. He'd come up and argue, but he'd be fair. He'd make his point, but in a reasonable way.

I was the first umpire in the National League ever to fly to an assignment. Reardon, Goetz and I had worked a series in Cincinnati, and then we had gone on by train to Pittsburgh. That's the longest train ride in the world, between Cincinnati and Pittsburgh. It's one of those "you can't get there from here" trips. We were on the train all night, and we didn't get to the hotel in Pittsburgh until eight o'clock in the morning. I went up to lie down for a while because you didn't sleep much on that train, and a little later I got a phone call from Ford Frick. George Magerkurth, George Barr and Lou Jorda had followed us into Cincinnati, but Barr and Jorda had both come down with the flu and couldn't work. Frick asked me if I could get right back to Cincinnati to help Magerkurth in the game that night.

I said, "I can't get there in time by train. The only way I could do it would be to fly." Flying wasn't such a common thing then. If you flew, that was an experience. I had never flown in my life.

"Are you afraid to fly?" Frick asked.

"I'm not afraid of anything," I told him.

"Okay," he said. "See if you can get a flight and let me know."

I phoned the airport, but the plane to Cincinnati had gone. They didn't have as many planes in the air in those days. I asked around and I found a fellow with a small plane who said he'd fly me to Cincinnati for $75. I called Frick back and told him, and he said to go ahead.

"Do you have enough money?" he asked.

"Just about."

"Go ahead, then, and I'll reimburse you."

I went out to the airport and I gave the fellow the $75 and we took off. It was an old single-engined plane, and it was a lovely flight. It's only about 250 miles from Pittsburgh to Cincinnati, but it took us hours. There were storms the whole way, and I bounced around that plane like a ball. I think the pilot was lost. He was white as a sheet when we landed at Cincinnati.

He taxied up as far as he could go, and I got out with my two bags and ran for a cab. I changed into my umpire's suit on the way and when we got to the ball park, I went right in and down

110

the runway to the Cincinnati dugout. There was one out in the first inning when I got there, and the bases were loaded. Magerkurth was behind the plate, Bucky Walters of the Reds was umpiring at first base, and Chuck Klein of the Phillies was at third.

Bill McKechnie said, "You're just in time, Jock. Go right out there."

I sat down.

"No, thanks," I said. "I think I'll just stay here until the inning is over. They may have a couple of plays." But one man struck out and the other popped up and nothing happened, so to speak. Neither Walters nor Klein had a decision to make. I went out then and relieved them. The next day Magerkurth came down with the flu and I had to umpire alone. I put Bucky back at first and Chuck at third, and we went through a couple of ball games like that. We got through it very well. They did a good job for fellows who didn't know where to position themselves and who had never umpired before. You know, it's amazing. I could take almost any ballplayer and ask him to umpire and I could say "Go to your position," and he wouldn't know where to go. Ballplayers don't know anything about umpiring. They know that a fellow stands down near first base or third base, but as soon as a runner would get on base, they'd be lost. They wouldn't know where to go or what to do in order to be in position to make a correct call. There is nobody, just nobody, who knows anything about umpiring except umpires. That goes for Commissioners, league presidents, owners, managers, coaches, players and bat boys. And the bat boy may know just as much as any of them. I forgot to include fans and sportswriters. Put them in that list, too. They don't know anything about umpiring, either.

I don't say this to belittle anybody, but they've never done the job. It would be like putting me in a dentist's office and giving me a drill. I'd probably break all the fellow's teeth.

It's a hard job umpiring. Sometimes you'll find older umpires are switched in their assignments so that they'll work what might be considered a tougher series, especially in a tight pennant race.

But I always figured every game was a tough one. You have to work just as hard umpiring a game between two cellar clubs as you do with clubs fighting for the pennant. The cellar clubs are in the league, too, and they deserve just as good umpiring as the club up in first place.

There are so many things. Even rubbing up the baseballs. They use six dozen baseballs in a game, and before the game the umpires have to rub them up. It's part of our job. New baseballs are very glossy and slippery, and we take a special clay and rub it on the balls to take that gloss off. Lena Blackburne, who used to be a shortstop and later managed the White Sox, came up with some clay he found along the Delaware River, I think. He takes one-pound coffee cans and packs them with this clay and sells it to the American and National Leagues, and I guess around the minors. They tell me he gets three or four dollars a can for it. There are a couple of cans in the umpires' room in each park. A can lasts nearly a year, I'd say. The clay is dusty but you add a little water to it to make it muddy and rub it all over the baseballs. They get all black and dirty, but after you go over them and rub them around in your hands and clean the clay off, they look fine. Once in a while you have to throw a ball out because sometimes the leather is different in certain spots and it will absorb the damp clay and get a dirty spot on it that you can't get off.

It doesn't take long. So that no one could duck the job or not do his fair share, we had a practice of having the man who was working the plate rub up all the balls for that day. If the pitcher had any complaints about a ball not being rubbed up right, he could only argue with one man, not four. So the plate umpire would rub up all six dozen baseballs before the game. It would take him about twenty, twenty-five minutes, that's all.

Umpires get their assignments about three weeks ahead of time, so that they can work out their travel arrangements. You are always moving. You seldom stay in a town for more than one series, and you almost never are in the same place more than two series in a row. But I recall one year when there was a tight pennant race—

which seemed to be the rule in the National League—and our team of umpires was assigned to one Brooklyn series after another. Every time the Dodgers looked up, there we were. They won sixteen out of the nineteen games we umpired over that stretch. All ballplayers are superstitious—I am myself a little—and because they were winning with us umpiring, the Dodgers thought we were the greatest umpires ever. The same guys, if they had gone on a losing streak when we were with them, would have been yelling, "Get rid of those umpires. They're no good."

Ball teams can be very unfair to umpires. George Magerkurth once called a balk on Hughie Casey and the Dodgers got beat. Brooklyn raised complete hell because Magerkurth called the balk. It was his turn to work the World Series that year, but the Dodgers were playing the Yankees and Judge Landis turned him down and substituted Pinelli. Landis said he was afraid there'd be trouble between Magerkurth and the Brooklyn club. He got the Series the next year, but I always thought he should have fought for it the year he was supposed to have it. George should have gone to Landis and said, "Look, I don't have anything against the ball club. I called a balk because it was a balk." Though, as I look back, Mage did seem to have a lot of trouble with Brooklyn, at that. Still, it was no reason to leave him out of that Series.

Magerkurth was a big rough-and-tumble guy, but he was as fair and honest as the day is long. He was a good umpire. Some people thought he made a lot of mistakes, but he never made any more than any other umpire did. He was such a big, rough man that everybody noticed him more.

You couldn't help noticing Magerkurth. He had that red meat face, and that big voice. He'd wave his hand and say something and that would be it. Charlie Dressen was managing Cincinnati one day, back in the middle of the '30s. Beans Reardon was behind the plate and Magerkurth was out on the bases. There were just the two of them, and Mage had the three bases to cover. There was a double play, or what should have been a double play. The shortstop took the ball and flipped it to the second baseman; as he did,

Magerkurth yelled, "You're out!" and turned to watch the relay to first. Only there wasn't any relay because the second baseman juggled the ball. Mage was looking at first base and when the runner crossed the bag he hollered, "Safe." But he had called the man out at second, and never saw that the ball had been juggled.

Dressen ran out and he said, "Mage! What was the call at second?"

"Out," Magerkurth said.

"He juggled the ball at second!" Dressen yelled.

Mage looked at him with that Wallace Beery face of his and he said, "Now I'll tell you, Charlie. He came down there like this—" and he pointed at second, smacked his hands together and then pointed to first—"and there it was."

Dressen said, "There what was?"

Mage looked at him and he did it again. He said, "Well, there, and he had the ball—" he pointed at second, smacked his hands together and pointed at first—"and there it was. Safe at first."

"Look," Charlie said. "Would you do me a favor, Mage? Would you ask Reardon?"

Sometimes an umpire, if he's not sure of his decision, will ask another umpire about it. But the other umpire won't volunteer information. You don't undercut a partner. Mage was positive he was right, anyway.

"Sure, Charlie," he said. He walked in toward Reardon at the plate and he said, "Beans, Charlie here asked me to ask you about that play. Now there the ball came down and it was second base and he was there—" and he did the thing with his hands again, slapped them together and pointed toward first—"and there it was."

Beans said, "Are you asking me or telling me?"

Magerkurth turned to Dressen and said, "There you are," and walked away.

Dressen screamed, "There I am what?" But he gave up and went back to the dugout.

Magerkurth worked with Harry Geisel in the minors. They

were completely different types. Magerkurth was big and gruff. Geisel was smaller and very smooth. I told Magerkurth that the pair of them reminded me of captain's men, as they called them in Chicago back in Prohibition days. There'd be two cops. One would be a big tough guy, and he'd go in and close down a speakeasy. Then the other guy, his partner, the smoothie, he'd go around and talk to the speakeasy owner and he'd arrange to have the place opened up again. And they'd take care of him. Then the two would go off and work the same thing on some other speakeasy.

I said to Magerkurth, "That's what you two reminded me of. You were the tough guy. Geisel was the smoothie. When you call them out, they're out. But Geisel, he's smoothing their feathers. When I was in the minors and Harry was umpiring there, I'd slide into second base and he'd call me out. I'd yell, 'He didn't even tag me! The *least* you could do is wait till he tags me.' Harry would say very calmly, 'He just had you, kid. Now keep quiet. I'm recommending you to the big leagues.' You were just like captain's men, the pair of you."

Magerkurth said, "Ah, I'll throw you through the transom, you little squirt." I loved to con him.

Those old umpires were colorful characters. Charlie Rigler, for instance. He was six feet four and he weighed about 260 pounds. When John Tener was president of the National League he told Rigler, "Any time you're in town, I want you to come up to my office and see me." Rigler was a great storyteller, and Tener wanted him to come in just so he could sit there and listen to him. He'd listen to Rigler tell stories, and he'd laugh all morning long.

Rigler had a big argument one day with a New York Giant player and he ended up by punching him. John McGraw wanted Rigler fired; he wanted him thrown right out of baseball. Tener called Rigler in and he said, "Charlie, how could you do such a thing? Hit a ballplayer, oh dear. Charlie, I'm going to have to let you out. Why did you do it, Charlie?"

"Well, I'll tell you, Governor," Rigler said. "I want you to know that I kept my temper when he called me an ugly, stupid this-and-that, and I controlled myself when he said I was a blind, no-good so-and-so and every other name you could think of. That was all right. I'm an umpire. I can take that. But when he said, 'You're just as bad as that blankety-blank Tener that you work for,' I couldn't hold back any longer, Governor. I let him have it."

Tener jumped up and yelled, "You should have *killed* him!" And he wasn't fired. He was suspended for a while, though.

Another umpire with a reputation for toughness was Bill Guthrie. He looked it. He was a bull, and he was a dese-dose-and-dem guy. But he was really a lamb, a big, kind, softhearted fellow. I don't think Bill ever read a rule book in his life, but he had tremendous judgment. In baseball you'll hear the expression, "It is or it isn't." Meaning it's either one thing or another, a ball *or* a strike, safe *or* out. There is no halfway. Guthrie had his own expression for that. When a batter or a catcher questioned him on a ball or strike call and asked "Where was that pitch?", Guthrie wouldn't say it was just on the knees or it just missed the corner. He'd say, "It's eider dis or dat wid me. Dere ain't no in-between."

He was a big, rough-talking umpire, but the players liked him. They respected him. He wasn't always looking to throw a player out of the game for nothing. He'd argue with them and talk back to them, but he could handle them. Sometimes he'd tell them they weren't much good and that they were lucky to be in the league. An umpire shouldn't talk like that, and it hurt Bill in his first year in the American League. Whitey Witt was at bat one day for the Yankees and Miller Huggins was the manager. Huggins was a little tiny man, only about five feet four, but he had great dignity and he commanded tremendous respect. Guthrie called Witt out on a third strike, and Witt ripped him up and down. He used really rough language. Guthrie was pretty rough with the language himself, but he finally threw Witt out of the game. When he did he used an inelegant expression. He said, "To da backhouse, bum. You're troo." Just then Bill saw Huggins running up to the plate to see what the trouble was, and he stuck his thumb out and said, "And take dat bat boy witcha."

Huggins stopped dead and all he said was, "Bat boy, eh?" The

Yankees were pretty important in that league, and Guthrie lost his job. He didn't get back in the league for six years.

He and I were umpires together in the American Association. He was in St. Paul one time when I was working across the river in Minneapolis. Guthrie's partner was a fellow named Polly Mc-Larry, who had been a good minor-league ballplayer. St. Paul was one run behind in the last of the ninth inning when the second baseman took a ground ball and threw to first for what should have been the last out. His throw went wild and was headed for the dugout, but the catcher, who had run down to back up the play, threw his mask at the ball and stopped it. And that held the runner to first base. Guthrie was working the plate and McLarry the bases. A fellow named Babe Ganzel was managing St. Paul, and he went out to McLarry and claimed that the runner was entitled to second base. That would mean the tying run would be on second, and a hit would tie up the ball game. But McLarry said No, the man had to stay at first. Ganzel ran in to Guthrie and said, "Bill, isn't that guy entitled to second base?"

Ganzel was asking Guthrie about a rule, but Guthrie didn't know the rules. He thought Ganzel was asking him an opinion about the runner's chances of making it to second. He said, "Kid, dey woulda trown him out by tirty feet if he went."

I used to go over to St. Paul at night and sit around with Guthrie and listen to his stories. He could be pretty funny. This night I said, "Anything happen today, Bill?"

"Yeah, kid," he said. Everybody was kid to him, whether they were young or old, big or small. And he was either Bill or Bull. "We had a play out dere today and Babe Ganzel came out." He explained the play—the wild throw past first, the catcher stopping it with his mask and the runner holding at first. "Ganzel asked if da guy coulda gone to second and I told him dey woulda trown the bum out by tirty feet if he went."

"Bill," I said, "that man was entitled to second base." I was a pretty good student of the rules. I knew them. It's surprising how few ballplayers or managers do. There were only a few that I can recall: Gil Hodges, who was the best of any player I knew; Charlie

117

Dressen; Jimmie Dykes; a few others. Jimmy Gallagher, who was a sportswriter in Chicago and then general manager of the Cubs before he joined the Commissioner's office, was great on rules. As a member of the Rules Committee, Jimmy did a lot to clarify them.

Anyway, I knew the rule and I told Guthrie the man was entitled to second base.

Guthrie said, "Why do you say dat?"

"Well," I said, "Rule So-and-So says a player cannot stop the progress of the ball with any foreign paraphernalia."

He said, "What kind of *nalia?*"

I said, "The mask. The mask is foreign paraphernalia."

"Dey make dem tings here," he said. "Whaddya mean, foreign?"

"No," I said. "I don't mean that, Bill. I mean, when he throws the mask, it's not legal. He can't throw it at the ball. It's against the rules."

"Oh, I getcha," he said. "I getcha. But dat's okay. Dem dumb dopes don't know da rules."

The next day I was working in St. Paul. Bill and Polly went someplace else, probably to Minneapolis. Before the game Babe Ganzel came up to me and he said, "Jocko, I want to ask you a question."

I knew what he was going to ask.

"We had a play here yesterday," he said, and he explained the whole thing. "Now, isn't that guy entitled to go to second base?"

I said, "Who was umpiring?"

"The Bull."

"What did he rule?"

"He said he wasn't entitled to second."

"What did you say to the Bull?"

Ganzel said, "What the hell can you say to him?"

"Well, there you are," I said, and I moved away from him. Babe went back to the bench and when he got there he turned and looked out at me. He said, "And I still haven't got any answer, not from you either."

I couldn't give Bull away. Loyalty to the partner.

11

NO SECRETS
AND NO SIGNALS

TIM HURST, ANOTHER ONE of the old-timers, used to tell young umpires not to let tense games and difficult situations affect their judgment. "Call 'em as you see 'em," he told them, and that has come down as one of the famous baseball sayings. Bill Klem improved it; he said to me, "See 'em first, my boy. Then call 'em."

In other words, don't be in too much of a hurry. Take a second or so. Some umpires take even longer than that, and they torture the poor fellows who operate the scoreboards in the ball parks. Those scoreboard operators are amazing, especially on balls and strikes. I don't know what I did when I was about to call a ball or strike, but those fellows would have it up on the scoreboard almost before I knew what I was going to call. They "read" an umpire, the way a ballplayer will read a pitcher to find out some little gesture or movement that indicates whether he's going to throw a fast ball or a curve. About the only one they couldn't read was Larry Goetz. A pitch would come in and Larry would call it a strike, so that the batter and the catcher could hear him, but he would be very slow to lift his right arm to indicate it. The scoreboard men couldn't read him and they would have to wait.

Still, it's better to be too slow than too fast. I can remember only once calling a play before I saw it, and then I was wrong on it. It was in St. Louis when Ed Stanky was managing the Cardinals. I was umpiring at second and young Guglielmo was umpiring at third; he'd only been in the league a year. Red Schoendienst was playing second and Solly Hemus short. Gil Hodges was the base runner on first base. There was a slow bounding ball through the pitcher's mound, and it was going directly toward second base. I was on the first-base side of second, in perfect position to call the play, I thought. Hemus came running in from shortstop to field the ball on the infield side of second, but he missed it. It went right between his legs and kept rolling. Schoendienst was standing on second by this time and the ball rolled right up to him just as Hodges was sliding in. But at that point, Hemus, who had really been charging the ball and who couldn't stop, ran right into me. He didn't crash into me, but he completely blocked my view of second base. I could see Red, but I couldn't see the ball and I couldn't tell whether it got there before Hodges did.

I called Hodges safe. It is the only time I can remember that I was not sure when I called the play. I've made a few wrong calls, maybe, but at the time I called them I thought I was right. This time I wasn't sure. I didn't know.

Stanky and a couple of the Cardinals came out of the dugout and started running toward me, and so did Red. But before Stanky got as far as the foul line, I yelled over to Guglielmo at third base, "Did you see that play?"

He said, "Yes."

I said, "Was he safe or out? Tell me the truth."

"He was out."

"He's out!" I said. And both sides took it. Nobody argued. Later, several players on both sides complimented me on it. A couple said, "Why don't more umpires do that?" Well, maybe more umpires haven't had plays like that, where they were blocked off. That's the only one I remember in my career. What I think the players were referring to is when they think an umpire missed an open-and-shut decision. Why doesn't an umpire ask another umpire his opinion then? Because if he does, he doesn't belong on the field. If he has to keep asking the other umpire all the time, he can't umpire. Call 'em as you see 'em. See 'em and then call 'em. That's all you can do.

The players often talk about umpires having little secret signals with each other to help out on tough calls. I never had any signals with my men. If there was any doubt, or if one of them looked at me and I could see the play, I'd holler right out: "No" or "Yes." Let everybody know. Let's not have any doubt about it with sneaky little signals. There's nothing sneaky about umpiring. It's right there. Why try to hide anything?

Players talk about signals particularly with what they call "half strikes," where the batter checks his swing on a pitch that isn't over the plate, one that will be called a ball if he hasn't swung. I don't believe there is any such thing as a half strike. What are you going to do, call one-half a strike this inning and the other the next? They say that the rule of thumb is whether or not the batter "breaks his wrists" as he swings. But that is a terribly hard thing to judge. To me, you're entitled to a full swing, an honest swing. Once or twice I wasn't sure if a batter had really swung—only once or twice, that's all—but when it happened I didn't hesitate, and I didn't signal. I stepped right out and yelled to my partner, "Did he or didn't he? Tell me right out. Did he swing? Yes or no?" If my partner said, "No," then all right, it's "No." Ball two. The point is, I did it so openly that I didn't get in an argument.

Vinnie Smith was umpiring behind the plate one day when Frank Robinson was up. Frank tried to check his swing and Smitty called a strike. Robinson had great control of the bat. He could start a swing and stop dead. He tried to stop this day, but Vinnie said he had swung. Robinson gave Smith a big argument about it, and when Frank came by first base later, where I was, he said, "Did you call that one?" I told him, "I call my own pitches. I don't give signals."

Frank Robinson was unpleasant with umpires when he first came up, but he got better. He's a tremendous ballplayer, but he was never too well liked. He was too much of a competitor. He got into a fight with Eddie Mathews once. They joke a lot about ballplayers' fights—how no one ever lands a punch—but that was some fight. Robinson slid into third base hard, Mathews said something, Robinson said something and they started to fight. Mathews landed one shot on the chin, and Robinson looked like he fell off a building. It was a short fight, but it looked like one of

121

Joe Louis's. It impressed Robinson, and don't let anyone ever tell you that Frank isn't tough himself or that he hasn't got guts. He still talks about that fight. He says, I really got beat in that one.

Eddie Mathews could have been a professional fighter. I used to fight a little myself, and I refereed and judged fights; I know something about it. I saw Mathews in two or three fights on the field, and I say he could have been an outstanding heavyweight. He's around six feet and close to 200, and he's built like a fighter with those sloping shoulders. Can he punch! Everybody he tags goes down. Yet he's a decent fellow, one of the best in the league. I always had a great deal of respect for him. He had ability, he handled himself well, and he always hustled. He was a real competitor.

The worst fight I ever saw on a baseball field was in San Francisco, and when I say worst I mean it was a lousy fight. Daryl Spencer of the Giants slid into Don Hoak of the Pirates at third base—the way Robinson did with Mathews. Spencer was a very rough slider; you had to tag him pretty good or he'd knock you right out of there. It was just the way he played ball. Hoak had a reputation for being pretty tough himself. When Spencer slid into him they had a few words and then they tangled. I was umpiring at third base, and I observed all this pretty well. They came together, got their arms around each other and fell down. They never threw a punch that I could see. And just like that, suddenly there were five other fights going on. A dozen ballplayers, all on the ground, all with their arms around each other. I looked at all six fights, and I still haven't seen a punch thrown. They were lying around on the ground hugging each other. It looked like a picnic. Danny Murtaugh was managing the Pirates and Bill Rigney the Giants. I called them over and said, "You know the rules in this league. Anybody who gets in a fight on the field has to leave the ball game."

They knew the rules.

"All right," I said, "if you can get these fellows back to the dugouts immediately, I won't put anybody out."

"You won't?"

"I won't. *If* you get them back."

"Everybody to the bench!" they hollered. Before you knew it, every one of those fighters was on his feet and on the way to the dugout. I didn't throw anybody out, and we went on with the game. Augie Donatelli was working with me and he said, "You know those guys were supposed to be thrown out. What are you going to tell the newspapermen? They're going to be asking you about it."

"I don't know," I said. "I'll think of something."

After the game we were in the dressing room and five news-papermen came in, fellows from both San Francisco and Pittsburgh.

"How come you didn't put any of those guys out of the game for fighting?" they asked.

I said, "I'll tell you why. If it was a good fight, I would have thrown a dozen of them out. But it was a lousy fight. I didn't see one punch thrown. Why put them out of the game for *not* fighting?"

They ran and put that in their papers, and a day or so later I got a phone call from Warren Giles. "I read about your big ruckus," he said, "and I'm still laughing."

"You should have seen the fight."

"Well," he said, "I think you did right in not putting anybody out."

Later he had the rule changed, the one that said a player had to be thrown out automatically if he got in a fight. Now, if it's just a little scuffle you can leave them in the game. You report it, and let the league handle it—fine them, or whatever. But don't spoil the color of the game. Don't hurt the clubs or the game just because a couple of guys took a swipe at each other.

It's just common sense, as Klem always said. An umpire has to have good judgment, and he has to think fast. I once told that to my friend, Judge Marovitz in Chicago. Abraham Lincoln Marovitz, a Federal judge. I've known him since I was a kid. If I had a ball game in Chicago, he'd come out to the park and we'd go have dinner together. This one day I called a close play against the Cubs, and I ended up chasing about three guys out of the game. Afterwards, the judge came to the umpires' dressing room to meet me. It was hot in there, and I'd been behind the plate and I'd lost about eight pounds. I was still perspiring, and I was beat. It had been a tough, hard game. Now the judge was a Cub fan. He looked in at me and he shook his head. He may have been kidding, but he said, "That was a terrible decision you made out there today, Jock."

I turned on him. This was my friend, you realize, but I snapped at him. I yelled, "Look, you! When you sit on a case, you hear first one side and then the other, and they give you three weeks to make up your mind. When I have a decision to make, I have to make it *now!*"

He was startled. Then he started to nod his head.

"That's right," he said. "I never thought of that. Yes, that's right. I'll wait for you outside, Jock."

Later at dinner he said, "Wasn't that a terrible thing I did, coming in there and criticizing you?" He was the kind of man who would admit it when he was wrong, a wonderful man, and a real baseball fan. But I kidded him anyway.

"That's all right," I said. "You didn't know any better. What do you know about baseball?"

Another friend of mine in Chicago was Tom Courtney, who had been state's attorney for Cook County back when they were breaking up the mobs in Chicago. He and Connie Mack were very close, and after Judge Landis died Mack proposed Courtney's name for Commissioner. He later became a Superior Court judge. He was a tough, fair man. And stubborn. I won a $20 hat from him because he got stubborn about something that happened in the 1945 World Series between the Cubs and the Tigers. Stan Hack hit a line shot to left to Hank Greenberg, who was a great hitter and a nice fellow but a lousy outfielder. The ball hopped over Hank's shoulder and went for a double, and the winning run scored.

124

It was an extra-inning game and getting dark, and a lot of fans and newspapermen thought the ball had gone between Greenberg's legs. But I was umpiring at second base, and I saw it clearly. I met Courtney after the game and the first thing he said was, "What a butcher that Greenberg is, letting that ball go through his legs." I said, "It didn't go between his legs. It bounced over his shoulder." Tom said, "Don't tell me. It went between his legs." And I couldn't convince him.

That winter they were showing the film of the World Series and I took Courtney to the special showing they always have for baseball people. I said to Tom, "Well, we'll be able to see the ball bounce over Greenberg's ——" He said, "Jock, it went through his legs." I said, "I'll bet you a new hat." He said, "You've got a bet." They showed the film and there was a slow-motion sequence of the play. The ball hit in front of Hank and took a nice big slow-motion bounce over his shoulder.

Courtney was disgusted.

I said, "What were you looking at that day, Tom?"

"There's the umpire for you," he said. "Never wrong."

We are wrong sometimes but, as I said to Abe Marovitz, we have to make the decision *now*. We can't wait six months for slow-motion films, or sit around a press box and argue about it for ten minutes. We have to act fast.

One hot summer day the Cardinals were playing the Dodgers in Ebbets Field. I took the lineups from the managers and was just about to start the game when I noticed a big, dark cloud beyond the left-field roof. The ball park was bright, the sun was shining and the players were running out to their positions. But I saw that cloud and I said, "Go back to the dugout. The game isn't starting yet." I called the head grounds keeper over and I told him, "Cover the field."

"What's the matter?"

"Just do what I tell you," I said. "Cover the field."

They got the tarpaulin out and they covered up the infield. Just as they finished, the sun disappeared and we had the darndest explosion of rain you ever saw. It rained for fifty-five minutes. The field looked like a sea. The rule was you had to wait thirty minutes before you could call a game, and I usually called them off at thirty-one minutes. Why keep everybody sitting around? Branch Rickey came over to me and said, "Goodness gracious, don't call it yet. Please wait a little longer." So we did, and finally the rain stopped. Ten minutes after it stopped, the sun was out and they took the tarpaulin off, and you never saw a dryer infield in your life. They played the game. Rickey came into the dressing room and said, "That's the best decision on stopping a game for rain that I ever saw."

The Dodgers were happy with the umpires that day because they didn't lose that big crowd. But there were other days. Like in 1951, when Brooklyn was blowing that 13½-game lead to the Giants. They were playing the Braves in Boston the last week of the season. Boston was nothing—a real dead ball club. They finished fourth that year but they were going down; the next season they fell to seventh and their attendance was so low that they moved to Milwaukee after that.

The Dodgers had already lost a lot of that 13½-game lead, but they still had a fairly good margin going into the last week—about three games. They went into Boston and lost a doubleheader to the Braves, but then came back and won 15–5. It looked like they were out of their slump. But in the ninth inning of that game Jackie Robinson stole home. That riled the Braves. They thought he was trying to show them up. I don't think that. He was a competitor. He played to win, all the time. He wanted every run he could get. But the Braves felt he was pushing it down their throats. They were yelling "showboat" at him and all that, and in the final game of the series they hustled like the devil and beat the Dodgers 4–3.

In that final game a Boston base runner was trying to score and Roy Campanella tried to block him at the plate. Frank Dascoli, who was umpiring the plate, was in beautiful position to call the play and he said the man was safe. The Dodgers screamed. They were jumping all over Dascoli, and Campanella was so mad he threw his catcher's glove at least twenty-five feet in the air. It landed out by the mound, and Dascoli threw Campy out of the game. Now, that meant Dascoli was the complete villain. The Brooklyn sportswriters said he shouldn't have put Campanella out, that he only dropped his glove, that it slipped. I'm a witness, and he threw it. When these arguments come up, you only hear one side, and *they* never did anything. You are always hearing or reading about players who have been thrown out of a game, and the player will say, "I didn't say one word to him." Ho-ho. Sometimes—only sometimes—they really don't say a word, but then they use gestures. When I recall some of the gestures I've seen maybe they would have been better off if they had said something instead.

That day in Boston the whole Brooklyn ball club went berserk. The ball game didn't end on that disputed run—but it was the winning run. The Dodgers lost, Campanella was chased and everybody was running around screaming.

After the game Dascoli, Bill Stewart, Augie Donatelli and I went up the runway to the dressing room. The Dodgers were still yelling and raging at Dascoli, and I had to push three or four of them away. They were calling him everything. We got into the dressing room and closed the door, and one of the Dodgers kicked a hole in the door. The press said it was Robinson, but it wasn't Jackie. He was blamed unfairly. It was Preacher Roe. Of all the guys. I liked Preacher, but he couldn't lick a postage stamp. Imagine him kicking down a door.

That Boston game was the start of the final decline by the Dodgers. They sagged through that last week and the Giants caught them, and they had to go into that play-off where they got beat.

I umpired in that play-off. The National League has had only four play-offs in its history, and I umpired in all four of them: 1946, 1951, 1959 and 1962. In 1951 I was working at first base when Bobby Thomson hit his famous home run. It was a sinker; it didn't clear the left-field wall by more than a foot. What I remember most after that ball went in was Eddie Stanky. He was in the dugout, where most of the Giants were. All the others ran up to home plate and were gathered around it waiting for Thomson, but Stanky streaked right past the plate and down to third base where Durocher was coaching. Stanky jumped up on top of Leo and pounded him and hugged him, and I think they both fell to the ground. I couldn't understand Stanky going out to hug Durocher because to me they were completely different personalities.

I did something that day that an umpire should never do. I did it when Charlie Dressen came out to change pitchers before Thomson batted. Charlie was taking Don Newcombe out, and he had Carl Erskine and Clem Labine and Ralph Branca in the bullpen. I walked in to the mound and I said, "Who are you bringing in?"

"Branca."

"Branca!" I said. "A *fast-ball* pitcher?" Charlie had two curve-ball pitchers warming up, who Thomson couldn't hit. But Bobby could murder a fast ball. I shouldn't have made the remark because it wasn't any of my business, but I was really surprised.

"Yes, Branca," Charlie said, and I caught myself.

"Okay," I said, and I waved toward the bullpen and called, "Branca."

He came in and threw two pitches, Branca did, and boom. I don't want to be a second-guesser, but in the Polo Grounds when the other team had the tieing runs on base you *had* to have a curve-ball pitcher. It was 4–2 and there were two men on, and Thomson's homer made it 5–4 Giants. I never thought he'd bring in a fast-ball pitcher at a time like that.

I don't think Branca ever got over it. In 1962 or so, when the New York Mets were playing in the Polo Grounds, they had one of those Oldtimers' Days and they brought back the Giant and Dodger players who had been in the 1951 game. I was the only umpire still around, and George Weiss arranged with the league for me to come into New York for that day. I worked behind the plate in the Oldtimers' game. Now this was all in fun, this game, but when Thomson came up to bat against Branca, Ralph was all business. It was his second chance, so to speak, and he got Thomson to pop up. Bobby said, "He's throwing harder now than when I hit the home run." Ralph even brushed Thomson back a little on the first pitch.

I had a nerve talking to Dressen like that, but I did the same thing years later, when Charlie was managing Milwaukee. He had this kid left-hander, Bob Hendley, who went to the Giants and then to the Cubs. The kid had a 1–0 ball game in the eighth inning. Two men got on base and there was only one out, so Charlie came out to the mound. He was going to take Hendley out. It was the boy's first start, and he had been throwing the ball very well. I was behind the plate, and I could tell. He had control and a good curve ball and a good fast ball. I walked out to the mound. Charlie said, "What do *you* want?"

"I just want to see what you're going to do," I said.

"Well," he said, "I'm going to make a change."

"What do you want to make a change for?" I said. "He's got good control, and he's pitching good. Why don't you leave him in?"

Charlie said, "You say he's pitching good?"

"Sure he is," I said. "You're not going to bring anybody in who's going to pitch any better."

Charlie looked at me and he said, "Well, I'll be damned. Okay, kid. Go ahead."

He walked back to the bench and let the youngster stay in. Hendley got out of the jam, shut them out in the ninth and won the ball game. He told me once, "I'll never forget you, Jock. I was on my way out of the game and you told Dressen how good I was pitching, and he let me stay in."

That is kind of like the time Casey Stengel went out to the mound to change pitchers. Tom Gorman was umpiring. Casey motioned to Gorman that he wanted a relief pitcher. When he did he waggled his left arm, because Casey was left-handed. He actually wanted the right-hander to come in, but Gorman didn't know that. He called in the lefty. Casey was busy talking at the mound and he didn't notice who the pitcher was until he got there. Then he said to Gorman, "I don't want him. I want the other fellow."

Gorman said, "Casey, you signaled with your left hand. That means you wanted the left-hander."

"But I didn't want him."

"Well, you got him," Gorman said. "He's got to pitch to one man."

That's the rule. If a pitcher comes in, he must dispose of one man—whether he gets a hit or makes an out or what. The fellow pitched to one batter and he didn't look too bad, so Casey let him stay in and he ended up pitching shutout ball in relief. The next day Casey made out his lineup cards and brought them up to the umpires. He had left a blank in the space left for the pitcher. The umpires looked the lineups over and one of them said, "Casey, you don't have any pitcher here."

"Well," said Casey, looking at Gorman, "he done such a good job for me yesterday, I thought I'd let him pick the pitcher again today."

I was an umpire in six World Series and in six All Star Games, and the best play I ever saw in any of them was the one Willie Mays made in the first game of the 1954 Series against Cleveland. I was umpiring at second base that day. You remember, Willie went straight back to the bleachers in right center and caught the ball over his head running away from the plate. That was a splendid catch, no question about it, though Mays made several catches in his career that were as good or better. But what he did *after* he caught the ball was something to behold. The score was tied 2–2, and there were two men on base and nobody out. Willie caught the ball no more than ten feet in front of the bleachers—that was by far the longest outfield fence in the major leagues, that one there in the Polo Grounds—and as he caught it he spun around and threw the ball, all in one motion. His hat fell off and he fell to the ground, but the ball came in to the infield on a line all the way from the center-field fence. It kept a run from scoring that would have given Cleveland the ball game. I watched that ball come in and I said to myself, "This has got to be the best throw anybody could ever make." The catch and the throw together was the play of the series, but the throw was even better than the catch.

I saw Mays make a play during the regular season one time where he ran across into right field to pick up a ground single. There had been a man on first and he was headed for third. Mays was running toward the foul line when he picked up the ball and yet he threw it on a line to third base and got the guy. He was the only man I ever saw who could run hard one way and throw hard the other.

There was another good fielding play by the Giants in that first game of the 1954 Series. The score was still tied, and the Indians had a man on third base. Somebody hit a terrible hard grounder down to Henry Thompson, the Giants' third baseman. There were two outs and the man on third took off for the plate, trying to score. Thompson knocked the ball down but it bounced away into foul territory. He didn't quit for a second. He charged after the ball, picked it up and really fired it to first, and he got the guy for the third out. I admired the way he stayed with that play. If he hadn't, the man would have beaten the throw, the run would have scored, the Indians would have won the game, and that whole Series could have been different. Even Mays's catch wouldn't have been as important.

I liked Henry Thompson. He was a tough little ballplayer, but he was always a gentleman with the umpires. He used to call me "the banty rooster." He'd say, "Look who's here. Look who's umpiring today. The little banty rooster."

There was a third impressive thing in that game. That was some ball game. Vic Wertz of the Indians gave about as fine an exhibition of hitting that day as I ever saw. He went to bat five times and every time he hit the ball right on the nose, tremendous hits. You could hear the bat go *crack!* every time he connected. He hit a triple, a double and two hard singles; he drove in both the Indian runs, and the only time he made an out all day was on the ball that Mays caught at the center-field fence. It was great hitting.

I saw Stan Musial have a day like that, too, though not in a

World Series. He went five for five, and I think he had a homer, a couple of doubles and a triple. I was umpiring at third base, and when he came in there with the triple I went over to him. An umpire shouldn't compliment a ballplayer, but I couldn't help it.

"Stan," I said, "you're a pretty good hitter."

He smiled—he has a pleasant smile—and he said, "Yeah, I guess I am." Musial could say that without sounding conceited. He certainly was a fine fellow, never complained about a pitch, never griped at all. It was a pleasure to know a man like that.

12

THE PEOPLE YOU MEET

WE MET A LOT OF NICE PEOPLE umpiring, mostly because we moved around so much and because there were only three or four umpires traveling together. When you're on a ball team there are twenty-five or thirty people on the squad, plus newspapermen and club officials, and you're always thrown together. You generally do all your socializing within the ball club. But when there are just three or four umpires together, you find yourself meeting people outside of baseball. And good people, kind people.

Harry Nolan in Cincinnati would give umpires a special rate at the Netherland Plaza Hotel. He'd charge us $2.50 and we'd go upstairs and find that it was an $11 room. Jack Loeffler and Broadway Sam, who had the Broadway Theater Ticket Company in the Piccadilly Hotel in New York, would see to it that we had tickets to the latest shows. Jack Loeffler was a devout Giant fan. Broadway Sam was always asking me to bring him a baseball. "Bring me in an apple," he'd say. "I've got a little kid up in the hospital." He'd take us with him to visit the kids. "Bring in an apple, Jock. Bring me two." I'd say, "We're not supposed to take any of those baseballs." Sam would say, "You bring them in. You're going to make some kids happy."

Big Sam was about six feet four, and he weighed maybe 220 pounds. He'd say, "What show do you want to see tonight?" I'd laugh and say, "Oh, *Annie, Get Your Gun.*" Or, "Mary Martin and Ezio Pinza in *South Pacific.*" Because you couldn't get tickets to those shows. Sam would say, "Don't worry about it. You got a ticket." And we'd get them.

We ate at fine restaurants. Tom and Jerry's in Cincinnati. Tom

Heffernan was a sportsman, a real baseball fan. In Chicago I'd meet Maurice Cullerton, the greatest friend I ever had, at Walter Staley's, a famous place to eat in Chicago.

In New York City my favorite restaurant was Dinty Moore's. Jim Moore was the best friend I had in New York, and one of the best friends I had any place. I met him in 1941. One day that season I ran into Ernie Stewart in New York. Ernie and I had been friends in the American Association, but he had gone up to the American League and I had gone to the National and ordinarily our paths would never cross. The major-league schedule was arranged so that in the towns that had teams in both leagues then— New York, Chicago, Philadelphia, St. Louis and Boston—the American League team was on the road when the National League team was home, and vice versa. But Brooklyn was considered separate from New York, and sometimes it would happen that both the Dodgers and Yankees would be in town together. When that happened once in 1941, Ernie was working in Yankee Stadium and I was in Ebbets Field. So we got together for dinner.

I told Ernie it was my treat, and we went to Moore's. I had eaten there one time when I played with the White Sox. We had a fine meal and then the waiter asked us if we'd like dessert. Ernie said he'd have a piece of strawberry pie.

I had a $20 bill in my pocket, and the check came to $16. I didn't have too much money in those days, and the check shook me up a little bit. I looked it over and I noticed that next to "strawberry pie" it said eighty-five cents.

"Did you make a mistake here?" I asked the waiter.

"I don't think so, sir," he said.

"It says, pie—eighty-five cents."

"Well, that's correct, sir."

I said, "My mother could bake eight pies for eighty-five cents."

I guess I raised my voice a little, because a man going past the table stopped and spoke to me.

"What did you say, young fellow?"

"Who wants to know?" I said.

"I happen to be the owner of this restaurant."

"Oh," I said. I had never even seen the famous Dinty Moore before. "Well. My friend here got just a little piece of pie and you charged him eighty-five cents for it. I happened to remark that my mother could bake *eight* pies for eighty-five cents."

"How was the rest of the food?" he asked.

"It was great. The best I ever tasted."

He sat down at the table with us. "I'm glad to hear you say that. Now, you think your mother could bake eight pies for eighty-five cents?"

"Yes," I said. "I know she could."

He leaned over toward me.

"My mother could, too," he whispered. We laughed and the ice was broken.

"What kind of work do you fellows do?" he asked. I was kind of skeptical about telling him, but Ernie said, "Go ahead."

"We're umpires," I said. "He's in the American League, and I'm in the National."

"Are you now?" he said. "I used to play ball. I played against Willie Keeler and all those old-timers. You see my fingers here?" He showed us his fingers; they were all bent and busted over. "That's what I got from catching them."

I said, "It looks to me like that's what you got from missing them."

"You're a fresh one, aren't you?" he said. "What's your names?"

We told him.

"Oh," he said. "You're that tough little Irishman, aren't you? I see you chased Durocher out of there today, hey?"

"Yes," I said. "I did."

We talked baseball for a while, and then he asked, "Do you fellows get paid much, just getting started?"

"No," Ernie said, "not too much."

"You umpires should get twenty-five thousand a year."

"I wish we did," I said.

"This restaurant is kind of expensive for you, isn't it?"

"Well, yes, it is."

He said, "Listen, I don't want you boys to stay away from this place. I want you to come in here. Can you afford to pay two dollars and a half for a dinner?"

"Sure," we said.

"Well," he said, "you come in here any time you want, and eat anything you want, and that's what the bill will be: two dollars and a half."

"That's great," we said.

"But don't stay out of here. I want you around. You're my type."

And that's how Jim Moore and I became friends. Maybe two or three years later he asked me, "Did you get a raise?"

"Yes," I said.

"Do you think you can afford three dollars and a half now?"

"Sure," I said, and so it became $3.50, for a great meal. I'd go in there and Jim would come over and sit down, and we'd talk baseball by the hour. He'd bend over and say, "This is the way I used to pick up those grounders." Everybody came to that restaurant, actors, people in sports, everybody. Moore was well liked; he did nice things. He thought very highly of Hank Gowdy, the old ballplayer who later was a coach with the Giants for a long time. When Hank retired, they gave him a day. Jim Moore said, "Hank always comes in and eats with me, and this is his last year. I think I'll give him a car." This was around World War II, when it was tough to get cars. He went out and found one, paid $2,500 for it and gave it to Gowdy.

The last time he ever ate in his restaurant before he died was with me. He lived upstairs over it, and he'd been very ill. I was in town, staying at the Astor Hotel, and he phoned me. He said, "I want you to come over here tomorrow. I'm coming downstairs, and I'm going to cook you a meal." He'd been a cook first; that's how he started. The restaurant was closed on Sundays, and he was in there alone. I came over after the game, and the two of us sat there in that big restaurant by ourselves and ate and talked baseball. After he died, his daughter kept the place going. It's a great restaurant. Whenever I'm in New York, I go in there and I always feel at home. The hat-check girl and the cashier and the waiters, they all remember me and they all say hello.

I like Toots Shor's in New York, too. Toots is a big loud guy, and he likes to talk rough to people. I heard him call a Postmaster General of the United States a crumbum. Everybody was a crumbum. Toots rubs some people the wrong way, but I like him. He's never nasty. He's a friendly, congenial fellow, and he can take it as well as dish it out. He knows good food, too. At least, I used to see him eating at Dinty Moore's now and then.

I was in Shor's one night with a friend of my brother Pete, a fellow named Danny Arnstein. Toots knew Danny and when he saw me with him he started out, "There's that crumbum, Conlan. He makes lousy decisions. Always calls the Giants out when they're safe." A lot of people were listening. I was eating soup. I looked down at it as though it didn't taste good, and I said to Shor, "Why don't you go over to Jim Moore's and learn how to make oxtail soup?"

Danny said, "Tell him, Jock. That's the way to give it to him." Toots just laughed. There never was any harm in him.

You met a lot of fine people. In St. Louis there was a man named Donnelly, who had a funeral parlor, the largest in St. Louis, I think. Many years ago he was at a game in Sportsman's Park at a time when the umpires had to walk through the crowd to get to their dressing room. Some fans jumped the umpires and began to hit them. Mr. Donnelly saw the commotion and he asked, "What's going on here?" Someone said, "Oh, they're beating up the umpires."

"That's terrible," he said, and he went and found a couple of policemen. He told them to get the umpires and bring them out to his car, a big limousine. The police all knew Donnelly, and they got the umpires and brought them out to his car and he drove them back to their hotel.

From that day on for something like forty years, Donnelly

137

always had one of his limousines waiting outside the ball park there in St. Louis to drive the umpires to their hotel. When we were leaving town, he'd have us driven to the railroad station or the airport.

We all chipped in one time and bought him a very expensive watch. We had it inscribed: "To Mr. Donnelly, our friend. From the National League umpires." He told us he thought more of that watch than any other gift he had ever received.

After he died, his son continued doing it for quite a while but they eventually got to the point where they were so short of available cars and drivers that they couldn't any more, which we understood. It was great of them to do it for as long as they did.

13

TRAVELS OF AN UMPIRE

BUT EVEN CONSIDERING all the friends and all the fun, traveling is the hardest part of an umpire's life. The single worst thing is being away from home so much. An umpire doesn't see his family for six months unless, like me, he happens to live in or near one of the cities in his league. Then he gets a chance to be home for a few days whenever he is assigned to work in that city. I was lucky enough to live in Chicago. After Milwaukee came into the league in 1953 that gave me an extra chance to get home. If we had a day game in Milwaukee followed the next day by a night game, I could leave right after the day game and drive down Route 41 from Milwaukee to Chicago and be there in an hour and a half. I'd be home in time for dinner and I could spend that night and most of the next day at home. I wouldn't have to start back to Milwaukee until about four o'clock in the afternoon. Of course, if we had a night game first and then a day game, I'd stay in Milwaukee overnight because I wouldn't have been able to get home until past midnight and then I'd have had to start back early in the morning.

But even getting home like that meant you'd see your wife and your kids only about a half dozen times a season. When our children, John and Nona, were small, we'd bring them down to spring training for a month. It's easy for an umpire to do that in spring training because he is usually based with one team most of the time. But during the season it's impossible for an umpire to have his family with him. When the team broke camp and started barnstorming north, the way they did in the old days, you'd send your wife and kids on home and that's the last you'd see of them until

139

October, except for those quick visits. It's lonesome for you, and it's very difficult for your wife.

My wife Ruth is a Chicago girl. We were both twenty-one when we met. She liked baseball, and before we had children she used to come and watch the games. After the kids came along, she stayed home with them until they were pretty well grown. Somebody asked her once if it wasn't kind of difficult having people sit alongside of her at a ball game screaming things at her husband just because he was an umpire. Ruth said, "Well, they always did holler at the umpires, didn't they?" Except I think she said "shout." She doesn't use words like "holler" and "shut up." She's very refined, except that she married me. She's been a tremendous help to me, a wonderful wife, and I think she did a great job with our kids. She always had a perfect attitude for a ballplayer's wife or for an umpire's wife. She didn't like me being away and traveling so much any more than any other woman would like it; but she said, "That's your job. That's what you have to do." She always understood. When she was sick, she never moaned or complained. I've always said, and I'll say it until I die, that there is no question about it—women have more guts than men. They can swallow pain. I think if it was me they could hear me complaining from here to Halstead Street, as they say in Chicago.

It was hard for both of us, and there wasn't much money, but we managed to bring up the kids and give them both a fine education. Nona graduated from Mundelein College in Chicago and then worked for Eastern Airlines as a stewardess. Her husband, Page Watson, is a pilot with United Airlines, and they have a fine family, three boys and a girl. The girl is named Ruth after my wife, and the oldest boy is named Johnny after me.

My son John graduated with honors from Northwestern University and Harvard Law School, and then he won a scholarship to the University of Cologne in Germany and has taught at two universities. He's quite a man. He was an Army captain and a paratrooper. (I said to him, "After me spending all that money on your education, what did you go in the paratroopers for?" He said,

"I wanted to be with the best.") He served in Europe, and whenever he had a leave he'd go traveling. He was behind the Iron Curtain twelve times. He's been in eighty countries. He traveled so much because he wanted to learn things, to see things for himself. By the time he came home he was fluent in German and knew something about several other languages. Once he hitchhiked alone all the way from Germany to Capetown, South Africa. He shot a leopard in Kenya. Then he worked his way home through South and Central America.

John passed both the Illinois and the Arizona bar exams, and he's been admitted to practice before the U. S. Supreme Court. In Arizona, where we live now, he became a state senator from Maricopa County. He's a Republican. I'm a Democrat, have been all my life. When John ran as a Republican someone asked me, "Aren't you a Democrat?" I said, "I was until John ran. Blood is thicker than water, you know."

We're very proud of him.

I haven't been to as many countries as John has, but I've moved around quite a bit, too. I don't mean just in this country, though I know just about every part of it except the Northwest. But I've been to Europe; I've been to Japan; Lefty Gomez and I went on a good-will tour to ten countries in Central and South America; I've been to Mexico to instruct umpires. When I was playing with Toronto we went on an 18-game exhibition tour across Canada, all the way west to Banff and Lake Louise. The players were supposed to share in the receipts but the weather was terrible and the crowds were tiny, and we got only eighteen dollars each. We saw a lot of beautiful country, though.

I've flown well over a million miles, and I don't know how many miles I traveled by train before I ever flew. I went to Europe three different times, each time to Germany to talk about umpiring at baseball clinics that were held for the soldiers stationed in Europe, and the Air Force gave us side trips to places like London and Rome. Artie Gore went with me the first time, in 1952, and Larry Goetz and I went in 1955. In 1958 I went by myself. In 1952 we

went to Nuremberg, and the next two times to Garmisch-Parten-
kirchen, where the 1936 winter Olympics were held and where
they have the bobsled runs. What snow. We made the trips in the
winter, in the off-season. People wouldn't believe me when I came
back from Garmisch and told them I walked in streets with 180
inches of snow.

We had men from all over Europe at those clinics. At the first
one, in Nuremberg, we had the soldiers there in a big quonset hut.
All our teaching was inside. We had college coaches with us and
major-league players and everybody taught his specialty. Artie
Gore and I had 500 men to teach. We split them into two groups
of 250. Artie took one group and I took the other, and we worked
for three weeks, morning and afternoon, long hours. I found out
later that a lot of those guys only said they wanted to become
umpires so that they could get a trip and a few weeks off, but anyway they sat in and listened.

That first trip was unforgettable. We flew over in a C-54. It was
what they called a bucket job, a cargo plane. On those bucket jobs
you had to sit on side seats, like on a park bench. Nobody knew
what the cargo was, but there were two Army captains who took
turns guarding it. Everybody was guessing what it was—the pay-
roll, or some kind of atomic stuff. We never did find out. Maybe
it's just as well, because I never went through a worse ordeal than
we did on that flight anyway. We took off from New York and
flew to Newfoundland. That was nice, going to Newfoundland, but
when we got there they said we'd stay overnight. It was 20° above
zero when we landed, and in the morning when we woke up it
was 20° below. The temperature had dropped 40° overnight. And
we woke up to find the ground crew and the plane crew arguing
over whose fault it was that the engines hadn't been covered the
night before. All four engines were frozen.

It took eight hours to thaw out each engine. Not eight hours for
all four; it was eight hours for each one, one after the other, thirty-
two hours in all. So we spent an extra day in Newfoundland. Then
we took off for the Azores, and there wasn't anything wrong with

that flight except that we were seven hours overdue. I noticed a couple of guys on the flight crew whose faces were white as my shirt. We finally learned that the compass—or whatever it was—had gone bad, and that we had been wandering around lost out over the ocean.

They got that straightened out, and we flew to Paris from the Azores. We were in Paris a couple of hours and then we taxied out to take off for Frankfurt. Now, there was a stewardess on board during this flight. She was a Polish girl and she was strong and tough. Early in the flight she was demonstrating how to use the Mae West, the life jacket, and there were a lot of Government people on board. There were generals and colonels and couriers with private papers, big attorneys connected with the Government, those two captains, and most of them kept right on talking when she demonstrated the Mae West.

Finally she said, "Listen, I don't care what your rank is or who you are. I'm in charge here and I'm supposed to demonstrate how this life jacket works. If this plane goes down, you're going to need it. If you're too dumb to listen, forget it."

"I'm listening," I said. "I can't swim."

Well, in Paris we were taxiing out for the flight to Frankfurt, and all of a sudden the plane turned, taxied back and stopped. And this girl, this stewardess, said, "Everybody off the plane. Right now!"

A couple of people started to ask her why, but I said to Artie Gore, "I'm doing anything that girl says. If she says get off, I'm getting off."

They got that door open and I went down the stairs in about three steps, bump, bump, bump, and you know what? The plane was on fire.

Gasoline had leaked and one of the engines had burst into flame. They put it out, but we stayed in Paris that night. It seemed about six months since we had left New York.

The next day we flew to Frankfurt. In the same plane. We got to Frankfurt and we met the general—I think his name was

143

Thompson. We were ushered into his office, a nice office; and there was an American flag in there waving—a little fan was blowing it, you know the kind. Everybody was standing at attention, and we were sort of lined up. The general came over—he was a friendly fellow—and he went down the line, saying hello and shaking hands and saying how much they appreciated our coming over. He'd ask each one, "Did you enjoy your flight?" Gore and the others nodded and said, "Oh, yes. It was fine, thanks."

He came to me and he said, "Jocko Conlan. Well, I'm glad to meet you. I've seen you umpire many a game in the Polo Grounds. Wonderful of you people to come over here and work with our boys. How was the trip? Did you enjoy your flight?"

I said, "It was horrible."

The other guys looked startled. The general said, "What?"

"General," I said. "I don't see how they can say they enjoyed the flight. We were scared to death three fourths of the way. We came in a bucket job. We had no sleep. Our engines froze in Newfoundland. We blew the compass going to the Azores. The plane caught fire in Paris. And we landed in Frankfurt two days late. You ask me how I like it? I'm telling you the truth. It was terrible."

The general said, "I appreciate your being honest with me. And I'll tell you something. You'll not go back in a bucket job. You'll go first class, with a cocktail lounge."

I looked at Artie and the others.

"There you are, boys," I said.

And they really treated us fine.

I think the best trip I ever made was the one to Japan with the Dodgers in the fall of 1956. The Dodgers needed an umpire along, and the league assigned me. They left from Los Angeles; I joined them there. We flew to Hawaii first and played four or five games there, and then we flew to Wake Island and on to Tokyo. The ballplayers were each paid the same amount of money for the trip, plus expenses. I was supposed to get the same thing, but I hadn't heard anything about it when we left Los Angeles. We were in Hawaii five days, and I didn't hear anything there, either.

When we were in the air on our way to Wake Island, Walter O'Malley came along and sat down next to me. O'Malley was always good to me, and I liked him.

"Jocko, I'd like to talk to you," he said. He got his cigar holder out and a big cigar and he lit it, and we sat there talking baseball and about different things that had happened. Finally, he said, "I've got something to tell you, Jocko. I've been holding off a long time on it and, frankly, I feel a little bad about it."

"What is it?" I said. "Let's have it. I can take it."

He puffed on that big cigar, and he said, "The Japanese people who are sponsoring this trip don't think the umpire should get as much as the ballplayers. They don't want to pay you as much as they're paying the fellows on the team."

"Oh, is that right?" I said, beginning to get a little sore.

"I'm afraid so," he said, and he went on talking about how bad he felt, that it didn't seem right to him, but that was what had happened, and that I just wouldn't be paid as much as the ballplayers would.

"Is that right?" I said. "That's the way they feel about umpires, hey?"

"Yes, it is," he said, puffing that cigar smoke up in the air.

"Well," I said. "I'll tell you what, Mr. O'Malley. We're landing at Wake Island in a few hours, right?"

"Yes," he said. "We lay over there a couple of hours and then go straight into Tokyo."

"Do me a favor when we get there," I said. "Arrange for a ticket for me right back to Chicago. If I'm not worth as much as these ballplayers, I don't want to go to Japan. And I won't go."

He gave me that O'Malley look for a minute, and then he started to laugh.

"That's just how I figured you, Jocko." He reached in his inside coat pocket and pulled out an envelope. "Here's your check, Mr. Conlan. Same as the ballplayers."

He'd had it all the time, all the way from Brooklyn to Los

145

Angeles to Hawaii to halfway to Wake Island. He just wanted to needle me, get my Irish up.

"Jocko," he said, "I wouldn't like you half as much if you hadn't taken that attitude."

In Japan, before every game, the ballplayers lined up along the base lines—the Dodgers on one base line, the Japanese on the other. Each player was introduced and so were different Japanese dignitaries and O'Malley and Walter Alston and the Japanese manager. When they did that before the first game they played, I was sitting on a little chair next to the dugout, just waiting and watching while the ceremonies were going on. And O'Malley stopped them. He said, "Just a moment." He told Walter Alston, "Go bring Jocko out here. He should be introduced, too."

And, do you know, I got the biggest hand of the whole crowd. They love an umpire in Japan. They respect him. The umpire is a big man. In Japan they called me "Ichi-ban." Ichi-ban means Number One, the best. That's all I got: Ichi-ban, Ichi-ban. Big Don Newcombe, the pitcher, got such a kick out of it that he started calling me Ichi-ban. Later on, I was working in Cincinnati after the Dodgers had sent Newk to the Reds, and he kept it up all one afternoon from the dugout: "Hey, Ichi-ban! Oh, Ichi-baaaaaan." Then he started saying, "Throw me out of here, Ichi-ban. Too hot here today, Ichi-ban. Throw me out of the ball game. Get me out of here, Ichi-ban." He aggravated me so much that I finally yelled, "Go on and get out. Get out of here."

Fred Hutchinson was managing the Reds then. I admired and respected Hutch, though he was a tough guy with umpires. He said, "What did you throw him out for?"

I said, "I just got tired listening to him. Ichi-ban, Ichi-ban. We're in America, not in Japan."

"I might need him for a pinch hitter," he said.

"Well, control your ballplayers then. You're the manager."

He went back. Didn't argue too much, either. I think maybe Hutch thought Ichi-ban meant something bad.

Hutch was a good man, a great man, but what a temper. There

146

was another time in Cincinnati when Warren Giles was at the game and Hutchinson came out to the mound to talk to his pitcher. When a manager does that, an umpire should always come out and hurry him up. Don't let the game be delayed too long just so the manager can hold a conference. This day, Mel Steiner, who was in only his first or second year umpiring in the National League, stuck his head into the meeting, and you could hear Hutchinson's voice all over the ball park. He yelled, "Get the hell out of here!" Steiner backed off. It looked like Hutch scared him, which he could do. "Just trying to get the game going," Steiner said. Ken Burkhart came in from first base then and had a few words with Hutchinson, and then I came in from third.

Hutch said, "I don't want anybody listening to what I have to say."

I said, "You've been out here long enough. I'm going back to third base, and if you're still here when I turn around, you're gone. And I'm not going to take too many steps." I walked away from the mound about five steps toward third and I started to turn around. Hutch said, "I'm going!" And he walked off. Warren Giles said later, "I don't know what you said to him, but I never saw a guy move so fast."

That trip to Japan was something. For years afterwards, right up until I retired, Pee Wee Reese and Gil Hodges and Duke Snider and Ed Roebuck and Newcombe and Roy Campanella— whenever I saw him at an affair—and Don Drysdale and Sandy Koufax, who were just youngsters with the Dodgers then, all used to kid me. They'd say, "Hey, Jock. How about that game you called off in the rain? What about that game in Osaka, Jock? You really called that one off, didn't you, Jock?" The wise guys.

It was about the seventh inning, and it had been raining all through this game in Osaka. Terrible weather to play ball in, but it was a big stadium and it was filled: forty-fifty thousand people. Some of them had come down from the hills on donkeys to see the game, and the Japanese officials didn't want to call it off.

The crowds were strange in Japan. They sat on their hands. They didn't applaud. If the play was good, they went, "M-m-m-m-m-m." A high-pitched sound. A weird sound. And if they didn't like something, they made the same sound, "M-m-m-m-m-m." It was eerie.

Now, they had a long press box right at ground level; it extended practically from one dugout to the other. You could have fitted one hundred writers in it. Before the game I had been over there talking to a handful of Japanese—officials, I guess, and newspapermen. They spoke English well enough. They were worried about the rain, and they said, "We'd like to play this game. It means so much to us. This big crowd."

"We'll get it in," I said. "Don't worry about it."

That's fine, they said. That's fine. But they kept asking me. They must have asked me at least five times about it.

I said, "Don't worry about it. I know about rain. I've had rainy days all my life in the big leagues. I'll get the game in for you."

Fine, fine.

It got to about the sixth inning. It was sloppy as the devil, and it was beginning to get dark. I decided to ask them to put on the lights. I went over to the press box, that ground-level press box, and I said, "Who's in charge of the lights?"

Nobody could talk English. All I got was, *"In-gow-oo-saka-mota. Gara-su."*

"Where did everybody go?" I said. "There were ten fellows here before who could talk English."

"Funa-saka-ga. Nika-tung-bow-du."

"Look, one of you guys can talk English, can't you? Who puts on the lights? It's dark! We need lights."

Nothing. *"Kow-too-nika-saka. Chichi-san-funa-doo."*

I almost blew my stack. Oh, I said, isn't this something. I went back to the plate and worked another inning, but at the end of the seventh it was raining too hard. I turned around and called time, and we went in the dugout. We waited, and it didn't get any better. The playing field was a mess, and now it was really dark. But nobody had left the ball park. Fifty thousand people, and every one is sitting there in the rain, waiting.

We waited a long time. Finally I stepped out of the dugout, raised my arms and signaled that it was all over. "This game is called," I said.

Oh, boy. Now the fellows who could speak English suddenly appeared. "No," they said. "Don't call it off. These people are here to see the whole game. You can't call it off."

I said, "You can't play in this. The game is off. I don't care what the people do. I called it off, and it's off."

They were arguing with me, and out of the crowd came that sound: "M-m-m-m-m-m." From all over the place, "M-m-m-m-m-m." They didn't like the idea of the game being called off. I can't tell you how strange that sounded, coming from all those people huddled in the stands, with the rain coming down, and the sky getting darker and darker.

I was standing in the Dodger dugout, out of the rain, and Roy Campanella said, "Jock, them people mean it. If we leave now, we'll all get killed."

I said, "I don't care. I called it."

They kept making that sound, and the Japanese officials were still arguing with me. Big Newcombe said, "Jock, old boy. We got to play." I said, "If you play, let the Japanese umpire. As far as I'm concerned, the game's over." Then Pee Wee Reese came over, and Gil Hodges. Reese sort of grinned at me and he said, "We're going to play it. Come on, John." And I gave in. I reversed my decision, I uncalled the game. We went back on the field.

It was dark and raining, and Duke Snider was the first batter.

"Start swinging, Snider," I said. I wasn't looking for any three-and-two counts in that rain. The first pitch came in about chin high, and he took it.

"Strike!" I yelled.

"Hey, that was high," Duke said.

"I told you to start swinging," I said. "You were the guys who wanted to play. Let's go. I called it once, and I'm not calling it again. You're going to finish. So you better swing."

They started swinging, to get it over with, and they end up hitting everything right on the nose and they scored six times! I thought they'd never stop scoring runs. And after that, for ten years, every time I went near the Dodgers I'd get, "M-m-m-m-m-m. You going to call the game, Jock? M-m-m-m-m-m."

I ran an umpiring clinic in Japan on that trip. The commissioner of baseball over there was a fellow named Isao Odachi. He spoke beautiful English, and he was a judo champion and everything. A wonderful fellow. He worked for an oil company, but baseball was what he loved. Ever since then I've sent him information on rule changes and things like that to keep him up to date. He asked me to conduct a clinic for the umpires. Dutch—they called him Dutch Odachi—interpreted for me. I spoke for four hours straight, using a blackboard to illustrate things. What an audience. They listened to every word. I never saw more intense listeners. They were interested in everything, every last detail. They're good umpires, the Japanese. They're very serious. They know how to position themselves. I don't think they take charge of a ball game the way they should, but over there it isn't as necessary because the umpire is very respected and his decision is accepted.

I spoke for four hours and then I turned to Odachi and I said, "I guess that's it, Dutch. I'm about worn out." He spoke to them in Japanese and they all started yammering and he turned back to me and said, "They want to know why you want to stop."

"Why?" I said. "They want to know why? I've been talking for four hours, that's why."

"I know that, Jock," he said, "but they want more."

I talked for another half hour. Four and a half hours straight, I talked. Oh, they love baseball there. We were pulling into a train depot one morning at seven o'clock and we passed a ball park, a beautiful park, and there were three ball games going on at the same time, at seven o'clock in the morning. Boys, twelve, fourteen years old, all in handsome gray and white uniforms. We call baseball our national game, which it is, but it's Japan's national game, too. They really love it.

150

14

JACKIE, LEO AND ME

I HAD A COUPLE of run-ins with Jackie Robinson on that Japan trip, which was nothing new for Robinson and me. He was the most difficult ballplayer I ever had to deal with as an umpire. I'm talking about ballplayers now, not managers. Leo Durocher was the all-time champion, but he was managing, not playing, when I was umpiring.

Jackie was one of those players who could never accept a decision. I give him credit for being a great ballplayer. He was a dangerous hitter, an aggressive player, one of the best base runners I ever saw in my life. Robinson kept an umpire on his toes when he was running the bases because he had such great reflexes. He could slide either way, and he could feint at the last minute, the last second, the last instant. He could start one way and go another. He was like Cobb that way. He was more like Cobb in temperament and style than any other player. He was very intense. Almost every time he was called out on strikes or on a close play on the bases there seemed to be a few words—the pitch was inside or it was high, or the fielder missed the tag or he wasn't on the bag.

This time in Japan, there was a little shortstop playing on one of the Japanese teams. Everybody liked him. He was forever bowing and saying, *"Mushi-mushi, mushi-mushi!"* He had everybody saying *mushi-mushi*. He was a good little ballplayer; he could run fast, he could field, he could throw pretty well. But he could not hit. He was an out man all the time: strike out, pop up, weak grounder.

Towards the end of the trip, one of the last games they played, this little shortstop came up with the bases empty, and he hit a ball down toward short to Pee Wee Reese. Pee Wee sort of took his time fielding it. He let it come to him, and he made sure he had a good grip on the ball before he threw it, and then he threw it not too hard to first. It was obvious that Reese was hoping the little guy would beat it out for a hit. And Gil Hodges at first base— a great fellow and one of the finest fielding basemen I ever saw—instead of stretching for the throw he took it right on the bag, and maybe even on the wrong side of the bag, to give the guy more time. They still had him out by a step.

I called him safe. It was the only time in my career that I ever called a man safe when I knew he was out. He was such a fine little fellow, that shortstop. But Robinson, who was playing second base, came charging over at me, waving his arms and yelling about the guy being out by five feet and so forth.

I said, "Just play second base, will you?"

He yelled, "Why don't you get in position? You're never in position to call a play."

He just galled me. Everybody else knew what was going on, and he didn't. I suppose it was because he was always such a competitor, but even so . . .

"You're *never* in position," he shouted.

I said, "I'm in a dandy position for you right now. Get out!" I chased him.

After the game I rode back to the hotel in the bus with the ballplayers, and as I walked down the aisle to my seat at least half a dozen guys, including Newcombe, Campanella, and Jim Gilliam, winked at me and smiled and nodded their heads. They all had great respect for Jackie, but he wore them out once in a while, too.

Another thing happened with Robinson on that Japan trip that I got a kick out of. I suppose I shouldn't have, because an umpire is supposed to be impartial, but it was so funny I enjoyed it. Jackie was at bat and the count was three and two, and first base was open. The Japanese manager stood up and pointed to first. In other words, walk him, make ball four intentional, give him the base. They feared Jackie—he was some hitter, especially in the clutch. The manager pointed, and everybody saw him do it. The catcher moved out a little to one side and held his glove out wide. Everybody relaxed as the pitcher started to throw because we all knew it was going to be ball four. Instead, the pitcher busted one down the middle, hard, right through the gate! They must have had a special signal. Maybe they did it with their teapot. They always had a teapot in the dugout instead of a water cooler. However they did it, the pitch was down the middle and the catcher hopped back in and caught it. Robinson was so surprised that he just stood there. "Sneak attack!" I yelled. "Strike three! Another Pearl Harbor!"

Robinson was a great ballplayer, but he certainly could bother an umpire. Still, he wasn't as bad as Durocher. Robinson can bat fourth on my all-difficult team, but Durocher is the manager. They're a great pair. When they were on television a couple of years ago, covering baseball games, you never saw two better friends. But you should have heard the things they called each other when Durocher was managing the Giants and Jackie was starring for the Dodgers. They were two pretty good mouths.

Durocher was a manager most of the time I umpired, but for a few years he was still on the active roster, listed as a playing manager. Leo had Pee Wee Reese playing shortstop most of the time, though, and he almost never put himself in the lineup. During the war, or just at the end of it, when Reese was still in the Navy, the Dodgers had a boy named Eddie Basinski playing shortstop. Basinski played the violin. He wasn't a bad fielder, but he hit like he had the violin in his hands. He was a nice kid; he wore glasses.

One day Branch Rickey asked Leo to play shortstop so that Basinski could have the day off. Durocher didn't want to play. He hadn't been a full-time player in five or six years. His legs were gone. But Rickey said, "Just spell the boy for today. It will do him good to be out of there for a day."

So Leo dragged himself out to shortstop. This could have been an exhibition game, maybe one of the last games in spring training before the season began. I can't remember exactly. Baseball sometimes seemed very informal back there towards the end of the war.

The Dodgers had a catcher named Ferrell Anderson. He was a big, blondheaded kid, and he had a wry neck. His head was always cocked to one side. He caught in a strange way, too, with one leg out stiff. He had a kid trick of catching bad pitches and pulling them into the strike zone. And holding them there. The idea, I suppose, is to fool the umpire into thinking the pitch is a strike. In the big leagues, all it fools is the crowd, and then they get on the umpire.

"Don't hold those pitches like that, Andy," I said. "Just catch the ball where it's pitched."

"I'll do what I want," he said. "I'm catching." Which was surprising because he was a good boy, Anderson, a decent fellow.

I said, "Andy, catch them where they're pitched. They don't pull pitches in the strike zone in the big leagues."

He did it again. A high pitch came in, and he caught it and snapped it down into the strike zone.

I said, "Look, you pull another pitch and hold it on me, and you're going out of here."

"Oh, yeah?" he said.

"Try it."

In came another pitch, high, and he grabbed it and pulled it down. I called it a ball and then I said, "Go on. Get out."

He argued a bit, and then he went. Now the funny thing was, Durocher never came in from shortstop. Can you imagine him not even getting involved when one of his players was being thrown out of the game? But he was dead. His legs hurt. He didn't move. He didn't even yell.

The Dodgers needed another catcher to take Anderson's place, so I called out to Durocher.

"Leo," I said, "who's the new catcher?"

"What?" You'd think he would have at least waved somebody out of the dugout, but he was so tired he didn't want to move.

I said, "Who's catching?"

"Why don't you guess?" he said. "You've been guessing all day."

154

"Okay," I said. "And you guess who's playing shortstop. Because you're through, too."

I think I did him a favor, though, throwing him out that day.

What do you think of when you think of an umpire? An argument. A ballplayer and an umpire yelling at each other, and the crowd booing the umpire. Everybody milling around, and finally somebody being thrown out of the game, and the crowd booing even harder.

That's the picture people have of an umpire, somebody always in trouble, or always causing trouble. In baseball, the umpire is always the villain.

I don't know where that idea got started. I don't understand why the fans boo the umpire. I know a lot of it is humorous, and it's part of the game, and the American way, and all that. But why is it? I wonder who the guy was who started it. Who started booing the umpire and calling him a blind bat and saying, "Kill the ump!" I wish I could find him. I'd like to tell him a few things.

I know a lot of it is kidding, but you ought to see some of the people who wait for an umpire after a game just to abuse him. They call you names, they insult you, they say things about your family. And then they expect you to have the perfect temperament on the ball field. Whenever an umpire gets a little hot under the collar, oh, isn't that terrible. He's lost control of the game, they say. He doesn't have the right attitude. Well, I'll tell you this, if they can find a fellow who can swallow all that stuff, then they don't have an umpire. I'm not talking about with a crowd. You're all alone then, one against the mob, and you have to keep quiet and take it. But when you're on the ball field you're not dealing with a mob; you're dealing with ballplayers, people you know, people you respect and admire for their ability. You can't take that abuse on the ball field.

My first year in the National League, I chased twenty-six fellows out of the game during the season. I chased twenty-six. That's a tremendous amount. But I wouldn't let anybody curse me. I've been very fortunate—and I'm grateful for it—that I never cursed a ballplayer in all the years I was an umpire. I had no right to and no reason to. Well, I had reason to, but I had no right to. And they had no right to curse me, or call me any of those names. I know all those names, and I'm none of them. And they're not going to call me any of them and stay in the ball game.

When I first came into the league Ford Frick asked me, "How much abuse will you take?"

"I won't take any," I said.

"None at all?"

"I don't think I should," I said. "I don't curse them and they're not going to curse me." If I let them, I'd have lost their respect. And if you're going to be a good umpire, you've *got* to have their respect.

They say a squabble with the umpire lends color to the game. All right, I don't object to an occasional argument. I kind of like one once in a while. I like a ballplayer who fights for his rights. It shows that he's taking the game seriously, that it means a lot to him. But that doesn't have anything to do with being called a filthy name. It doesn't have anything to do with all the phony arguments and rotten abuse you get from some of these so-called colorful characters. Like Durocher.

Durocher? You can have him. I umpired in the minor leagues for five years and in the National League for twenty-five, and I never saw anyone else like him. He is the king of the complainers, troublemakers, arguers, moaners, the ones who can never, never, never accept a tough decision that goes against them.

There aren't very many of them. A few years ago a couple of us umpires went over the rosters of all the teams in the league, and we picked out the troublemakers. I don't mean the fellows who get in an occasional argument or who get thrown out of a game once in a while. That happens. That's part of baseball. We picked out the ones who go out of their way to stir things up, who are always bickering, always finding fault, always making trouble, the ones who play to the crowd to get the fans down on the umpire.

There was only about one per team, two at the most. But they can make an umpire's life hell.

Durocher was the worst. He is king of the hill. He comes up oozing charm. He doesn't fool me. I've known him too long.

I remember a time in the early '50s, when Leo was managing the Giants. I was in St. Louis when I got a telegram from Ford Frick. The Dodgers were going into the Polo Grounds for a five-game series with the Giants, and Frick's wire said, "Change of assignment. You are to go to New York for the Dodger-Giant series. You will open the series behind home plate."

I was supposed to go to Chicago next, which would have meant being home for a few days, something I always looked forward to during the season. But it was a compliment to be assigned to the Dodger-Giant games, because it was an important series. That was the Giants of Sal Maglie and the Dodgers of Jackie Robinson, and it seemed that they were fighting for the pennant every year. Some umpires don't like to work a tough series, but I felt proud at being assigned to it. And proud to be assigned to the plate for the first game. Usually when you get a change of assignment and join another team of umpires you go to third base for the first game. An umpiring team rotates. You umpire at third one day, second the next, first the next and finally home plate, and then back to third again. But Frick said, "You will open up at home plate, and that will give you two games behind the plate out of five."

I had had plenty of trouble with Durocher over the years, and he knew how I felt about him. He'd heard me tell him often enough. But before the first game when we were standing at home plate, he and Charlie Dressen of the Dodgers came up with their lineups, and he started right in with the old ooze.

"Hello, boys!" he said. You would have thought we were his dearest friends.

"Well," he said, looking at me. "I'm certainly glad to see that the best umpires in the league were assigned to this important series. I really have to hand it to Ford Frick for doing that."

I said, "Just give me the lineup."

157

Usually, the umpires and the managers go over the ground rules before a game, but Durocher and Dressen both knew the Polo Grounds better than they knew their own front yards, and so did the umpires. All Durocher did was make speeches then, anyway. So I took the lineups, checked them and said, "Everybody knows the rules. Let's go." Then I walked about ten feet out in front of home plate and left Durocher standing there. I wasn't about to take any of his bullthrowing.

Great umpires. What a phony he is. Managers don't come up and praise umpires before a game. And an umpire doesn't look for praise. He looks for respect. Once in a while you hear a player or a manager say, "You're a good umpire" or even "You're a great umpire." But I never thought of it in terms of being great. It was just a job, that's all it was, and you worked hard at it. You had to. You had Durochers around.

Great umpires. He never bothered to call me a great umpire when I made a good call that went against his team. I had trouble with Durocher ten years before he pulled that "Hello, boys" con, and I had trouble ten years after. Back in the early '40s, he kicked dirt on me at home plate at Ebbets Field in Brooklyn because of a decision I made, and it was a great decision. I was umpiring behind the plate. The Cubs and Dodgers were tied 1–1 in the bottom of the sixth. Bobby Bragan walked for the Dodgers and Goody Rosen was hit by a pitch. There were two out, and Frenchy Bordagaray came up to bat. Bordagaray hit a long single to center and Bragan, who was one of the slowest base runners I ever saw, tried to score from second. Rosen was going from first to third, and he wasn't the fastest man in the world, either. The throw went to third, and they got Rosen for the third out. I didn't call that play; that was the base umpire's call, and nobody made any objection to it. As the plate umpire, I had to see whether Bragan crossed home plate before Rosen made the third out, and Bragan didn't. He hadn't reached home plate, so the run did not count. Everybody in the park was watching the play at third, and practically nobody saw me signal that the run did not score. They have all sorts of telephones and public address systems now, but at that time the umpire had to report substitutions and rulings on plays like this to the official scorer up in the press box. I turned and waved my arms and screamed, "The run does not score!"

Durocher was on the lines coaching, and he came running up to the plate cursing and swearing and yelled, "Did you say that run doesn't score?" I said, "It doesn't score," and I chased him out of the game for his language to me.

"Why, you lousy so-and-so," he said, and he kicked dirt on me. There was always a lot of soft, granular dirt around home plate in Ebbets Field; we were forever sweeping off the plate, because just a flick of the foot could cover it with dirt. When he kicked dirt on me, he spattered me from head to foot. It was all over me. He kicked the dirt and then he turned and went toward his dugout, and I followed him. I was wearing an inside chest protector, under my coat, so I couldn't take that off, but I tossed my mask away. That was kind of dumb on my part; if I was going to have a fight, I should have kept it on and let him break his hand against it.

I yelled, "Hey, turn around."

He stopped and turned.

"Take a punch at me," I said. I was boiling.

"Why?" he said.

"So I can knock you out," I said, "right here."

He turned and kept going, into the dugout.

Meantime, the fellows who run the scoreboard thought the run had come in, and they had put a big 1 up on the scoreboard. When they put up a run on the scoreboard in Ebbets Field it didn't matter whether it counted or not. That was their run. Never mind how it got there. It was theirs.

But it had to come down, and a big 0 was put up instead. When the run came down, so did everything else in the stands: sandwiches, pickles, hunks of salami, tomatoes. And bottles. There must have been at least a hundred bottles, all aimed at me. They called it a pop-bottle barrage in the newspapers, but all I saw were beer bottles—Schaefer's and Rheingold and a couple of those other

159

brands they sell in New York. I was standing near home plate, and those bottles kept flying out of the stands. Charlie Grimm was managing the Cubs and he came running up.

"You hardheaded Irishman," he said, "get out to second base before you get hit with one of those bottles."

I said, "I'm staying here, *watching* the bottles. I'm not running for anybody."

I liked Charlie, but I didn't want just one manager coming out and standing there with me. That didn't look good. So I said, "If you don't get out of here, you can join that other punk."

"Not old Charlie, boy," he said, and he ran like the devil for the Cub dugout. You remember how Charlie Grimm used to run, with that waddle, with his arms down straight and his hands spread? That's the way he ran. It was funny, and maybe that helped ease things because after awhile they stopped throwing bottles. Of course, just about the same time, four policemen appeared on the field and plenty more started moving through the stands, and I think that had more to do with it. Either way, I was very happy to see the bottles stop. It's not a very comfortable feeling to be standing at home plate while people you don't know are throwing beer bottles at your head. They stopped selling beer and soda in bottles after that; I'm the guy who put paper cups in the ball parks.

We got the game going again and the Cubs scored in the seventh. That's the way it ended, with the Cubs winning, 2–1. Then the crowd got sore all over again. At Ebbets Field the umpires used to get on and off the field through the field boxes down along the right-field line. That was so we wouldn't have to mingle with the players. I started down that way after the game ended, but the captain of police over there at that time, a big Irishman named Murphy, met me and said, "Come on, Jocko. We'll go out this way." Meaning through the Dodger dugout and down the runway that was fenced off from the crowd.

I said, "No, I'm going out the way I came in." I was a little stubborn and I didn't want them to think I was scared.

Murphy was very patient. He smiled and said, "No, Jocko. We're going this way. Don't worry about a thing. There'll be policemen outside and you'll have nothing to worry about." He led me and the other umpires right along with the players and up to the umpires' dressing room. I was working with George Barr and Dusty Boggess. The newspapermen came in and asked questions about the fuss, and I never in all my career closed my door to the newspapermen. I always gave them an answer. And they were pretty fair to me. One or two I didn't like, but most of them were fair.

But answering their questions delayed me a little in getting dressed. I was just taking off my second shin guard when Barr and Boggess patted me on the the back and said, "We'll see you tomorrow, Jock." And they were gone.

"I'm alone," I said to myself. "How could they get dressed so fast? Or did they dress? Did they go out of here in their umpires' clothes?"

I was alone, and I could hear the crowd still yelling and milling around outside the ball park. I got dressed, and I walked along to the rotunda where the main entrance to Ebbets Field was, and I went outside. I was staying at the Astor Hotel in New York, and the way I went back there from Brooklyn was to walk three or four blocks to the subway station at Prospect Park and take the subway to Manhattan. I came out of the ball park and there must have been three or four thousand fans out there, just waiting for me, and I couldn't see a policeman anyplace. I knew the crowd was waiting for me because I could hear my name, and I could hear things like "that blind so-and-so." It was August, and I had on a very handsome light tan suit, a panama hat, and brown-and-white shoes. I was kind of a dude then. I edged out and walked right through the middle of the crowd, and none of them knew me. They were looking for a guy in an umpire's cap and a blue suit.

I walked down Sullivan Place toward Prospect Park, and it was darker there than it was outside the ball park. I was feeling sort of cocky, but then these two bruisers started to move toward me.

161

They had on white shirts and I could see them plain. They began to follow me. I started to walk faster, and they followed right along, maybe twenty or thirty feet behind me. I figured they were going to wait until I got to the subway because it was a long way down those subway stairs, and it wouldn't take much of a knock to send me all the way down them and ruin me. I looked for a cop, and I couldn't see one. I thought, "Well, I'm not going to let them get me on the subway steps," and I turned around and faced them. I figured, let them try to get me up here; at least I have a chance. I said, "If I'm going to get it, let's go." They came toward me, and I took a swing at one of them, but the other grabbed me. He handled me like a toy. He said, "Take it easy, Jocko. We're policemen. The captain told us to keep an eye on you."

Oh, what a relief. They were big, rugged-looking guys, and I had never realized they were cops. They stayed with me all the way back to Manhattan, right to my hotel. When we got there, I dug down in my pocket and I took out a ten-dollar bill and I said, "Here, boys. Have a cup of coffee and a sandwich on me."

They said, "Not a chance, Jocko. It was a pleasure. We were only hoping someone would try to lay a hand on you so we could go to work on them for you."

I said, "Fellows, thanks. They call the police 'New York's finest.' I go for that. Thanks again."

But the thing is, the whole point is, the entire situation was caused by Durocher. He could not accept the decision. It was his base runner who was slow. It was his base runner who got put out at third. It was his base runner who failed to score before the third out. I didn't do any of it. I didn't prevent the run from scoring. I didn't put the run up on the scoreboard for the people to see, and then take it down. It never belonged up there in the first place. All I did was call the play the way it happened, and all Durocher did was cause all the trouble. Typical of him. Typical.

He caused me a lot of trouble again in 1961, just a few years before I retired, when he was a coach with the Dodgers in Los Angeles. He kicked me. This is what it said in the paper: " 'Conlan kicked me and I kicked him back,' said Durocher. Leo said his intentions were peaceful. He just wanted to kick dirt on the umpire's shoes. 'I've kicked dirt at umpires a thousand times,' he said, 'and Conlan was the first who ever kicked back.' "

Well, I say, who is he to kick dirt on me to start with? I'm not scum. And he didn't just kick dirt on me; he kicked *me*.

It started with a pop fly that went up near home plate. The Dodgers were playing the Pirates, and Hal Smith, the Pittsburgh catcher, went out to catch the pop. But he missed it. He missed it clean. It hit fair about three feet inside the foul line, and then bounced foul. Norm Larker had hit the ball and he ran to first base, but when it bounced foul that meant it was a foul ball and Larker had to go back to the plate and bat again.

All of a sudden, Durocher had a brainstorm. He decided that the ball had hit Smith's glove. I was right on top of the play—I was the plate umpire and I ran down the first-base line to watch it. Durocher was nowhere near it. But he decided it hit Smith's glove. If it hit the catcher's glove first and then rolled foul it would have been a fair ball, and Larker would have been safe on first base. But it didn't hit the glove. It didn't come anywhere near hitting the glove. It bounced foul, and it was a foul ball. Period.

But Durocher came out yelling: "It hit his glove. It's a fair ball."

I said, "It didn't come within three feet of his glove."

"The hell it didn't," he said.

Nobody else complained. *Nobody*. Walter Alston didn't. Larker didn't. Nobody. Only Durocher. He came running out with his mouth flapping. One of the guys said later, "Oh, he's on Dinah Shore's show tonight, and he was just raising a fuss to get publicity." You know, so that people listening in or reading the paper would say, "Gee, he's on TV tonight. Let's watch." I don't know if that was so, but I wouldn't put it past him. Be typical of him. So he claimed it hit the catcher's glove, and I said it didn't. He didn't have much of an argument, and he knew it, and he turned away to go back. As he did, he tried to kick dirt over my shoes, but when he did that, he kicked me, good. He may not have meant to kick me that first time, but he kicked me. You could hear it sound off the shin guards under my trousers. I was working the plate, and I had mask and chest protector and shin guards on.

Naturally, I kicked him back. I'm not going to take that from anybody, especially Durocher. I kicked him pretty good, too. I had the plate shoes on, the ones I wore when I worked behind home plate. They were reinforced with steel over the toes. After I kicked him, he came right back at me and gave me a hard kick in the shin, but I never felt it because of the shin guards.

I kicked him a second time. I kick left-handed, or left-footed. I'm left-handed, and I can't kick with my right leg. So I shifted like a fighter and threw the left. I got him in the right shin the first time, and when he turned back and kicked again he left his left leg open, and I got that one real good. I got both his shins. I didn't kick with the side of the shoe either. I kicked him with the point, real good strong kicks.

I took my mask off, and when he kicked me I tossed my protector away. I had my hands up, all ready for him, though a funny thing is, all through this he had his hands in his pockets and he never took them out. I was ready to tag him, and I heard Augie Donatelli yelling, "Hit him!" I was just cocking my left hand, measuring him, when Chris Pelekoudas grabbed my arm and said, "Don't do that, Jock." Don Drysdale, the Dodger pitcher, ran out from the dugout, and I was going to throw him out of the game. I thought he was going to start something, and I yelled, "What do *you* want?" But he was just getting between Durocher and me to make sure nothing happened. He said, "Jock, I didn't want you to get in trouble."

Some people said it was a pretty childish exhibition. Maybe it was. But what do you do when a man who has galled you all through your career kicks you in the shins? Blow him a kiss?

I didn't kiss him, that's for sure. A couple of the Dodgers told me that he still had marks on his shins a month later. I really got him good that time.

15

CONLAN, THE GREAT ACTOR

DUROCHER WAS always trying to do things. He didn't deliberately break rules, but he would strain them. He would go as far as he could, just to see what he could get away with. When he couldn't get away with it, he would make it look like the umpire's fault.

One time in Chicago, they had a packed house. Leo was managing Brooklyn then. He was always hanging around with actors and theatrical people, celebrities. This day in Chicago, just before game time, I noticed a guy sitting in the Dodger dugout. He was wearing a beautiful camel's hair coat. Durocher came up to home plate with his lineup, and I said, "Who's the fellow sitting on your bench?"

"Oh, a wonderful fellow, Jocko," he said. "A great guy. That's Rise Stevens' husband."

I said, "Well, he'll have to go now, you know. The game is about to start."

He said, "Jocko, I haven't got a seat for him. It was too late to get a ticket. The place is full. Everything is gone."

"You know the rules. He can't sit on the bench."

Charlie Grimm of the Cubs was standing there, too.

"I'll get an okay from Charlie," Leo said. "Charlie, this fellow is Rise Stevens' husband. He's a great friend of mine and a real high-class fellow."

"It's okay with me," Grimm said.

"Well, it's not okay with me," I said. Here we go again. Conlan, the mean umpire.

"Jocko, he's not going to bother anybody," Leo said.

"You know the rules as well as I do," I said. "Nobody is allowed on that bench except the manager, the coaches, the eligible players and the trainer. Not even the owner can sit on the bench. You know that. Tell your friend he has to get out."

"I don't know where he's going to sit," Durocher said.

"I don't, either. But I know where he's not going to sit, and that's on the bench. Get him out."

Leo went away grumbling, but the fellow left, as he had to. It was the rule, and Durocher knew it was the rule when he invited him down, but he thought he could stretch it a little. That's exactly why they have that rule. If they didn't, guys like Durocher would have so many actors and friends and celebrities down on the bench the ballplayers wouldn't have room to breathe.

He was just making a big show, a big deal. Leo is bigger than the rules. Leo tried the same thing another time with Danny Kaye. Danny Kaye is a good fellow, a very likable guy. I met him several times when he was playing theaters in New York—the 46th Street Theater, the Music Box. I used to go around to see him backstage. He kept a catcher's glove and a finger mitt there, and when it was intermission or when he wasn't on stage himself, he'd get me to play catch with him. I'd put the catcher's glove on, on the wrong hand of course, because I'm left-handed, and he'd put the finger mitt on, and we'd stand behind the back curtain, at the very back of the stage, and we'd have a catch. I think the audience could hear us sometimes. Danny knows baseball, and he likes it. He threw pretty well. Not like a professional, of course, but he impressed those people backstage. When he threw the ball I'd let it go *pop* in the catcher's glove the way you can, and the people backstage would say, "Oh, Danny, that was a fast one! Boy, you really threw that one." To me, he was throwing pumpkins. But it's like everything in life when the big shot is in the middle. They build him up to build themselves up, I guess. I always found Danny to be a real likable fellow, and he seemed to enjoy baseball very much.

But this one day he was on the Dodger bench before the game. Leo came up with the lineup and said, "You know Danny, don't you?"

"Yes, I know him," I said. "Nice fellow. Great actor."

"I'm going to have him sit on the bench today. It will give him a big thrill."

"It may give him a big thrill," I said, "but you can't have him sit on the bench. You know that."

Leo got a little mad and he said, "Well, he's *going* to sit on the bench."

"Oh, is he?" I said. "Listen. If you want me to, I'll tell Danny myself that he has to leave, because I know he'll understand. But if he insists on sitting there, you are going to go and he is going to go with you. I don't need Danny Kaye up here, and it's a cinch I don't need you. So if you want to manage this game today, you better get rid of him."

He went back to the bench and Danny left, and then Leo came up to the plate again.

"You're not a good fellow," he said.

"Good fellows are a dime a dozen," I said. "I'm a good umpire."

Durocher didn't like me doing that, and I don't suppose Danny Kaye did, either. But I couldn't help that. It was Durocher's fault, not mine. He knew better. But he was always making theatrical moves around these people, always shining up to them. I have to laugh. Once in Cincinnati I ran into Frank Sinatra in a hotel lobby. He was making a picture—or else he had just finished making one —across the river in Kentucky. I had met Frank Sinatra before, and I liked him. He was just as regular, a real swell little guy. He came up to me and put his arm around me, and he said, "Jocko, how are you? It's good to see you."

We talked for awhile and then he said, "Come on, I'll take you to dinner."

"I'd love to," I said, "but I'm working a ball game tonight. I have to leave for the park."

"That's too bad," he said. We talked a little more, and then he said, "How are you getting along with Loudmouth?"

I said, "Who?"

"Loudmouth."

167

I said, "Who's Loudmouth?"

"Durocher," he said. "That's what we always call him."

I roared laughing. I said, "Boy, you sure named him right."

"Well, you can hear him all over the place, can't you?"

"Right," I said, "and you could have put a couple of other names on him, too."

Durocher got me once, though. He really put one over on me, and I didn't even know what was happening. I was working with George Barr at Ebbets Field that day, just the two of us. Incidentally, one of the reasons I never cared for Durocher was the way he used to ride Barr. George was excitable. He could get very worked up, very tense. When George was umpiring behind the plate, Durocher would get his whole ball club on Barr with the very first pitch of the game, whether it was a strike or a ball or whatever it was. They'd all yell "Oh-h-h-h-h!" as soon as George made his first call. They'd have him worked up even before the second pitch was thrown, screaming at him like that. They did it just to upset him. They didn't care about the pitch.

I wouldn't let them pull that on me, and Durocher knew it. I remember coming out of a ball park one day when Arky Vaughan caught up with me. Arky was a superb ballplayer with Pittsburgh, and he went to the Dodgers when Larry MacPhail was picking up good older players to help rebuild the club. Vaughan was a high-class man. He drowned later trying to save another man when their boat capsized.

Arky caught up with me, and he said, "How are you, Jock?"

"Fine, Arky," I said.

"I want to pay you a compliment."

"Now don't start that, Stan." I used to call him Stan because to me he was a dead ringer for Stan Laurel, with that straight, dead-pan face.

"I'll Stan you," he used to say, and he'd pretend to take a swing at me. He could fight, Vaughan could, really handle himself. He used to spar with Harry Greb in Pittsburgh.

This day he said, "No, I mean it. I've got a compliment to pay you."

168

"What?"

"Durocher had a meeting today and he told us, 'This is an important game, and I don't want anybody put out of it. Conlan is umpiring, and the quickest way to get put out is to curse him. Nobody gets put out today, including me, or I'm going to take some of your money.' " Arky said, "I thought that was a compliment to you, Jock, coming from a guy like that."

The day Leo put one over on me I came out on the field before the game, and as I was walking in toward home plate I saw a fellow in a Dodger uniform having a catch with one of the players. I said, "That guy isn't a ballplayer. He doesn't even know how to roll his pants." He had a little fat pouch on him, and the hat looked funny on his head. As I got near the plate the fellow spotted me and came running toward me, waving his hands and yelling.

I thought, "What is this?" I said, "Go on. Get out of here. Get away from me. What are you doing in that suit anyway? You're no ballplayer. Go on, get out of here."

"I'm not allowed out here?" he shouted, sticking his face into mine. "I'm with Leo Durocher!"

"If you keep this up, you're going out of here and Durocher is going with you. Get away from me!"

He yelled, "This is terrific, Jocko. This is great. Now wave me out of here. Chase me out of the ball game."

I thought the guy was crazy. I said, "Who are you?"

"I'm one of the ballplayers," he shouted.

"The hell you are," I said. "Get out of here!" And I gave him the heave-ho. I was really getting sore. The guy was still yelling, but he began walking away.

Durocher came running up then and he said, "What's the matter, Jocko?"

"What's the matter?" I said. "Where did you get *that* creep?"

"Don't you know who he is?" Leo said.

"No, I don't know who he is. But he doesn't belong out here."

"That's Bill Bendix," he said.

I said, "Who is Bill Bendix?"

169

"The actor," he said. "The movie actor. He made *The Babe Ruth Story.*"

I was confused. I didn't know who Bill Bendix was. He was over in the dugout by then and he called out, "Couldn't have been better, Jocko. The action was great."

I didn't know that they had had a camera on us and that they had been shooting the two of us arguing. I just wanted to get the game started. Bendix was leaving the dugout and he called over, real nice, "Thank you, Jocko." And he left.

The game was on then and I had a lot to do, and I didn't think any more about it. I believe it was a Sunday and probably a doubleheader, and after the last out of the second game we had to hustle to catch a train. I never thought about it any more.

A month later, we were rained out of a game in Philadelphia, the last game of a series, and I went downtown to catch a train. I was early and I had a couple of hours to kill so I wandered around the station. Finally I dropped into one of those newsreel theaters. You know the kind. They show an hour's worth of news and shorts and cartoons. I was sitting there, watching, and this short started, starring William Bendix. The name still didn't click with me. It meant nothing. In this short Bendix was going around telling people how to do things; he went up to the White House to tell Harry Truman how to run the country, things like that. He was always marching from one scene to the next, trudging along to the next person he had to see. There he was, walking across the Brooklyn Bridge, right in the middle of the road, with buses and trucks and cars passing him on both sides. Then he was in the center of Brooklyn, and then all of a sudden I spotted the rotunda of Ebbets Field. It was getting interesting. This guy busted right through the gate and disappeared inside. Then they showed the field and two umpires walking in toward the plate, and it began to dawn on me. I said to myself, "Why, that's me." And then there was Bendix in a baseball uniform and now, finally, I recognized him. There was a lot of crowd noise and Bendix and I were having a big argument, and then you could hear me yell, "Get out of here!"

There I was, sitting in that newsreel theater in Philadelphia, and I started to laugh. Oh, how they had put one over on me. I was laughing as though this was the funniest picture ever made. A fellow sitting next to me sort of looked at me and said, "How about that?"

I said, "Do you know who that umpire is up there?"

"Yes," he said. "That's Jocko Conlan."

I said, "That's me."

He said, "That's you? Yes, that is you. Well, how about that? How are you? I'm glad to meet you."

I think he was relieved I wasn't crazy. I told him what had happened, and we had a good laugh together. But score that one for Durocher. I never knew what was going on until I saw it up on the screen. He beat me that time.

16

NICE AND NOT-SO-NICE GUYS

Most ballplayers don't give an umpire trouble. When I say trouble I don't mean when a ballplayer turns around and says a pitch was too high or too low. I don't call that trouble. Trouble is a ballplayer who puts you on the spot, who gets you a razzing or a booing from the fans and who gets things so stirred up that his ball club is riding you on every pitch.

And yet I can recall a day when one of the pleasantest fellows ever to play big-league ball did just that to me. It was Stan Hack of the Cubs. He was a fine ballplayer, a .300 hitter, a good third baseman. Later on he managed the Cubs for two or three seasons, and he had the Cardinals for a short time, too. He had the warmest smile you ever saw; he was a very pleasant man.

It was my first year in the league and we were in Chicago. The Cubs were getting beat 1–0 in the ninth inning. A big crowd was there. The Cubs were still a good ball club in those days, though they weren't as good as they had been. Hack was the lead-off batter in the last of the ninth, and the crowd was yelling for a rally and a run or a couple of runs. The first pitch was right down the middle, and Stan took it. I called it a strike.

Stan was considered a good fellow with umpires. He was a professional; he didn't complain about balls and strikes. He took this pitch, I called it a strike, and he turned around to me and said, "Isn't that a shame, Jock? That I have to take a pitch like that."

He was under orders from the manager, of course. Lead-off hitter in the ninth. Take a couple of pitches. Wait the pitcher out.

Try to get a walk. Make the pitcher work. But a hitter hates to see a fat pitch go by him.

Hack shook his head in disgust. He banged his bat on the plate, and he said, "I don't see why I have to take a pitch like that." And when he said it, he was looking right at me with an angry look on his face. Now the crowd started to boo. Who did they boo? Me.

They thought Hack was griping at me. I hadn't had a word with anybody the whole game. I had what I used to call a perfect ball game going, no trouble at all, and now Hack had thirty thousand people screaming at me. He kept chewing about having to take that pitch.

"That's too bad, Stan," I said, "but why don't you get in and hit now?"

"Yeah, but to take a pitch like that," he said.

"I don't have anything to do with that," I said. I was getting angry. "All I know is you're telling thirty thousand people that you didn't like the strike I called."

"I didn't say anything about the strike!" Hack said. Now he was getting a little sore at me.

"That's right, because it was a good strike. But those people hollering at me don't know that. Get in and hit."

"The hell with you," he shouted.

Voom!

"Get out of here," I said.

He nearly died.

"Damn," he said. "I get chased and I never said one word to you about that strike."

"You told *them.*" The crowd was really giving it to me now. "Go on. Beat it."

I went home that day—this was in Chicago—and my brother Pete called me up. He had been listening to the game on the radio, and naturally the announcer assumed that Hack had been griping about the strike call. Pete wanted to ride me a little bit about it.

"Had a rough day today, didn't you, kid?" he said.

"From *you,* too?" I yelled. "Look, you! I told you before, don't pay any attention to newspaper write-ups and radio broadcasts. Just let me umpire, and you mind your own business."

That's how things can happen sometimes.

Another nice guy who gave me trouble but in a different way was Ernie Lombardi. There probably never was a ballplayer in the major leagues who was better liked by everybody than Lombardi. Just a big warmhearted guy. What a hitter! And what a thrower! But he was so slow on his feet that he could hit a line drive that another fellow would get a triple on, and Lom would end up with a single. Hard grounders that would go through the infield for hits for other fellows would be ground outs for him, because the infielders always played way back on the grass for him, he was so slow. Yet despite that, he won the National League batting championship twice. Everything he hit was a line drive, a low line drive that would carry five feet above the ground all the way to the fence. If he could have raised the ball up he might have broken Ruth's record. Even though he was slow, he beat out a bunt once or twice because the infield was so far back. He got a headline for it once: LOMBARDI BEATS OUT BUNT.

Lom had bad knees, especially towards the end of his career, and it hurt him to get into a squat, the way catchers usually do. When nobody was on base he'd catch kneeling down. When somebody got on base he'd stand up, so that if he had to throw he'd be in position. When he knelt, it was fine. An umpire could see over his shoulder and call the pitches. But when he stood up it was terrible. Lom was six feet three or four and he weighed about 240, and when you were five feet eight, like me, you couldn't see around him.

Lom was with the Giants his last few years, and this one day Carl Hubbell was pitching. Hubbell liked to throw that low breaking pitch at the knees, a tough pitch to call. A man got on first base with two outs and Debs Garms, a good hitter—he won the batting championship one year—came to bat. Lombardi stood up. Hubbell was throwing those pitches down there at the knees—this way, that way—and I'm jumping all around in back of Lombardi trying to see. The count went to three and two. I said, "Lom, get down. I can't see."

He said, "I can't, Jock. I'd kneel except there's a man on first."

He stayed up. I stood on tiptoes to look over his shoulders. I peeked under his arm. I didn't know what to do. Hubbell was out there with that nonchalant motion of his, and as he pitched the ball the runner on first took off for second. The pitch was a screwball down low and big Lom was all spread out waving his arms to stay in front of it and get hold of it. I couldn't see. I was getting panicky. Just before the ball got to the plate I shoved Lombardi off to one side—I still don't know how I did it—and got my head in on the side of him. The ball was right over the plate, knee high, but Lom was so far to one side he had to reach over and catch the ball backhanded. Garms took it, and I said, "Three!" Strikeout. The inning was over.

Lombardi said, "Gee, Jock. Why did you push me?"

I yelled, "I got to see the plate, too, Lom!"

"Don't get mad, Jock," he said. "It's just my knees are killing me."

You couldn't get mad at him. He was too nice. Just the opposite of Harry Danning, another catcher the Giants had back then. I guess Harry was personally a decent enough guy, but when I knew I was going to be working the plate for a Giant game I used to hope, sometimes pray, that Terry or Ott, whichever was managing, would put somebody else in to catch. Danning would pull pitches on you, like Ferrell Anderson. He'd take high pitches around the shoulders and low ones down around the ankle, and he'd pull the high pitches down and the low pitches up and he'd yell, happy as anything, "That's it! That's a strike! That's the way to put 'em in there!" He had a terrible screechy voice; it would go right through you. He'd pull the ball and hold it right there, in perfect strike position. He never got to the point where he was nasty, but he could show you up before a crowd. Danning wore me out. I can still hear that voice. For nine innings, every ball a Giant pitcher threw: "Good pitch! That's it! That's a strike!" I think maybe that's why I chased Ferrell Anderson so fast.

A lot of catchers give umpires trouble. There was a play in the 1961 World Series that I remember. Elston Howard, the Yankee catcher, was at bat and he hit a ball that bounced in front of the plate, a fair ball. Howard started to run to first and as he did the ball came up and hit his bat again before he could toss it to one side. The Reds fielded the ball and threw him out at first base, but I ruled that he was out automatically and that there was no advance by the base runners. If a ball hits the bat twice, the batter is out.

Ralph Houk was managing the Yankees and he came up to argue. He said, "What kind of a decision is that?"

"A good one," I said.

"I never saw anything like that before."

"I never did, either," I said, "and I've been umpiring twenty-five years. But I saw it today, and I knew what to do with it. He's out."

Houk grumped a little bit and then he left.

After the game I was going through the runway behind the Yankee dugout on my way to the umpires' room, and I saw Elston Howard there, waiting for me. I thought he was going to give me an argument. Instead, he turned out to be one of the nicest fellows I've ever met in baseball. He said, "Mr. Conlan, I'd like to ask you a question. Could you explain your ruling on that play where I was out?"

I explained it, and as I did he asked me various questions about the situation and the rule and the possibilities—good questions, smart questions. He said, "You understand, I'm not complaining. It's just that I never saw that play before. If it ever comes up again, I want to know how to handle it." I told him I had thought he was going to give me an argument.

"I try not to get into arguments," he said. "I just go out and play baseball."

"That's great," I said. "I wish there were a lot more like you." It was a real pleasure talking to him.

And then there were other catchers, like Buddy Rosar—what a

pain in the neck he was, always moaning. And Smokey Burgess, Andy Seminick and Joe Garagiola. I used to call them the three worst umpires who ever caught a ball game. They were always trying to help the umpire. Once a sportswriter asked me what catchers gave me the most trouble, and I told him those three. It was kind of a joke, but Smokey Burgess got a little annoyed by it. "Why did you have to tell them that?" he said. "What a thing to put in the paper. I don't give you any trouble, Jock."

"I don't let you," I said. Smokey was never satisfied. If he was batting and he took a pitch, it was a ball. If he was catching and the batter took a pitch it was a strike. It was very simple, the way Smokey umpired.

Seminick and Garagiola got a kick out of the story. They knew it was really in fun. Seminick would jump around there behind the plate; he'd box you. You had to have good footwork. Andy was over the hill as a ballplayer when that story ran, and he'd been working mostly in the bullpen. When he saw me, he said, "Jock, thanks for mentioning my name. I've been in the bullpen so long my friends didn't know I was still with the ball club."

Garagiola said, "That's great, Jock! Great! Keep my name in the papers."

"Joe," I said. "You are the worst of the lot. You have absolutely no conception of a strike. You don't know what the strike zone is."

"Hear that, you writers?" Joe said. "Attaboy, Jock. Keep telling them. Keep 'em writing about me."

Garagiola was a lot of fun to kid with. He kept an umpire company. He was always talking behind the plate. Joe was a better ballplayer than he gives himself credit for being, you know. People forget that he was the first-string catcher on the Cardinals when they won the pennant and the World Series in 1946.

Joe's pal, Yogi Berra, was a moaner. Back in the early 1950s, Larry Goetz called the Yankees "crybabies" because they were always moaning about decisions. Larry was criticized for saying that, but he was absolutely right. They were crybabies. They cried about everything, every pitch, every call. Berra was always complaining, moaning in that big heavy voice of his. I never could understand him half the time. I remember in 1950, when I was working the first game of the World Series, the Yanks against the Phils. That was the game I was hurt in, when my elbow was hit.

Despite the pain, I was going along fine in that game. I didn't have anybody question me about a ball or a strike. Vic Raschi beat Jim Konstanty 1–0, and they both pitched great. It's easy to umpire great pitching. Whenever you see a man umpire real well, you can bet the pitcher turned in a good ball game. What makes a hard game is when you see sixteen or seventeen bases on balls and errors. It's not that the umpire works a *bad* game then; it's a hard game. You're getting complaints all the time. The pitchers can't get the ball over, and the umpire gets blamed for it. When a pitcher is getting the ball over, the umpire has a rocking-chair job. The game practically umpires itself.

This game in 1950 was like that. A beautifully pitched ball game and no problems. The ninth inning came along, and I called a high pitch a ball. Yogi jumped up and growled something like "Ohrrurghrumugh." I couldn't make out what he was saying, but I knew he was complaining about the call. There wasn't any question about that. He walked out a couple of steps, the way he always did, and threw the ball to Raschi and then came back.

"Remember, it's the ninth inning," he said, meaning don't choke up now just because it's the last inning; this is the Yankees you're umpiring today, don't get nervous now. What do I care if it's the Yankees? Or anybody else?

"Look," I said. "If you're scared because it's the ninth inning, I'm not. Don't give me that stuff. You just catch, and I'll umpire."

Raschi got the side out—he was some pitcher—and then Yogi said, "Good game, Jocko." Later, when I was going through the runway, Raschi said, "You worked a fine game, Jock." I said, "Thank you. You pitched a fine game." But it's like the old saying about winners making jokes. Winners always say you worked a great game.

Yogi was a good guy, but he *was* considered a whiner. Richie

Ashburn, over in the National League, moaned a lot, too. Whether the ball was over or not, he'd always ask whether it was outside or inside, or too high or too low, or he'd make that great remark of all ballplayers: "Where was it?" I used to say soberly, "Can't you see it, kid?" Richie was a good guy, though, and one day I had some fun with him. He moaned about a pitch, so I said, "Okay. *You* umpire. You call the next pitch. I'll wait till you tell me what it is, and whatever you decide, that's what I'll call it." Del Crandall was catching, and Ashburn said to him, "He can't do that, can he?" Crandall said, "You don't know Jocko." Ashburn looked at me and said, "Do you mean it?" I said, "Yes! I want to see how good you are." He said, "Okay." The pitch came in, and it was belt high but about a foot inside. Ashburn looked at it and then he said, "Strike." I put my right arm up and said, "Strike," and then I called time and walked out to dust off the plate. As I did, I said, "Richie, you have just had the only chance a hitter has ever had in the history of baseball to bat and umpire at the same time. And you blew it. That's the last pitch you call. I'm not going to have you louse up my profession."

Another guy who used to be a whiner but who later turned out to be wonderful with umpires was Ed Bailey, also in the National League. When he was a kid, Bailey was terrible, but later he was a delight, a very funny guy, a conversationalist. He had a good arm and when there was a man on first he'd yell to his pitcher, "Don't hold him on. Let him run, let him run. I'll give him a head start." Clyde McCullough used to do that, too. He'd holler down to a base runner, "Go ahead. Take a lead. Take a big lead. Watch old Clyde throw you out." And then he'd throw him out.

There are a lot of catchers it was fun to work behind. Fellows like Gabby Hartnett or John Roseboro. Roseboro never complained, never. Just great.

I was there when Juan Marichal and Roseboro had that fight, when Marichal hit him with the bat. I was retired then, but Giles phoned me and asked me to go to San Francisco and observe the series. Just observe and report. I was sitting in the first row

179

directly over the Giants' dugout. I didn't see anything until Marichal turned and then hit Roseboro on the head. Why John didn't go down I don't know, but it was a good crack, enough to open his head. I'll say this for Roseboro, he threw the glove off and the mask away and started punching.

Before I knew it, Tito Fuentes, the Giants' shortstop, came running out of the dugout, carrying a bat and waving it like a machete. He didn't hit anybody, though. Then Orlando Cepeda—he was still with the Giants then—started out with a bat. I yelled, "Orlando!" and he turned and looked at me.

"What you want, Jocko?" he said.

"Don't go out there with a bat. Stay where you belong."

He said, "Okay, Jocko," and he put the bat down. I think he went out anyway, without the bat.

It was a confusing affair. I know that Shag Crawford, the plate umpire, got right into the middle of it and did a tremendous job in breaking it up. The other umpires were coming in, but Crawford didn't hesitate. He went right in between Roseboro and Marichal. He was knocked down and when he got up he was full of dirt, but I give him the credit for stopping a lot more brawling. He's a great young umpire. Willie Mays did a lot to stop it, too, grabbing Roseboro and saying, "John, you're hurt," and calming him down and leading him off.

Marichal lost his head. If you're going to fight on a ball field, fight with your fists. I always found Marichal to be a nice young fellow and a marvelous pitcher. When Juan was first in the league, Charlie Dressen tried to upset him by claiming that he was pitching illegally. When a pitcher goes to a full windup, he has to have one foot on the rubber and one behind it. Marichal pitched off the end of the rubber, one foot on it and the other off to the side—off to the side but behind the line of the rubber if you extended it. Dressen claimed it had to be directly behind it.

"He isn't on the rubber with one foot behind it."

"He's behind it for me," I said.

Charlie sent Bob Scheffing, one of his coaches, into the clubhouse to get a rule book. Now, you don't flash a rule book at an umpire, not in front of the grandstand you don't. I had never had anyone do that to me.

Dressen told Scheffing, "Go on up there and read that rule to him." Scheffing started up to the plate and I stopped him when he was no more than ten feet out of the dugout.

"Don't you come out here and pull a rule book on me," I said. "You do, and you're gone. I know the rule and I don't have to read any book."

Scheffing didn't want to be put out of the game, so he turned away and headed toward Ken Burkhart, who was umpiring third base. "Come here a second, Ken," he said. "I want to show you this rule." Scheffing was well liked, a high-class guy, and almost automatically Burkhart started toward him.

I shouted, "Ken, if you read that rule book and you don't unload him, you and I are through."

Burkhart stopped and he said, "Don't come near me. If Jocko won't read it, I won't, either." Scheffing went back to the bench, and Marichal was never bothered after that. It was only an incident, but it stuck in Marichal's mind, and he said afterwards, "You are my friend. You would not let them change my pitching." I said, "All I did was let you pitch legally, which is what you were doing."

Batters can get an umpire's goat, and not just by complaining over strike calls. Harry Walker was a terrible nuisance. He didn't complain, he didn't give the umpires a hard time, but he fidgeted all the time. They called him The Hat because of the way he fooled with his cap when he batted. Every pitch, he'd have to adjust his hat. He'd put the bat down, take hold of the peak with one hand and the back with the other and adjust it. Then he'd touch the peak again, and then the back. And then he'd do it all over again. It was aggravating. You were out there trying to concentrate on the strike zone and do your work, and here was this fellow fiddling and fiddling and fiddling with that hat. I used to yell at him, "Hold still! Leave that hat alone." He evidently had a little psychology going with it because it used to gripe the pitcher, too, and Harry led the league in hitting one year. I imitated him once, one day in Philadelphia. I stepped to one side and fidgeted with my umpire's cap and touched the peak and the back and adjusted and readjusted it. The crowd got quite a kick out of it. Harry laughed.

And Pee Wee Reese. Pee Wee was a wonderful person to know, a real friend, but he was the toughest man I ever had to umpire behind at the plate. Pee Wee was what they call a two-strike hitter, maybe the best two-strike hitter I ever saw. He was hard to strike out. He'd always get a piece of the ball. He would invariably take the first pitch. Once in a great while he would swing at it and when he did he'd hit it hard—a base hit, or right on the line to somebody. But mostly he didn't swing. Sometimes you wondered why, because the pitchers knew he was going to take it and they were always trying to get that first pitch in there.

Reese used to stand close to the plate and lean over it a little bit; it seemed to me they threw more close pitches to him than anybody else. And he had a slight crouch, not one that was out of line or an attempt to fool the umpire, but a crouch. He made it difficult for a pitcher to throw strikes to him. They couldn't pour one down the middle because Reese was a pretty good hitter. They had to be careful, and before they knew it there they were at three and two. Reese could work a pitcher up to three and two better than anybody. When he came up to bat you called more balls and strikes than you did on any other batter. He made you work. He'd wear you out. When we were on that good-will trip to Japan he was the same way.

I said, "What are you, still looking for a walk over here?"

He said, "I can't swing at that first pitch, John. I can't hit bad balls."

"They're not bad," I said. You might call a ball on him on a pitch barely an inch outside the plate. He'd take it. Another fellow would swing at a ball six or eight inches outside and get a base hit. Not Pee Wee. It had to be a strike for him to swing, and then usually it had to be the third strike. He'd drive you crazy.

Eddie Stanky was that way, except that he wasn't as good a hitter as Reese. But he had a good eye and he drew a lot of bases on balls. He could foul off pitches, too, one after the other. Stanky tried to crouch, but I straightened him up pretty quick. He'd stand at the plate and when the guy pitched he'd go into a crouch and kind of drop his head. It took pretty near a foot off the strike zone. I called a couple of strikes on him that looked very high the way he was crouching.

"That's not a strike," he said.

"It would be if you stood up in your natural stance," I said. Some guys hit out of a crouch, like Stan Lopata, the catcher the Phillies used to have. Stan crouched, but he stayed in the crouch when he swung. He was a good hitter, too, that Lopata. Give him a low ball and he'd tag it. But when Stanky swung at a pitch, he'd straighten up first.

I had no favoritism as an umpire, but I had a little soft spot for Stanky. I admired his heart. He wasn't a great player, but I don't think anybody ever tried harder or thought more about how to play the game. When he first broke in, he had a reputation for having been an umpire baiter in the minors. The first time he came to bat when I was working the plate he stood in the batter's box with his right foot way behind the back line of the box. I walked out and leaned over and dusted off the plate. Then I stood up and looked Stanky right in the eye. I said, "In the big leagues, you stand in the batter's box. Do you hear me?"

"Yes, I hear you."

"Well, that's what you're to do," I said. "Either get that back foot inside the batter's box, or get out of here."

He said, like a kid, "If that's the case, I'm going to stand way up in front."

"You might be a better hitter if you did," I said.

He got way up in the front of the box, and he found out he liked it there. I don't believe he ever changed after that, and he was in the big leagues for quite a while. He told me once, "You know, I think you helped me."

183

Andy Pafko used to put his foot out of the box. He'd scratch out the line, and then put his toe where the line was. But his foot would be outside. Andy was such a fine guy—he never bothered anybody, and he was a solid ballplayer—that I let it go. I always said whether you're in or out of the batter's box a couple of inches won't make you a better hitter. I didn't want to get too technical because I didn't think a guy could improve himself as a hitter doing that, anyway.

Johnny Temple was a terrible guy with most umpires, but never with me. Or almost never. He'd always try to get on base. He'd crouch and move up in the batter's box and then back. One day I called a strike on him and he said something I had never heard before, though you hear it a lot now. He said, "Where was that, on the black?"

"What?" I said.

"That pitch must have been on the black."

I said, "What are you talking about—black? Get up and hit. Don't give me that."

He backed out and he said, "I'm not mad at you, Jock. I just asked you was it on the black."

"Where's the black?" I yelled.

He leaned over the plate and rubbed the dirt off the edge of it, and where the plate bevels down it was black.

I said, "Well, I'll be. That's the black." I had been playing and umpiring for, I don't know, thirty-five years then, and I had never heard of that before.

Temple used to give umpires trouble when he was in a rundown on the bases. He'd put his hands on a fielder and then yell he'd been obstructed. He pulled that on me one time, and he got away with it. He fooled me. I called obstruction and let him go back to the base. The ballplayers knew what he had done. It was against Brooklyn, and when I made the call Pee Wee Reese shook his head.

"Not you, John," he said. "Anybody but you."

That's all he said, but the instant he said it I realized I had been suckered. No more than a week later, I was working another Cincinnati game and Temple pulled the same thing. But I was watching him like a hawk this time, and I saw him grab the fielder. I said, "You're out."

"Last week you called obstruction on that," he argued.

"That was last week," I said. "This is this week. You're out."

Reese called me John, and so did Gil Hodges and Duke Snider. I guess they picked it up from Reese. Big Frank Howard did, too. I was always amazed at Howard's shyness. He'd walk up to the plate with his head down, sort of tucked under his wing, so to speak. I didn't do this to many guys in my career, but I always spoke to Howard when he came to bat just to see what he'd do. I'd call out, "Hello, Frank!"

"Hello, John," he'd say, all embarrassed. He wouldn't even look at me. What a huge fellow—what is he, about six feet seven?—and what a pitiful case on curve balls. But when he got hold of one, good-bye. Like that one he hit off Whitey Ford in Chavez Ravine in the 1963 World Series. It was like he fired a rifle into the upper stands.

17

FELLOWS YOU HAD FUN WITH

SOME OF THE FELLOWS you seem to be having trouble with are really a lot of fun. You get a lot of laughs on a ball field. There was a time when Danny Murtaugh was playing second base for Pittsburgh and I called him out on strikes. He called me a name.

"Not even for you, Murtaugh," I said, and I put him out.

"Now wait a minute, Jock," he said. "Wait just a second."

Murtaugh could be a very funny guy, and he had put this soothing voice on.

"No, go on," I said. "Get out of here. You're through."

"I'll go," he said. "I'll go, Jock. But just let me say something, will you?"

"All right," I said. "Say it and get out of here."

"I want you to look around, Jock," Murtaugh said. "I want you to notice that there are two Polacks out there, Shuba and Hermanski. There are three colored guys, Newcombe and Campanella and Robinson. There are two Dagos, Furillo and Ramazzotti. And there are two limeys, Reese and Hodges. There are only two Irishmen here, Jock: Murtaugh and Conlan. Do you realize you're putting half of us out of the ball park?"

I said, "Shut your mouth and get back to the dugout. You're still in the game."

Frank Frisch was the prize, though. I threw him out of more ball games. He was in Dinty Moore's one night with Bill Corum, and Corum was asking Frisch about all the run-ins he had had with umpires. Corum said, "Did Jocko Conlan ever put you out of a game, Frank?"

186

"Let me see," Frisch said. He sat there thinking. Then he said, "I think Jocko holds the record."

There was a time in Brooklyn—so many things seemed to happen in Brooklyn—when Frisch was managing the Pirates, and they weren't too hot a ball club. It was a rainy sort of a day, with a thin drizzle coming down—not enough to keep you from playing but enough to be annoying. Pittsburgh was losing 1–0 in the third inning. If the game went into the last of the fifth it would be a legal game and if it was called then because of the rain, the Pirates would lose. So Frisch started agitating for me to call the thing off.

"Come on, Jock," he'd yell. "It's raining. Call the game."

He kept it up.

"What do you want? You want my players to catch pneumonia? They'll get their death of cold in this weather. Call the game, Conlan."

"It isn't raining hard enough," I said. It was unpleasant, but you could play in it. I'd seen worse.

Finally Frisch yelled, "You haven't got the guts to call it." Meaning I was afraid of being criticized by the club, because they'd lose the paid admissions if the game was called before the legal four and one-half innings were played.

"Oh, is it guts now?" I said. "It's a question of guts, is it? Maybe you haven't got guts enough to play it. It's only 1–0, you know. If you had any guts, you'd try to beat them."

That didn't stop him. He kept yammering. In those days photographers were allowed to work on the field. Later, the National League barred them and made them stay in the stands or in special coops that they had. But that day there were two or three photographers down on the field shooting the game. Frisch was always good copy, and when the photographers saw him yelling at me from the dugout they ran over as soon as the inning was over to get his picture. One of them was wearing a raincoat—I admit it *was* raining—and he had an umbrella with him.

I turned around to the ball boy to get some more baseballs and, as I did, Frisch, with his bright ideas, grabbed the photographer's umbrella and walked out to the third-base coach's box with it. When I turned back to start the inning, the top of the fourth, there he was standing in the box, holding the umbrella over his head. I glared at him. He held his hand out and looked up at the sky and said, "It's raining, Jock." The crowd started to laugh.

"Take it with you," I said.

"What?"

"Take it with you when you go."

"Ah, come on, Jock," he said. "Can't a guy have a little fun?"

I said, "Have all you want, Frank. But not at my expense. Get out of here."

"Ah, in your hat," he said, and he left. Frisch always said that when you threw him out, but he'd also say, "So long. See you tomorrow."

Frisch once gave me a textbook decision to make in Chicago, when the Pirates were playing the Cubs. It wasn't raining this day, but it had rained during the night and the field was wet, slippery. The Pirates had a ballplayer named Frankie Zak, a very fast runner, leading off first base. Frisch was coaching at third for the Pirates. Eddie Stanky was playing third for the Cubs. And I was umpiring at third. Jim Russell, a good batter, hit a shot to the outfield for extra bases and Zak ripped around second. There was no doubt, he was going all the way to the plate and score. But as he went around third Stanky gave him the hip. Zak went flying past the base onto his belly and skidded halfway to the Cubs' dugout.

Now Frisch was a great ballplayer—look up his record sometime—and a successful manager; he won a pennant and the World Series with the Cardinals in 1934. But, believe me, he never knew a rule. He didn't know one page in the rule book from the next. He was jumping around Zak screaming, "Obstruction! Interference! Blocking the basepath! I don't know what the hell it is, but it's something. He scores, doesn't he?"

I was holding my hands up to calm him, and I said, "He scores, Frank. He scores." Then I looked back, and here came Jim Russell; he was trying to stretch his hit into a triple. Frisch was still standing by Zak, but he started running toward third—after all, he was supposed to be coaching there. But instead of just going to the coach's box he ran past it and slid into third base. He made the most beautiful hook slide you ever saw in your life. He slid into third, Russell slid into third, and the ball came into third.

"Russell is safe," I said, "and Frisch is out. Of the game."

Frisch looked up at me. When he was playing he was famous for being a head slider. He always slid into a base head first. Now, lying there in the mud, he said, "The only time I ever made a hook slide in my life, and you put me out of the game."

"That's right," I said.

"It was a hell of a slide though, wasn't it, Jock?"

"It was a beautiful slide, Frank. Now get out of here."

"Ah, in your hat," he said. "So long, Jock, old boy. See you tomorrow."

Gee, Frisch had fun. His squabbles with umpires were seldom because of a decision or his griping about it. It was always some nutty thing that he did or said. There was no meanness in him. When he did argue about a decision, it would be in a 1–0, 2–1, or 3–2 ball game, where it was important. When the score was one-sided, Frisch never came out of the dugout. In a tough ball game he would. Some guys getting beat 10–0 come out and make a big stink just to put the hat on the umpire. Frisch never gave what we call a lousy beef, a pointless argument. But he could do crazy things.

One day in New York, a hot summer day, about 90° in the shade, with the humidity higher than that, he was managing the Pirates against the Giants. Frank lived in New Rochelle, which was only ten or fifteen miles from the Polo Grounds. He had a lovely house and a beautiful garden, a couple of dogs. He was always talking about it.

This was a doubleheader on a weekday, I think. There were only about five thousand people in the stands. The Giants weren't much good, and neither were the Pirates. Neither of the clubs was going any place that season. The game was dull. One of the teams got a big lead, and that was it.

Then, all of a sudden, here came Frisch out of the dugout. He was waving his arms and yelling, and I went toward him to stop him. Nobody was going to come out yelling at me like that.

When we came together he was still waving his arms, but he said, "Jock, old boy. I want you to do me a favor." The crowd was starting to make some noise now. This was the only thing interesting that happened all day. He said, "Jock, I want you to throw me out of this ball game."

"What are you talking about?" I said.

"You know my house up in New Rochelle, Jock. It's a lovely place. It's got trees and green grass and beautiful flowers. And I've got a nice little keg of Schlitz, all iced up, sitting down in the cellar. Jock, this ball club is driving me insane. I can't stand watching these .220 hitters any more. And it's hot. It's too hot. If you ever did me a favor, Jock, throw me out of this game. Let me go home."

Oh, boy.

"Frank," I said. "You're right. It is hot. It's terrible. This isn't much of a ball game. And the second game is likely to be just as bad. But you're sitting over there in the dugout in the shade next to the water cooler. I'm standing out here in the sun in a dark blue suit, in a mask and shin guards and a chest protector. I'm dying up here. And you're going to die with me. If you think I'm going to throw you out, you're crazy. Go back and suffer."

"Ah, in your hat," he said.

Once in Philadelphia I was working with George Barr and Lou Jorda. Barr had the plate, Jorda was at first base, and I was at third. There was a good-sized crowd there, and it was a tight game. Frisch came running out to kick about a decision at first base. He argued with Jorda, nose to nose for three or four minutes. Then he turned and he stomped into home plate, and he argued with Barr. Finally, he sort of shook his head in disgust and he came walking down to third base to me. I started walking away.

"Don't come down here," I said. "There's nothing here for you."

But he came all the way down to me, calm as could be, and

190

before I knew it he had his arm around my shoulder and he's talking to me real confidentially, just like two old pals.

"Where did you ever get those two old bastards you're working with?" he said.

"Get out!" I said.

"What did I do to you?" he said. His feelings were hurt.

I said, "You're going to tell fifteen thousand people how bad those two are, and then come down here and put your arm around my shoulder and tell them I'm your old pal? Get out of here!"

"Ah, nuts," he said. "I can't have any fun."

Bill Klem liked Frisch. "He's an honorable man," he used to say. Once, back in the '30s, several managers in the league got down on one of the umpires; they wanted to get him fired. They asked for a meeting with Ford Frick in the National League office. This umpire had just thrown Frisch out of a game, so Ford Frick asked Frisch to come to the meeting, too.

Frank walked in and he said, "What did you want, Ford?"

"Well," Frick said, "some of the managers here don't like So-and-So as an umpire, and they think we ought to let him go. What do you think?"

"What are you talking about?" Frank said. "He's the best umpire in the league. If you guys think you're bringing me into a meeting to knock an umpire, you've got the wrong guy. So long." And he walked out. Ford Frick told me that story himself.

Charlie Grimm was another manager who enjoyed life. Charlie was funny. It's hard to describe what he used to do because it doesn't *sound* funny, but it *was* funny. He'd coach at third base, and he'd exaggerate the signs to his hitters or he'd stick out his belly and walk in little circles. He was a great clown, and he could play to an audience. The crowds loved him. He had a little outfielder named Dom Dallessandro, who was only five feet six inches tall. Dom would slide into third base, and Charlie would pick him up bodily, dust him off, pat him on the back and stand him up on the base.

Charlie had his Cubs in Cincinnati one day for a Sunday doubleheader, and it was hot, at usual. That town to me was always the worst for heat. The Cubs were beating the Reds in both ends of a doubleheader, and when a home team is losing the fans can get pretty grumpy. But they liked Charlie so much, and they were laughing at him so hard, that they didn't seem to mind. I called a close play at third against the Cubs, and Charlie gave me an argument. The crowd booed me, and we jawed at each other for a few minutes. It wasn't a very big argument, but George Barr, who was umpiring at the plate, came down the line and said, "Come on, come on. It's hot. Let's get the game going."

Barr turned and walked back to the plate, and Charlie followed him, imitating his walk. George was little, and Charlie was big and it was hilarious, this great big fellow right behind the little umpire, imitating the little steps he took. The crowd was roaring. Barr didn't know what was going on, and he turned around. There was Grimm right behind him. Barr threw him out of the game.

Now Charlie was mad and he started yelling at Barr. I went in and said, "Come on, Charlie. You're through. You better leave."

"Oh, I know," he said. "I'm gone. But we were only having fun. What did he have to throw me out for?"

"Well, in any case, you're out," I said. "Why don't you go?"

And then he pouted, just like a kid. "I'll go for you," he said, "but I won't go for that so-and-so." And then he left. He was going to go anyway, but it made him feel better to say that.

I like it when fans have a good time at a ball park. Most fans have fun. Of course, some have too much fun, like that foreman at Hazleton. Or in Philadelphia—I don't know why it should be, but Philadelphia is the noisiest ball park in the National League and probably in the majors. An hour before game time, with nothing going on, there is more noise coming down from the grandstand than you'd hear in another ball park in the seventh inning. They are the noisiest people I ever heard. And the most rabid. There was a lady in Philadelphia who used to write to the umpires all the time. She'd tell us exactly what we did wrong and she would call us down for throwing this ballplayer or that one out of a game. And there was Big Pete in Philadelphia. Big Pete and his brother. They were hucksters, fellows who sold vegetables in the street, yelling, "Potatoes!" What voices they had. One of them would sit by first base and the other by third and they'd get you in a crossfire. They could get on you better than anybody in the whole baseball world. They'd find out things about ballplayers, their personal lives, and they'd holler them out. Or they'd nag on one thing. Terrible.

They were there in Philadelphia for years, back when Connie Mack was still alive and managing. The ballplayers complained to Connie and asked if he couldn't bar them from the park. Connie said, "There aren't many people coming to see us play these days, and those two pay a dollar and half a day to come in. They can holler anything they want."

But they were terrible, Big Pete in particular. He'd get down as close behind the dugout as he could. One day he pretty near started what could have turned into a riot. When Jackie Robinson first came into the league he drew big crowds everywhere he played, and he drew lots of colored people to the ballpark. This day in Philadelphia maybe half the crowd was colored, and a lot of Brooklyn fans had come down from New York for the game, too. Big Pete was getting on Robinson. He wasn't yelling anything racial, anything about Jackie being colored. He was just yelling, but he could be so irritating and so annoying and so nagging, he'd drive anyone crazy. Jackie didn't exactly have a high boiling point anyway, and he was about ready to go into the stands after Big Pete. He didn't, thank the Lord, though I don't think I would have blamed him. But if he had, what a mess that would have been: a Brooklyn ballplayer fighting a Philadelphia fan, a Negro fighting a white. That whole place could have exploded.

One day Big Pete got on Larry Goetz and started swearing at him. Goetz stopped the ball game. He said to the special police, "Take him out of here. There won't be another pitch thrown until he's gone." And the cops took him out.

The brother died, I believe, and Big Pete stopped going to the games. He moved to Florida, somebody said. I know I saw him down there at a ball game one day in West Palm Beach, still hollering things at the players.

Not all the oddball fans were like Big Pete. There was a fellow in Brooklyn named Eddie, who had one of those sweet potato whistles. He had a little accent, and he never could say my name right. Whenever I came out on the field, he'd blow that whistle of his and he'd call, "Umpire Conley! Umpire Conley!" He'd keep whistling and calling my name until I looked over and waved and said, "Hello, Eddie." That's all he wanted, just for you to recognize him. "My friend, Umpire Conley," he'd say. Then he'd go around and get Charlie Dressen at third base. He'd whistle and call, "Charlie Dressen! Charlie Dressen!" until Charlie would wave back and say, "Hello, Eddie." Then Eddie would say, "My friend, Charlie Dressen." They say the fellow had a lot of money.

It's funny how fans can make mistakes about ballplayers. Some players have a reputation with fans for being nice guys, and others have a reputation for being real bums. Sometimes the fans are right. There never was a nicer fellow than Stan Musial, and Gil Hodges was great. But there are others who got a bad rap. Rogers Hornsby, for instance; he never was particularly popular, but the umpires loved him. And Bill Terry of the Giants. He used to walk in from that center-field clubhouse in the Polo Grounds and be booed the whole way in. Most of that was from Brooklyn fans who were there, but Bill was never popular with Giant fans the way Mel Ott and Carl Hubbell were. And he was a splendid fellow, a very thoughtful and considerate man.

Or Ted Williams. The fans loved to ride Williams, hoot him, boo him, drive him to distraction. And yet I would say there has never been a ballplayer who behaved better toward umpires than Ted Williams. You'd think a player like Williams, who was supposed to be tense and irritable and high strung, would blow up when he got a bad call at the plate. He knew the strike zone perfectly. He knew it better than any other ballplayer. Yet he'd never say a word. He never complained.

I met Ted Williams when he was a minor-league player with the

Boston Red Sox farm team at Minneapolis. I was working in the American Association and I had been assigned to Minneapolis for spring training. That was a strange setup. Here I was an umpire, and they had me rooming with a ballplayer, a kid named Robert Robertshaw, a left-handed pitcher. This was in Daytona Beach. Williams had just been assigned to the team and he was in the next room to ours. There was a connecting door between the rooms.

I was in bed sleeping one morning, my face pushed down into the pillow, and Williams came into our room and jumped on top of me.

"Get up, Bush," he said. "Let's go!" He always called people "Bush," all through his career.

I pushed him off and rolled over and said, "Get out of here, you big skinny punk. What's the idea of jumping on me?"

"You're not Bush," he said. "You're not even a ballplayer. You're too old to be a ballplayer."

"Who are you?" I said.

"I'm Ted Williams," he said. "I hit twenty-three home runs in San Diego. I'll hit forty home runs in this league."

"You better wait till the league gets started. Maybe you won't even be here."

"Is that so? You watch me. I'm a great hitter." He was. He hit forty-three home runs that year.

I liked Williams right from the beginning. He seemed awfully cocky, but he was a nice kid. I was in the hotel one morning when Mike Kelly called me. He owned the Minneapolis ball club. This was my first year umpiring in that league, but I knew Mike from having played ball in the Association.

"I want you to come out and take a look at a boy we have. Tell me what you think of him." I went out with Mike to watch morning practice. The ball park wasn't the one in Daytona Beach that's near the ocean. It was back inside someplace and it had a tremendous long fence. Williams came up in batting practice and he hit three or four balls out of the park that looked as if they were shot out of a cannon.

"How do you like him?" Mike whispered.

"He's great," I said. "I never saw a more even swing. And the timing."

"Yes, he'll do," Mike said. "He's great now, but he's going to be greater."

Mike and Ted had a warm feeling for each other, a mutual admiration society. But Donie Bush, the Minneapolis manager, couldn't stand it when Ted would walk after a ball in the outfield, which he would do now and then. Williams was such a great hitter that the crowd always expected him to hit, every time. That went on all through his career. Whenever he made an out, they booed him. I know that at Minneapolis he could hit home runs his first two times at bat, but if he struck out or popped up the third time the crowd would get on him. He was just a young kid and his feelings would get hurt. If a ball was hit to him in the outfield the next inning, he'd walk after it. I saw Donie Bush pull him right out out of a game when he did that. But old Mike called Donie in, and he said, "Don't you ever take that boy out of a ball game again. You can't take a player like him out. Where will we ever see another like him?"

Then Mike got hold of Frank Bowman, the trainer, who later worked with the Giants, and he said, "Tell the boy I want to see him." When Ted came up to his office, instead of bawling him out about walking after the ball Mike put his arm around his shoulders and said, "You know, I used to do the same thing when I was a kid." And he would talk so gently and so skillfully that by the time Ted left the office he was practically crying. Williams often told me, "There was nobody else ever like Mike."

They had a special promotion one night in Minneapolis. They called it Centennial Night, and they had thirteen thousand people there in that old Nicollet Field. How they got thirteen thousand in that place I don't know. They were hanging from the eaves. Oh, it was jammed. Williams hit two home runs, and they were tremendous. They landed on the building across the street from the outfield fence. And then in the last of the ninth he came to bat with the bases loaded, two out and Minneapolis behind by a run. The count went to three and two. I was umpiring behind the plate. The crowd was yelling for another home run, or any kind of a base hit, or even a walk to force in the tieing run. And I ended the ball game by calling Williams out on strikes on a pitch right at his knees.

Donie Bush was coaching at third base and he came running in. "Ball?" he yelled. "It was down by his ankles. It was on the ground." A low pitch is always on the ground, and a high one is always over the head. The crowd was furious. Bush was yelling at me, and the fans were booing.

And then Williams did something I'll never forget, and it is one of the reasons I consider him a great friend of mine in baseball. He looked at Donie Bush and he shook his head.

"No, Donie," he said. "It was a good pitch. It was a perfect strike, right at the knees. I should have hit it."

I could have thrown my arms around him. I walked off the field and I thought, "What a man that is." I never had anyone else in my career do anything like that.

Another time, in the 1947 All-Star Game, I called Williams out on strikes again. It was in the Cubs' park in Chicago. I think Ewell Blackwell was pitching, and I called Ted out on a low pitch, a bad pitch. As soon as I called it, I knew I had made a mistake. The pitch was too low. I should have called it a ball. Here I called Ted Williams out on strikes on a bad pitch in an All-Star Game. You know what he did? He put his bat on his shoulder and he walked away. He didn't say anything.

I've always felt bad about calling that one wrong on Williams, but he has never said a word to me about it. All through his career, for all his temperament and his difficulties with the fans and the press, he had the same reputation with umpires that Musial had. I'd ask American League umpires, "What kind of a guy is this Williams?" To a man, they said, "Jock, he's the greatest." He never complained. He never argued, not a word.

Eddie Dyer was another decent fellow with umpires. He managed the Cardinals when they won the pennant and the World

Series in 1946. I made a call once on him that should have made him blow his stack. It cost him a ball game and maybe a pennant, and it brought about a change in the rules. In 1949 some of the players who had jumped to the Mexican League in 1946 were reinstated, and one of them was a left-handed pitcher with the Giants named Adrian Zabala. He was a Cuban and he had pitched in the United States and in Mexico. Wherever he had been pitching, he apparently had been allowed to do anything he wanted with his pitching motion. I don't want to go into all the technicalities of the balk, but when a man is on first base a pitcher is supposed to come to a stop in his pitching motion—if he doesn't pitch from a full windup. He brings his hands down, pauses for a moment, and then pitches. Every now and then we have trouble with that because pitchers get careless and ignore the rule more and more until finally the umpires have to crack down on them, straighten them out a little. That happened in 1949 and it happened again at the beginning of 1963. Everybody screams, but the pitchers come around after a while.

Anyway, in 1949 this Zabala was pitching for the Giants against the Cardinals. When there was a man on first base, he would bring his hands down to his waist, the way you do in the set position, but he didn't stop. He just kept right on going with his delivery. He didn't pause at all. I called him on it. Bill Stewart, who was umpiring the plate, called him on it. He was called on it three times in the same ball game, three straight times when there was a man on first base. Durocher was managing the Giants then and on the second balk he came running out to ask what was wrong.

"You better tell him to come to a stop," I said.

"I can't tell him," Durocher said. "He doesn't understand English."

"He doesn't have to understand anything," I said, "if you showed him the correct way to pitch."

The next inning there was a man on first again for the Cards. Nippy Jones was the hitter. Zabala pitched, didn't come to a stop

198

and I called another balk. But Nippy Jones swung anyway at the pitch that Zabala threw and he hit a home run. But I had called the balk, and the pitch therefore did not count. The home run was nullified, and Nippy Jones had to go up and hit again.

Eddie Dyer came out to ask about the decision. He was a little disturbed. It was a tight ball game, and his man had hit a two-run homer, and here was an umpire taking it away from him.

"When did you call the balk?" he said.

"Long before he let the ball go." I turned to Terry Moore, who was coaching, and I said, "Did you hear me call 'Balk'?"

Terry said, "Yes, I heard it. He called it before he threw."

That was good enough for Dyer. He accepted it. He was one of the few who could accept a decision like that, a decision that cost him two runs. He was a fine man, Dyer.

The Cardinals lost that ball game 3–1. And they lost the pennant that year by one game. That balk hurt, and especially since it had been called against the other team. So they changed the rule. Now, if a pitcher throws a ball illegally and the batter swings at it, the team at bat has the option of taking the balk or the hit, if there is one. It's their choice.

Sometimes you call a balk on a pick-off throw a pitcher makes to first base. The pitcher must throw in the direction he steps. For instance, if he steps toward the plate he must throw to the plate. And he cannot make a deceiving move. He has to stay pretty much in the same pitching pattern. Some pitchers have amazing moves to first base. Whitey Ford was great. So was Warren Spahn. Spahn rarely balked. His timing was terrific. Spahn was a marvelous athlete. Compare Spahn and Koufax, two of the greatest left-handers ever, two of the greatest pitchers ever. Spahn was a ballplayer. He could pitch. He could hit. He could field. He could run bases. He could knock you out of a ball game by picking a runner off first base. Koufax had much better stuff than Spahn. But Sandy had a poor move to first base. He wasn't much of a hitter. He was a slow runner. He was an ordinary fielder. Koufax was strictly a pitcher. But what a pitcher!

Sherry Smith, a left-hander who pitched for the Dodgers back around 1920, had one of the greatest moves to first. You know they say of some pitchers that they can look over at first base and if the runner happens to be tapping his foot on the bag, the pitcher will get him between taps. They used to say about Sherry Smith that if the base runner was only thinking about taking a lead Sherry would throw over and get him between thoughts.

Hughie McQuillan was another. He had pitched with the Giants and then he joined the Newark team I was with in the International League. They told us that when Hughie was with the Giants and it was a close game, if the other team got a man on base in a late inning McGraw would yank his pitcher and put Hughie in. Hughie would pick the runner off base, and McGraw would send another pitcher in to finish up. It was a good story, but it seemed fantastic to me. Yet Walter Johnson did exactly that with McQuillan at Newark when I was there. He took Hughie right out of the dugout—he didn't even warm up—and sent him out to the mound. Hughie took his five or six practice pitches from the mound, and then got ready to pitch. There was a base runner on second. Boom. McQuillan caught the man off second, and then Johnson took him out. I saw it happen.

A relief pitcher has to dispose of one man before he can be taken out. Ordinarily, this means he has to pitch to one batter for his complete time at bat. But if he picks a man off base, that's disposing of one man.

Bob Feller had a good pick-off play to second with Lou Boudreau. In the 1948 World Series, Phil Masi was on second for the Braves, Feller threw back to Boudreau and caught Masi off base—or, I should say, he did or he didn't. Bill Stewart made the decision and he called Masi safe. Then someone got a hit, Masi scored and that was the only run of the game. Feller got beat 1–0. There was a big controversy about it, because photographs—which you seldom can prove anything with—seemed to show that Masi was out.

I argued with Bill Stewart later that he was on the outfield's

200

side of second where he couldn't get a clear look at the play. In other words, he was behind the play. We have it in the National League now that the second-base umpire must be in on the grass when there are base runners. That is, inside the base lines. I put that in. I fought for it with Warren Giles. If you're on the grass, about fifteen feet down the line toward first base, there is nothing to obstruct your clear view of both the base and the tag on a steal, a double play or a pick off. If you're on the outfield side of the base, you're behind the play. You can't always get a clear view of the base or the tag.

The spring after that pick-off controversy in the 1948 Series I was working second base in an exhibition game in Los Angeles between the Cubs and the Indians. Feller and Boudreau worked that pick off twice that day, and the first time they did it Feller came running at me. He hadn't seen me call the man out. Boudreau yelled at him, "He's out! He's out!" Feller stopped then but he said, "Can I ask you a question? Boudreau and I have that pick off working pretty smoothly, but we feel we're not getting all the calls that we should. Where do you stand to call that play?"

I told him, and both of them said, "I wish the American League would start doing that."

But the American League won't. It has its way of doing things, and the National League has its way. It goes back to Tommy Connolly and Bill Klem, and the rivalry between them.

Umpiring should be uniform for both leagues. And I feel strongly that in both leagues the second-base umpire should be inside the base lines. I read recently that some of the general managers were saying that they thought four umpires were too many and that maybe they should go back to three, and get rid of the one at second base. That's foolish, but it's typical. In baseball there's a lot to worry about, but they're always worrying about the wrong things.

18

THE SPITBALL
AND THE BEANBALL

THEY KEEP TALKING about the spitball nowadays, the way the pitchers are getting away with it, and the way the umpires don't call it. Baloney. The spitball is a false issue. It doesn't exist. I umpired in the National League from 1941 into 1965 and I saw a spitball thrown exactly once. It happened in Brooklyn, but it wasn't Preacher Roe. After he retired, Preacher confessed that he threw the spitter. I say he didn't confess, he *claimed*. I say he didn't throw it. He couldn't throw hard enough. A spitball is a fast pitch. You've got to have speed to throw one.

When I was in the Midwest League in Chicago we had a pitcher named Lefty Sullivan. He couldn't field bunts, and if he did manage to pick one up he couldn't throw it to first. He must have become dizzy when he leaned over. The White Sox gave him a chance and he was bunted right out of the league. But he had a million-dollar arm. He could really throw hard and—this is the point—he threw a spitter. Every good spitball pitcher that I ever saw back in the old days threw hard. Preacher Roe had a little left-handed sinker ball and a slow curve and a slower curve and a slower curve. He was a clever pitcher. I liked him; Preacher was a good competitor. But he didn't throw a spitball. I think they should reinstate the spitball, if only to eliminate all the protesting. But even if they did reinstate it, there wouldn't be six pitchers in the league who could control it.

I know what a spitball is. Most of these guys talking about the spitter today don't know what they're talking about. They never saw one. They see a real good curve, a good sinker, and they swing and miss, and they complain, "Hey, take a look at that ball. He threw me a spitter."

Listen, when you see a spitter, there's no question about it. I know. I played ball when it was a legal pitch. I batted against it. When they banned it, around 1920, no new pitchers coming into baseball were allowed to throw it, but the old-timers who regularly used it were permitted to keep using it until they retired. One of the last of the old spitballers, Red Faber, was still around the White Sox when I played with them in the '30s. When an old-timer like Faber threw a spitter, sometimes you could see flecks of saliva flying off it when it was hit. It was really wet. There's a story about Burleigh Grimes, who threw the spitter, being ineffective in the 1920 World Series because the Cleveland team knew when he was going to throw it. Every time he got the sign to throw one, his shortstop would reach down and take a little dirt in his hand. See? The spitball was so slippery that an infielder wanted a little dirt on his throwing hand to make sure the ball didn't slip out of his fingers. You don't see a ball wet like that today.

The only pitcher I ever saw throw a spitter when I was umpiring was Whitlow Wyatt, who was a great star for Brooklyn when they won the pennant in 1941. It may be a coincidence, but Wyatt was on that White Sox club with Red Faber. It was the third out of an inning, and Wyatt really broke one off. The batter swung and missed it a mile. He didn't say anything. He didn't know what it was. They didn't yell as much about "spitters" in those days; it wasn't the fashion.

But I knew from its action what it was. As Wyatt went past me toward the dugout I called out to him, "Make that the last one of those you throw."

"What?" he said. "What? What?"

"You know what I mean," I said, and he kept going toward the bench. I walked out toward the mound and picked up the ball. The catcher had rolled it out there after the out. But if there had been anything on it, the catcher's glove and his hand and rolling it through the grass had cleaned it off.

Every pitcher in the majors has been accused of throwing the spitter, but except for that one of Wyatt's I never saw one thrown, not a real old-fashioned spitball. They accused Lew Burdette. He was always fidgeting on the mound and going to his mouth with his fingers. They were always claiming he was throwing a spitter, and they were always asking the umpire to look at the ball. I must have called for the ball from Burdette and examined it fifty times. And every time I asked for the ball he threw it right to me; he didn't roll it on the ground. It was always as dry as could be. I never saw Burdette throw anything but a sinker. It was a good sinker, but when the batter missed it, invariably he'd yell "Spitter! Spitter!"

There have been several pitchers who threw good downers. Clem Labine, who was at Brooklyn when Roe was there, had both a sinker and a good curve ball, a downer curve. The sinker broke straight down to a right-handed batter, maybe even in a little; the curve broke down and away. He was a strong pitcher. Rosy Ryan and Freddie Fitzsimmons had curves like that, and Cliff Markle and Walter Beall. Beall had one of the greatest curves you ever saw—just like it dropped off the table. George Earnshaw, who was a 20-game winner three straight years with the Philadelphia Athletics, had a great curve ball. The nearest thing to him in recent years was Koufax. Sandy threw his curve overhand; he was the only left-hander who threw the curve ball overhand to make it drop off, straight down. There was no question that his was the greatest curve around. You couldn't hit it any distance. It was a ball you beat into the ground. That was the reason for all his victories. He struck out a lot of men, but those that got the bat on the ball hit it on the ground.

You never hear the batters talk about a low pitch being a spitter when they get a base hit off it. From the way they talk, you'd think the spitter was a pitch nobody ever hit. If that was the case, those old guys liker Faber would have thrown it all the time. It was a good pitch, a hard pitch to hit, but it wasn't all-powerful. Its effectiveness was when it was used with other pitches, like a fast ball, the way Koufax used to mix that curve with his fast ball. The old-timers used it as a decoy, so to speak. Red Faber probably didn't throw more than twenty spitters a game, but he always came up to his mouth with his glove and bobbed his head as though he was spitting on the ball. He kept the batters guessing. Even Burdette said that. "Let them think I'm throwing one."

They used to accuse Whitey Ford of throwing a spitball all the time. Every time he struck out a tough hitter with a low pitch in the clutch, you'd hear that same old cry, "Spitter! Spitter!" Ford was a smart pitcher. He had a fast ball that he used to set up his curve and his sinker, that so-called spitter. After Yogi Berra, who caught Ford for years, went over to the Mets somebody asked him about Whitey's spitball. Yogi said it wasn't a spitter. He said Whitey used dirt, that he'd get some dirt to grip one side of the ball. I don't know if that's so or not, but it certainly sounds reasonable. It goes back to the shine ball. If you held the shine ball rough side up, it would sink; and there was no question but that Whitey had a great sinker. Of course, that's another thing they said about Ford: he threw a "dry" spitter.

I've heard some people say that a spitball is a sort of fast knuckle ball, that it moves the same way, except faster. What they mean is the knuckler is thrown without a spin, but slowly; because of the way you hold it, it doesn't spin. And that because of the slippery saliva, a spitball is also thrown without a spin; it slips out of your fingers without spinning. But the two pitches are not the same at all. The knuckler is erratic; it breaks left or right, this way, that way. You can never be sure. Don't let anyone kid you about that. If you could stand there and watch Hoyt Wilhelm throw a knuckler, you'd know what I mean. Wilhelm had the best knuckler I have ever seen, though Dutch Leonard had a good one, too. Wilhelm's knuckler was so erratic that his own catcher couldn't follow it. I was working a game in New York one day when Wilhelm was with the Giants, and his catcher, Ray Katt, set a new record for passed balls: four in one inning. Katt never touched any of them. Two of them hit him in the mask, and the other two went right past his shoulder. Katt said, "Get me out of here before I get killed." He hung in there, but what an ordeal. I have always contended that a knuckle ball is the hardest pitch for an umpire to call. You have to wait on a knuckler longer than you do on a fast ball or a curve or a slider or any other pitch. It has no pattern. It is much harder to call than a spitter would be, because a spitter can go only one way: down.

Sometimes you'll see a pitch go wild and almost hit a batter or go flying past the catcher back to the screen. Someone is sure to say, "That was a spitball that sailed." But a spitball doesn't sail; it drops, straight down. Those sliders they throw now will sail sometimes. A slider is nothing more than a fast ball that slides sideways a little. Casey Stengel always called it a nickel curve. That's what they called it in the old days: it was considered a bad curve ball. Today it's an effective pitch because there are so many more fast balls thrown; a batter expects a fast ball and a slider looks like one and then it moves just enough to upset his timing.

But a slider will take off and sail now and then, the way a shine ball would sometimes in the old days. You hear people mention the shine ball fairly often when they discuss the spitball and other old-time pitches, but I don't think many of them really know what a shine ball is, either. But thinking about Whitey Ford and all the complaints about sinkers, I have a suspicion that what they throw today is a lot closer to a shine ball than it is to a spitter.

The way they used to throw the shine ball, they'd rub it against the side of their pants and they'd get a glossy finish. The other side, they'd scuff up a little bit. When you held the shiny part up and the rough side down, the ball would sail up. It looked like a perfect pitch coming in and then it would sail up and throw the hitters off. If you held it shiny side down, rough side up, it would sink. I can see how wetting a ball a little could gloss one side a bit, and wetting the fingers can give you a better grip to impart spin. But that still isn't a spitter. The shine ball was dangerous because if you threw it with the shiny side up it could take off and hit a man, even though the pitcher had no intention of coming anywhere near him.

That's why they use so many baseballs in a game today—to keep the pitcher from fooling with the ball. Pitchers still do, when they can. You ought to see what a major-league pitcher can do with a roughed-up ball from infield practice. In a game, if a skillful pitcher happens to find a ball that's got a nick or a mark or a rough spot, he wants to keep it in play as long as he can. That's the reason batters ask to see the ball so often; they aren't claiming a spitter on every pitch. There may be a grass stain, or a dirt mark, or a mark where the bat hit the ball.

When I first was umpiring in the National League we started a game with twenty-four baseballs. Later it went to forty-eight, and now they begin with sixty. Once in a while all sixty will be used, and the umpires have to call for more. Any ball with a mark or a scuff or a tear goes out of the game, and the home club uses them later for batting practice. Of course, they lose a lot on foul balls into the stands, too. Years ago they used to go after the fans and take the ball away from them, and then they finally realized that it was good advertising, good public relations to let the fans keep them. There isn't a happier expression in the whole world than when a little boy in the stands gets a hold of a ball. And grownups look pretty happy, too. I like to see that.

Sometimes a ball can stay in play for a long time. When I was behind the plate I used to carry five baseballs in my pocket. I'd put a new ball in play as it was needed and get more balls from the ball boy to keep a supply of five with me. I worked the plate when Carl Erskine pitched a no-hitter, and I remember marveling that we went through three full innings with the same baseball. The ball was never thrown out, nobody even asked to see it, and there were no fouls into the stands. The ball was hit and fielded and thrown in to the pitcher and used again. For three innings I never went into my pocket for another ball. Never saw that happen before or since.

Sometimes a ball can be thrown out for no reason, or for no apparent reason. Sometimes a pitcher just doesn't like the feel of a ball. I've heard that when Ken Raffensberger, who pitched for the Phillies and the Reds, went to warm up he'd go through a dozen balls in the ball bag before he found one he liked. He'd say he was looking for a small one. Jack Sanford, who was a star with the Phillies and the Giants and the Angels, used to gripe me the way he kept asking for a new ball. He was always asking for a new one. I said one day, "What's wrong with this one?"

"It's too heavy."

I said, "It's too *heavy?*"

"Yes," he said.

"How much do you weigh?" I said.

"One hundred ninety pounds."

I said, "You're six feet tall and you weigh one hundred and ninety pounds, and this five-ounce baseball is too *heavy?* You ought to quit."

"I've got small hands," he said.

I got fined $25 once because of a pitcher like that. I was umpiring in the American Association and it was a hot, muggy day, the kind of a day when anything can get you irritated. There was a pitcher with Minneapolis named Walter Tauscher. He was a pretty good pitcher, but he was like Sanford—he was never satisfied with the ball. This day he has a ball out on the mound, and I have five in my pocket. He said, "Can I have another ball?" "Sure," I said, and I threw him a ball. He fidgeted on the mound and fingered it. He didn't like it, so I gave him another. The ones he didn't like I put back in my other pocket. He walked around the mound for a while and rubbed it up a bit and looked up into the stands, and then he got on the mound and gripped the ball, and then he backed off. It still wasn't right; he wanted another one. That was four, and he hadn't thrown a pitch yet. I said to the catcher, "What's the matter with the fellow? There's nothing wrong with the balls. Those baseballs are all perfectly good." The catcher shrugged and said, "That's Tauscher." I said, "Oh, that's Tauscher." As if that explained everything. It was hot and it was muggy, and Tauscher spent a little time rubbing up that ball. Then he shook his head and lobbed it in. "Give me another," he said. I threw him the fifth ball without saying a word. Sure enough, he didn't like that one, either. When he asked for another one, I took all five of the baseballs I had in my pocket and threw them all out to the mound. "Pick one out!" I yelled. The crowd laughed.

Tauscher said, "You're trying to show me up."

I said, "You're showing the game up."

The crowd got a kick out of it, but I got fined $25 by the league president for "not conforming to standard practices of the game" or something like that. It was worth it.

But to get back to the spitter and illegal pitches. It isn't the spitball they should be worrying about today. It's the beanball. That's the pitch they all say nobody throws, and it's just the pitch they do throw. It's not only against the rules now, it always has been against the rules, which is more than you can say about the spitball.

And don't tell me pitchers don't throw it. The managers make them throw it, even nice-guy managers, even managers I've respected in every other way. George Stallings used to say, "Hit him in the head. If you can't hit him in the head, hit him in the navel. But get him."

Times haven't changed. Every manager I played for, except for Walter Johnson at Newark, had their pitchers throw at hitters. Johnson was the one guy who could have intimidated batters by throwing at them, but he always told his pitchers, "If you can pitch, you don't have to knock anybody down."

They don't call it the beanball now. They get around that so cozily. They've got nice words for it. They don't say, "Throw a beanball." They say, "Brush him back." "Dust him off." "Pitch him tight." "Loosen him up."

All those words mean exactly the same thing: Hit him. Or come so close to hitting him that he has to scramble to get out of the way. He *has* to fall down. I heard Durocher one day yell, "Stick it in his ear." It didn't mean anything. Just an expression. "Loosen him up." "Brush him back." "Stick it in his ear." It's a common saying in baseball now, though I never heard it before the day I first heard Durocher use it. I stopped the game that day, took off my mask and said, "If he does, you're going out of here first and he's going to join you. Now let me see whether he does it or not." And he didn't.

I'm not singling out Durocher now. Every manager I played for did it, except Johnson. Stallings, Tris Speaker, Casey Stengel, Jimmie Dykes, men I otherwise admired, men I liked, good friends of mine. Every one of them said, "Knock him down." They claim it's part of baseball. Keep the batter loose up there. Don't let the horse get out of the barn, don't let him get a jump on you and beat you. Knock him down. Push him back.

What happens if the batter gets hit? In 1920 Ray Chapman got hit in the head, and he died. Other men have had their careers ended, like Mickey Cochrane. He was a great ballplayer, but he was hit in the head when he was only thirty-four years old and he wasn't worth a dime after that. Others have become gunshy. Joe Medwick was the best hitter in the National League when he was beaned; he was a run-of-the-mill ballplayer afterwards.

That's baseball? To risk a man's life or his career? And what about the umpire? What about the legal aspects of it? The umpire is supposed to warn the pitcher if the pitcher throws a knockdown pitch. He's supposed to say, "Don't throw another." And if the pitcher does throw another, he's supposed to be put out of the game, automatically.

I've warned them. I've warned lots of them. I warned Durocher that time. I warned Casey Stengel in the 1957 World Series. Casey was managing the Yankees and he brought Art Ditmar in to pitch against the Braves. Ditmar was all right. He wasn't vicious. But he knocked Aaron down and he knocked Crandall down. I walked out to the mound and I said, "It's a little rough up there at the plate, and I don't want you throwing at anybody any more."

"Jock," he said, "it slipped."

I said, "If another one slips, you're going to slip out of the game."

Casey came trotting out waving his arms. "What's the matter, my boy?" he said to me. Then he said to Ditmar, "Art, are you and my boy having words?"

I said, "Look. There'll be no more of that knockdown stuff. It's tough enough to follow the ball umpiring. You know what the shadows are like in this ball park. No more knockdowns."

Stengel said, like they all say, "That one just slipped."

"I already heard that," I said. "And I told him if another one slips, he's going to slip out of here. And I'll tell you, Casey, you're liable to slip with him."

"All right," he said. "Now, Art, if my boy says that, he means it. Let's go along now."

It's funny, sure, but what about the umpire? He warns a pitcher if he feels that the pitcher threw at the batter deliberately. The umpire is supposed to be an expert judge of that by virtue of his experience; and he is. Now, suppose the pitcher does it again and hits the batter and kills him or maims him or ruins his career, makes him gunshy. Suppose the batter or the batter's family brings suit. The basis of the suit would have to be the umpire's action— that he had already in public accused the pitcher of deliberately throwing at the batter. They have evidence of intent. What a nice spot for the umpire to be in. The stigma is all on him. He's the one who called it a beanball.

Why should it all be on the umpire? Suppose he ignores it and sits back and lets the pitcher throw at everybody. Somebody is liable to get killed. Especially now with so much night baseball. Nobody knows how differently a ballplayer's eyes react at night compared to day; at least, I don't know of anybody who has proved anything one way or another. But, as an umpire who has worked day games and night games, I *know* that it's harder to judge the ball at night. Throwing at a batter at any time is terribly dangerous, but especially at night.

They say that because batters all wear helmets now, there's no danger. Sure, batting helmets have probably saved a few lives, but did you ever get hit in the head with a pitched ball while you were wearing a batting helmet? It hurts. It hurts plenty. And you can get hit under the helmet, in the ear, on the cheekbone. A fast ball travels 90 to 100 miles an hour, and there are more big powerful guys throwing fast balls today than ever before. You can't have pitchers like that throwing at a man's head.

An umpire can't ignore beanballs. He has to step in. And then everything falls on his shoulders. Why does he have to carry the bag? Particularly when beanballs can be stopped like *that*. It's the managers, not the pitchers, who throw at the batters, the gutless wonders sitting over there in the dugout, sitting on the bench, telling their pitchers to knock somebody down. The manager can't get hurt. He doesn't have to come to bat. He doesn't have to run the bases, or tag a guy sliding in hard. He's like the old fight manager telling his fighter to get in there and mix with him, he can't hurt us.

The ballplayers don't like it, because they know that when their manager orders a pitcher to throw at an opposition batter, then the opposition manager is going to order his pitcher to throw at them. Naturally, the other club retaliates, and players on both sides get shot at. The managers are immune. No wonder they got so much guts.

There are a lot of pitchers who don't want to throw at the batter, but the managers make them. Or else they throw at the batter because of a custom that has come into being because of the beanball. A player says, "My pitcher has got to protect me. He has to throw at the other team." Nuts. The great pitchers don't do it. I didn't like Robin Roberts, but he was a great pitcher and I never saw him throw at a batter. Bob Feller never did. He'd have been afraid of killing someone. Koufax didn't throw at hitters, though now and then he'd lob a ball over a batter's head, as if he was doing something he was supposed to do but didn't really want to.

They argue that some pitchers were never effective until they began to brush hitters back, get them loose. I say they never were pitchers in the first place. You can pitch inside and outside, up and down, keep a batter off balance, keep his timing off, without trying to hit him in the head. If you're a pitcher.

It's so pointless, too. The good hitters—ones like Musial, Mays, Aaron, Frank Robinson, that type—if you throw at them, it backfires, because the good hitter gets mad and hurts you twice as much with his bat. Anyway, what they usually do when a man hits a home run is knock down the next batter. What is that supposed to do? Scare the first guy into not hitting any more home runs?

It's stupid. The managers can stop it, and they will stop it if the owners tell them to. I can't figure out why the owners don't. They have all these million-dollar ballplayers—Mays, Aaron, Brooks and Frank Robinson, Richie Allen. At the prices they're giving bonus kids today, don't you think a great player is worth at least a million dollars on the open market? Suppose one of them is crippled by a knockdown pitch and ruined? Or a pitcher is run down and hurt on the base paths in retaliation? There's a million dollars down the drain. You'd think the owners would protect their investment. You'd think they'd say, I have four players on my club worth a million dollars or more apiece, and every other club has a few. Great ballplayers are hard to find, but they're the ones who attract the crowds. Why ruin them by throwing at them?

All the owners have to do is get together and give a group order, a command, to all major-league managers: "We do not want anybody hit or knocked down or thrown at. If any of your pitchers throws a knockdown pitch, *you* will be suspended for thirty days. If it happens a second time, you're through."

Tell the managers that, and they'll stop. Sure, there will be occasions when a ball really does slip and hits a batter or comes very close to him. A pitcher can lose control, but you can tell that. And you can tell when it's deliberate. Anybody who watches the game closely can tell when it's deliberate. But the umpire is the one who has to call it. He is the one who has to accuse a man of doing such a terrible thing.

And it is a terrible thing, a very dangerous thing, and they ought to do something about it. Forget about the phony spitter. Worry about the real beanball. If a man like Walter Johnson can say, "You can win without throwing at a batter," then you don't have to do it. It's not a game when they do that. They're not throwing a baseball then. They're using a weapon. It's like having a knife and a gun.

213

19

THE UMPIRES' STRIKE

CONSIDERING THEIR RESPONSIBILITY and their importance to the game, umpires have always been poorly paid. It's no wonder the umpires went on strike that time, or almost went on strike.

When I broke in as an umpire in the minors in 1936, I made $300 a month and the season ran no more than five months. I had a little money saved up for my family to live on; otherwise, we couldn't have made it. In the winter I always worked. I was a playground director for the city of Chicago, and later on I opened a florist shop. But you had to cut every corner you could. When I went back for my second year of umpiring in the New York-Penn League—they changed its name to Eastern League that year—I bought a little Pontiac coupe for $150. We were paid five or six cents a mile for gasoline and maintenance, and that helped. That was a great car. I had a puncture the first day of the season, and a puncture the last day, but in between it took me every place I had to go. And when the season was over I sold it for $150.

When I moved up to the American Association in 1938 my salary went up to $500 a month and our expense allowance was a little higher. But it was still only for five or six months: maybe $3,000 for the year. The minors were five years of struggling and hoping that the Lord would take care of your health and keep you safe and sound and someday give you the chance to get to the big leagues where you could make a decent living.

But even in the big leagues my salary was terrible at first. I have always been grateful to Ford Frick for giving me my chance in the National League. But the money was awful. I got paid $3,600 my first year and $7 a day for expenses. That's $7 a day for food, hotel and incidental expenses. When I look back on it, I wonder how we made it. The cheapest decent hotel room you could get in those days was $3. Which left you $4 to eat three meals with, take care of your laundry, keep your clothes cleaned and pressed and get yourself to and from the ball park. We were allowed a little extra for taxi fare the first day in any new town; that's because we had our big equipment bag with us, as well as our own suitcase.

They raised me $900 my second year, but then World War II came and after the 1942 season they sent me a contract with— imagine this—a raise of $250. This was the major leagues. I wrote and said, "Either I'm a better umpire than this, or I'm no good at all." Frick wrote back, "Well, there's a war on, and we may have to shut down. We don't know if we're going to play or not. President Roosevelt is liable to tell us to stop." I wrote him and said, "If he stops you, then you won't have to pay me at all."

I think I got $500 then. But that seemed to be the maximum. Once or twice I got a $1,000 raise, but $500 seemed to be the biggest raise an umpire ordinarily could expect. I used to fight with them. When I sent my contract back unsigned one year, Frick sent me a letter. He said, "Year after year after year after year—" he said it four times—"you keep sending your contract back. Can't you understand the terms of it?" I wrote him, "I understand it, but I can't see the figures. They're too small."

I can't say that I was well paid under Frick. I repeat that I'm grateful for the chance he gave me, because it wasn't easy to make the big leagues, but in turn I felt as though I gave him good service. I was a good umpire for him, and I earned whatever I made. But my first few years under him, I was making less than I had as a minor-league ballplayer fifteen years before.

I had been in the league eleven years when Giles came in as president, after Frick was made Commissioner. From then on, it was much better. Warren Giles was the best friend the umpires ever had. He saw to it that we got better pay—not that we've ever been overpaid by any means, but my first raise under Giles was $1,000 and he raised our daily expense money to a more realistic figure.

He gave young fellows decent salaries to start out with, which was good, and he saw to it, too, that umpires who had been in the league a long time, and who had started out at much lower salaries than the newer fellows, got bigger raises to even things out.

I don't say he over-raised us. I do say he raised us real good, and today the National League umpires get more money per man than the American League umpires. Bob Addie, the Washington sportswriter, had a story in *The Sporting News* talking about the low salaries umpires get; he said tops was $15,000. That's for the American League. I'd say there's a $3,000 or $4,000 difference between the top salary in the American and the top salary in the National. It's now $20,000 and over in the National. Rookie umpires start at $9,500. I was working in the league nearly ten years before I got $9,500.

When you talk about the low salaries back then they keep giving you that old story about how you could buy a lot more with your money in those days. I can't see that argument. I couldn't buy *anything* with my money back in the old days. I can buy a lot more now. I'll take a little more money any time.

Giles arranged for us to have travel cards so that we could charge our plane and train fare. It used to be that we had to carry lots of cash with us all the time. It was seldom that a hotel would accept a check, and it was almost impossible to pay for transportation with a check.

Giles fixed it for Railway Express or Air Express to pick up our equipment bags at the ball park after our last game in a city and deliver them right to our dressing room in the next park. The clubhouse boy would unpack them and hang our things up so that everything would be ready for us when we got there. Each umpire in a team would tip the clubhouse boy $4 or $5 each trip; the clubhouse boy would take care of things if you needed any laundry done or if anything needed cleaning or pressing. What a difference from the old days when we had to lug those equipment bags ourselves from the park to the railroad station, and then from the station to the hotel and then from the hotel to the ball park. Giles changed that, and you have no idea how much it meant to an umpire.

He did things like seeing to it that in places like Los Angeles or San Francisco, where it's difficult to get a taxicab sometimes, there'd be rental cars available to us that we could charge on our travel card. Warren Giles made umpiring a decent job, and every umpire owes him a vote of thanks.

Giles was really so much better than Frick. Frick was a nice man, but he never did anything. He didn't seem to have much interest. You very seldom saw him at a ball game, except at the World Series or opening day or at an All-Star Game. Giles is at ball games all the time, in whatever city he may be in at the moment. Frick to me was just a guy who got his pay. What did he ever do? Whenever a problem came up when he was Commissioner he'd say, "That's a league matter." And he always seemed worried about spending money, even on little things. For instance, they give the players and the umpires in a World Series a little memento—a ring, or a cigarette case, something like that. Nice, but nothing extravagant. One year—it was 1957—Frick met with the umpires and he asked each one what he wanted, and he didn't ask me. I said, "What about me?" He said, "There isn't any for you this year." I said, "Why not?" He said, "You've been in enough World Series. You don't need any memento this time." I said, "If all these guys are entitled to a memento, why aren't I?" But he wouldn't give in, and I never got one that year.

And then in 1961, I was in the Series again, and we had the same meeting and this time he asked me what I wanted. I said, "Well, I don't know. You turned me down the last time I worked a Series. How can I ask you for something now?" He said, "Do you want a ring?" I said, "No. I don't want a ring. I got a ring." He said, "I'll send you a pin then." I said, "I'll take it." He sent it to me, and it's a beauty, I'll say that. But I still don't understand why he wouldn't give me anything that other time.

Frick did another thing to me in that 1957 Series. He fined me $100 and I still think he had no right to. He had issued an order that no outsiders were to be allowed in the dressing rooms before the games, whether it was the players' dressing rooms or the umpires' dressing room. By outsiders, he meant anybody who was not in that particular World Series. He said that he would see to it that there would be a guard at the door of the umpires' dressing room, just as there are always guards at the doors of the players' dressing rooms. I guess the idea was that they didn't want anybody talking to the umpires—hoodlums looking for information that would help them make bets or set odds or anything like that. Frick wanted to keep the game at a high level all the way through, which is right, and the way it should be.

But I was in the washroom in the umpires' quarters in Yankee Stadium. I had just got through rubbing up the baseballs for the game, and I was washing the dirt off my hands when Beans Reardon and Larry Goetz came busting into the room. There hadn't been any guard at the door, but even if there had been he probably couldn't have stopped Reardon and Goetz, anyway. The kind of men they were, they wouldn't have cared if it was Frick standing there, or Judge Landis, or anybody.

"We just want to get a couple of baseballs for Hal Stevens," Reardon said. The umpires always had a few extra baseballs, and old Hal Stevens of the Stevens concessions family was one of the grandest men anyone could ever want to meet. A fine, warm man, and he loved the umpires. Bill Klem and the Stevenses had been tremendous friends. It was Klem back in the early days who was one of those who helped make the Stevens family business what it eventually became. In those days old man Stevens sold scorecards and pencils, but he came to Klem and he said, "On doubleheader days, if I could have five minutes between games I could sell some peanuts, too." At that time, one game of a doubleheader followed right after the other. The starting pitchers for the second game would be warming up in front of the dugouts along about the eighth inning of the first game, and as soon as the game was over the second game began. There was no more interval than there would be between innings today. Stevens asked Klem if he could give him five minutes between the games, and Klem did. The fans enjoyed the break. It gave them a chance to get a hot dog and a drink, and Stevens put in different things and really built it up. Now there's a half hour between games, and when you have a crowd of fifty thousand the sales between games are tremendous. Concession revenue is a very important part of a ball club's income. And for it, baseball can thank Klem's consideration for Stevens way back then.

The Stevenses were always grateful to Klem, and they were close friends after that, and it continued with other umpires, too. It was a natural thing, then, for Reardon and Goetz to come in for a couple of baseballs to give to old Hal Stevens. I said, "Help yourself, but you're not supposed to be in here, you know." They took the baseballs and left. Mel Allen, the announcer, was sitting in there, too, drinking a Coke, and I told him. Allen was a good friend of the umpires, but I said, "Mel, nobody is allowed in here today."

"Who says so?"

"Frick," I said. "Those are his orders."

"Oh, who cares?" he said. "I'll be going in a little while."

The next day, just before the second game was to start, Charlie Segar came in. He was Frick's assistant. It was ten minutes to one, and the game started at one o'clock. I was working the plate.

"The boss wants to see you," Charlie said.

"He wants to see me?" I said. "Now?"

"Yes, now." I went out on the field and walked over to Frick's box. The first thing he said was, "I'm fining you one hundred dollars."

"For *what?*"

"You let two umpires in your dressing room, and I told you the order was nobody allowed in the dressing room."

"I know that," I said. "But I didn't let them in. They came in. I was in the washroom. All they wanted was a couple of balls for Hal Stevens, and then they left."

"Well, that's it."

I said, "You mean you'll take one hundred dollars off me for that?"

"Who were the umpires?" he said.

"If you know I let two umpires in, you must know who they were."

"Reardon and Goetz," he said.

"I want to tell you something, Mr. Frick," I said. "I broke in with Reardon and Goetz. I never knew two more honorable guys in all my life. They served you and baseball well for more than twenty years. If I can't give them a baseball, as decent and loyal as they are, then I don't care. You can have the hundred dollars. Keep it."

And then I had to go up and umpire behind the plate. A World Series game, and I had to go through this ten minutes before it began. It was in that game I called Ditmar on the beanball. And I also turned the lights on that day. Early, two o'clock in the afternoon. Nobody had ever turned lights on that early before, but it was just too dark around the plate and I went over and told them to turn the lights on. The next day, after we'd gone to Milwaukee, Frick complimented me. He complimented me for stopping the beanballs and for turning on the lights. They were telecasting the game in color, and the TV people were having trouble with their picture before the lights went on. Frick said the TV people had called him to thank him, and he passed the compliment on to me. But he never gave me back my $100.

Umpires don't get paid enough for working a World Series, anyway. You only get in a Series about once every six or seven years on the average, though it used to be a little more frequent before expansion, when there were fewer umpires. In my twenty-four full seasons, I worked six Series—1943, 1945, 1950, 1954, 1957, 1961. Roughly once every four years. In the old days, four men would work the plate and the bases, and they'd assign two more as alternates, in case one of the regular men got sick or hurt. I was an alternate in 1943, my first Series.

They always hold a meeting before the Series to discuss things,

and at the meeting in 1943 Joe McCarthy of the Yankees mentioned that he had seen games won and lost on disputed decisions
over balls hit right down the foul lines. He suggested to Judge
Landis that they take the two alternate umpires and station them in
the outfield, along the foul lines. Landis glared at him with those
little pointy eyes of his, and he snapped, "Four men on the field
are enough. Is there any other business to discuss?" Landis liked
to be fast and decisive even when he was wrong. He had people
looking up at him; he had them scared of him, too. A lot of
matters were never brought to his attention because of that; he
could shoot down a good idea, like McCarthy's about the alternate
umpires.

When Happy Chandler became Commissioner after Landis died,
McCarthy's idea was put into effect and the alternates were put to
work in the outfield. Now all six umpires rotate during the series.
In a six- or seven-game Series, every man works every position at
least once: plate, bases and outfield. The umpires wanted that for
a long time.

In the beginning, the regular four umpires got paid $2,500
apiece for a Series and the two alternates got $1,000 each. It was
that way when I broke in, and it had been that way for, oh, twenty
years, I guess. We thought we should get more, and in 1945 I spoke
to Chandler about it. I suggested that they pool one winning share
and one losing share and split it evenly for each two umpires. The
Commissioner and the two league presidents decide on things like
that, and the two presidents then, Frick and Harridge, voted against
it. They said it was the players' money, and the umpires couldn't
touch that. I said, "Players' money? It's the people's money. It's
supposed to go to the participants. Umpires are participants just
as much as the players are." But they said No. I said, "Well, we
ought to get more than $2,500 and $1,000." Chandler said, "What
do you think you ought to get?" I said, "If you want to give us a
raise, give us $4,000 and the alternates $2,000." He said, "I think
that's fair." But he didn't have the power to authorize it.

He did get us a boost in our expense money, though. I think we

221

were getting $15 a day then for the Series when the question came up about getting more. This was 1945, just as the war ended, and Art Passarella of the American League spoke up and said, "In the Army, I got by on a dollar a day."

"Who's asking you?" I said. "This isn't the Army. It's the World Series. We got to pay for hotels, meals, taxicabs, everything. Don't tell me about your dollar a day."

So Chandler raised it; I think he made it $25 a day for the Series, and now I believe it's $30. But they wouldn't raise our fee, not then. Around 1950, I think, it went up to $3,000 for the regular umpires and $1,500 for alternates, and later on to $4,000 and $2,000. Now it's $4,000 for all six, since none of the umpires are considered alternates now.

That guff about the World Series money being the players' money has always annoyed me. They used the same argument when they put the Player Pension Plan in after World War II. One of the great injustices in baseball was leaving the umpires out of that Pension Plan. But that's the way it always is. I don't think baseball people are deliberately mean and unfair to umpires; they just forget about us all the time. They say a good umpire shouldn't be noticed, that it's only when something goes wrong that people become aware of him. If that's the case, we must be awfully good because we're not noticed most of the time. They build ball parks, and they don't provide for umpires' dressing rooms. They put in a pension plan, and they leave us out of it. I always felt that if Ford Frick, as president of the National League, had insisted that the umpires be included back when they were drawing up the plan, there never would have been any question about it. It wouldn't have affected the size of the players' pensions by much. Heck, there were only a couple of dozen umpires in both leagues at that time, and there are only about forty now.

In the 1950s and '60s we tried several times to get the player representatives to suggest that we be brought into the plan. We talked to different fellows—Ted Williams and Stan Musial and Gil Hodges and others—and they came out openly and said they thought it was only right. Robin Roberts was the head of the National League player representatives at the time. Somebody told me once that Bob Carpenter, the owner of the Phillies, said that Roberts ought to end up with a million dollars, he was such a tough negotiator about money. "He's as cold as ice," Carpenter said. I believe it. I collared Roberts after one of the players meetings one year.

"Did you fellows decide anything about the umpires?" I asked him.

He looked right through me with those blue eyes of his.

"What?" he said.

"I hear you talked about the pension plan," I said.

"Why, yes, we did," he said.

"Did you decide anything about the umpires?"

He gave me one of the most disgusted looks I ever saw in my life.

"We didn't even discuss you fellows."

"Isn't that nice," I said. "Great guys like Williams and Musial and Hodges say the umpires belong in the plan as much as they do, but you don't even discuss it."

The umpires had a pension plan of their own, of course, the same one Harry Grabiner told me about back in 1935. You got $100 a year pension for each year you served as an umpire. Beans Reardon retired in 1950 after twenty-four years of service, and he received a pension of $2,400 a year without putting a penny of his own into it. The league did that. But in 1950, a pension of $2,400 a year didn't sound quite as good as it did in the 1930s. It was still the same $100 a year per year of service, and it was never changed until Warren Giles succeeded Frick as president.

Giles raised the pension the first year he was in office. He upped it from $100 a year to $150 and then later to $200, and he made the increase retroactive for umpires who were still in the league. We contributed 5 per cent of our salaries to the pension, but it was worth it because the pension was doubled.

We still didn't like it too much, though, because it couldn't compare to what the ballplayers were getting. And there were other things we wanted—insurance and hospitalization and things like that. We had Blue Cross, but we paid for it. So we organized an umpires' association in the National League. It was really started by Augie Donatelli and myself in 1963. We planned a meeting in Chicago on an off-day because Chicago was the easiest place for umpires traveling east and west to new assignments to get together. We elected five directors: Tom Gorman, Al Barlick, Shag Crawford, Augie Donatelli and myself. We had decided that we wanted a lawyer, and because the meeting was to be held in Chicago, where I had lived for so long, they asked me to suggest one. I knew a lot of lawyers in Chicago, and we settled on John J. Reynolds, a young fellow I knew, a very intelligent man. I got in touch with Reynolds, and he was interested, so he came to the meeting and sat down and talked to us. He listened to what we had to say, and he explained some things to us. He told us what he thought he could do, and he told us what his fee would be.

We talked it over and we decided to retain him. The following winter the major-league meetings were to be held in Los Angeles. We agreed to have a meeting of our own there, because Reynolds thought it would be good for us to be in Los Angeles then. We would be there more or less like a lobby, working for our interests and trying to get the owners to do something for us.

I think we made a mistake in not telling Giles in the first place that we were hiring a lawyer, because anything we got would have to be got through Giles anyway. But after we retained Reynolds, he went down to Cincinnati and met Giles and he made a good impression. It shows you how fair Giles is that he agreed to let Reynolds talk to the league's executive board at Los Angeles. Buzzie Bavasi of the Dodgers was on that board and John Holland of the Cubs and Bill DeWitt of the Reds.

Reynolds spoke to the board and asked for certain things for the umpires. He asked for hospitalization, life insurance, increased pension benefits and things like that, very similar to what the ballplayers were getting. The main thing was the pension. We wanted it raised to $300 for each year of service. We figured that a man who had umpired twenty years deserved a $6,000 pension. We thought that was fair.

When Reynolds was through talking, the executive board recommended that he be given the opportunity to present his case to the pension board. I believe Bavasi made the motion, and Holland seconded it. The pension board had John Galbraith of Pittsburgh as chairman, and men like Don Grant of the Mets and Walter O'Malley of the Dodgers were on it and a few others. Giles arranged for Reynolds to talk to the pension board, and he seemed to be pretty well received. It was encouraging. They said they'd take his proposals under advisement.

But nothing happened, and the umpires got restless. We had another meeting in Chicago in May of 1964. About the same time, Giles got the pension base raised from $200 to $250. He didn't know about the May meeting; he just did that on his own.

But the umpires wanted the $300 base, and they wanted the other benefits. They felt the owners were giving them the runaround. We met in May at the Union League Club in Chicago and took a vote and decided to go out on strike on July 4. I was against the strike. I thought it was a mistake, and I said so. I said, "You cannot go on strike without giving the league president a chance to negotiate."

They said, "We're going out on strike."

I said, "Look, whatever you decide to do, I'll go along with it, because I'm an umpire and I'm all for the umpire getting everything that's coming to him. But you're doing it the wrong way. You're trying to bulldoze them. Why don't we send the lawyer down to talk to Giles again and explain our position? That's what we hired the lawyer for."

If you have ever been in a meeting with twenty umpires, I guarantee you that when the meeting was over, nobody had gotten any place. Because there would have been twenty different motions and twenty different seconds. It's the damndest conglomeration you ever heard in your life when umpires get together. That was the reason we hired the lawyer, to get something done. One man can talk for twenty, and that's the proper way to do it.

"We're going out on strike," they said. "We're going on strike on the Fourth of July."

"What a day," I said. "One of the biggest days of the year in baseball, and you're going out. You're really going to defy them."

About a month later I was working a ball game in Los Angeles. It was in June, getting close to July. Buzzie Bavasi came to me, and he said, "I want to ask you a question about something that's just beginning to dawn on us. Are the umpires really going out on strike?"

I said, "Yes, they are."

"Are *you* going out on strike?" he said.

Buzzie was always a big help to the umpires, and a good friend to me. But I said, "Buzzie, I'm an umpire. I have to go along with them. It's the only thing I can do. I don't like it. I think we should have gone to Giles again. But that's the way it is."

Buzzie said, "Gee. Everybody is beginning to think about this. It's a bad thing. It's pretty serious."

I said, "I know how to stop it."

"You know how to stop the strike?" he said. "How?"

"I *think* I know," I said. "At least, I have an idea."

The All-Star break that year was the 6th, 7th and 8th of July, and the strike was due on July 4. All the major-league clubs are represented at the All-Star Game and they usually have a meeting.

I said, "If you can get our lawyer, Reynolds, representation at the All-Star Game—if he could present our case to *all* the owners there, as to what we want—I think the strike would be postponed."

"That's all?" he said. "It's that simple? You think that would do it?"

The thought had just come to me, but I said, "If he can talk to them, I think we'd vote to put it off."

Bavasi phoned Giles, and Giles promised that Reynolds would have the opportunity to speak to the owners at the All-Star break. When the umpires heard that, the strike was called off.

It was important because that was the only chance Reynolds had of getting our case before all of them. They came to an agreement. We didn't get everything we wanted, but we got the big thing. The pension was raised to $300 for each year of service up to the age of fifty-five—you can work past fifty-five but your pension doesn't get any bigger. There were other details. Instead of paying 5 per cent of our salaries into the pension fund, we paid a flat $350 instead. Each umpire's life was insured for $20,000 ($50,000 in case of accidental death). Hospitalization is still being argued about.

But the main thing was, the strike was off. The umpires' demands, which were reasonable, were recognized.

Maybe the owners recognized, too, that baseball without umpires is nothing. They can't play without us. They should remember that.

20

RETIREMENT AND RETURN

IN 1962 WARREN GILES SAID to me, "Jock, listen now. You're getting up there in age, and you've been up here quite a while now. More than twenty years. When you feel you've had enough, or when you feel you can't umpire any more, I want you to let me know. I know you'll tell me the truth: either that you don't think you can go any more, or that you don't want to go any more. When you quit is up to you."

I said, "All right, Warren. I'll tell you."

I umpired that year, and everything went fine. But the next year, 1963, I had an unfortunate thing happen to me, and it bothered me quite a bit. When I was a player I was always considered very fast on my feet, and I was considered fast as an umpire, too. I'd move out there. I'd move quick. You have to run as an umpire. You can't stroll around.

But in 1963 I somehow came up with a spur on my heel. I found out about it in Pittsburgh. I ran to get into position to call a play at second base and—I don't know just how to explain it—but the pain that ran through my foot and up my leg was like an electric shock. It shot through me. The pain was excruciating. When it hit me I let out a scream, right on the field. Pete Runnels was playing second base for Houston, and he said, "What's the matter?"

I said, "Oh, my God, my foot. I don't know what it is."

I tried to put it down and put my weight on it. Runnels said, "Take your time, Jock. There's no hurry. It's more important that you're all right." He was very kind. I've always remembered how considerate he was. They held up the ball game for a few minutes and the pain eased off. I went back to my position, but the very

228

next play was another force at second. I ran over to call it, and the same thing happened. The same terrible pain.

I called time, and I said, "That's it. I can't make it." And I walked off the field. Except I didn't walk. I was helped off, limping. I phoned Giles and he told me to come from Pittsburgh to Cincinnati to see a doctor there, and then I went home to Phoenix. It didn't get any better, and I missed the last seven weeks of the season. Every time I stood flatfooted, it hurt like the devil.

Finally, I went to Dr. Kurland in Los Angeles, the same fellow who took care of the Dodgers—Sandy Koufax and all the rest. He looked at the foot and ordered a $\frac{3}{16}$-inch metatarsal bar to be put on the soles of my shoes. That took the pressure off my heel, and I could do things again. The heel still wasn't right—if I stood for a long time, I could feel it—but it was nothing like it was. With the rest, I felt fine and I went back umpiring again the next season, my twenty-fourth straight in the majors.

But I kept thinking about my foot, and I was thinking of other injuries, too. I had broken my collarbone twice. I had smashed my elbow that time. I had been hit in the larynx. And there was a thing that happened in the Coliseum in Los Angeles when the Dodgers were still playing there. Jim Coker was catching for the Phillies, and the batter dribbled a ball down the third-base line. It was a question of whether it was going fair or foul. Coker went out after it, and I went right after him to call it. He whipped off his mask and flipped it in back of him, and the mask hit me right on top of the head. It stung, and I yelled at him, "What's wrong with you? Don't you know where to throw the mask when you want to get rid of it? Throw it to one side."

He was a busher then. He didn't know. He said, "I'm sorry. I didn't realize." I put my hand up to my head and the first thing I knew my hand looked as though it was painted in blood. Blood was coming down all over. That mask had split my scalp. They stopped the game and clipped my hair and put a patch on my head. I was thinking about this when I decided to retire: when you're a plate umpire and you get sick or hurt, you don't find too many umpires who'll say, "Take him inside. I'll take over for him." Some of them don't like that plate too well. So they put a patch on me and said, "It's okay now, Jock," and I umpired six more innings with my scalp split and a patch on it and my mask rubbing against it all the way.

Afterwards, in the dressing room, the doctor put three stitches in it and put a big bandage around my head. I didn't take an anesthetic—too dumb to, I guess—and Johnny Podres and Don Drysdale held my arms and talked to me to keep my mind off it while the doctor put the stitches in. I put my hat on, on top of the bandages, and I looked like a circus clown. I went outside looking for a cab, and there was a limousine with a driver. "Step in here, Mr. Conlan," the driver said. Inside the car was Walter O'Malley. "We'll take you to your hotel, Jocko," he said. "You've got to ride like a big leaguer."

Well, that was fine, but I was getting too old to get injured like that any more. I went to Giles before the 1964 season began and I said, "Warren, I'm telling you in advance. This is my last season. I've had a long run. I don't want to go on and maybe injure myself for the rest of my life."

He said, "Okay, Jock." And so, at the end of 1964, I packed it in. They gave me a solid gold lifetime pass for both major leagues, signed by Giles and Joe Cronin of the American League. It was inscribed, "The National and American Leagues of Professional Baseball present this lifetime pass to John B. 'Jocko' Conlan in appreciation of his long and meritorious service as an umpire in the National League." Of course, when I go to ball parks, I don't even have to pull the pass out, because they all know me.

Towards the end of that last season something happened that I don't think ever happened in baseball before. It was my last trip around the league, and it started in Shea Stadium in New York. They stuck a message up on the big scoreboard that said: "Jocko Conlan, 44 years in baseball, is retiring at the end of this year. He participated in six World Series, six All-Star Games and in each of the four play-offs in the history of the National League." The public address announcer said, "Let's give him a big hand." That new breed of fans at Shea Stadium, the ones who had been hollering at everybody, they tore the place down. They gave me a tremendous ovation. Oh, I enjoyed that.

I went from there to Pittsburgh and in the seventh inning of the last game I worked there, they did the same thing. Made the announcement and the fans gave me an ovation. From there I went to Cincinnati, and they did the same thing.

From Cincinnati I went to Chicago, and there they had a Day in my honor. Mayor Daley—I've known Dick Daley since we were kids; he still lives in the same neighborhood he grew up in—presented me with a beautiful console TV set, and there were other gifts. The Cardinals were playing the Cubs that day, and Red Schoendienst gave me a sterling silver beer mug engraved, "From a Dutch second baseman to an Irish umpire."

I went to San Francisco, and there was an announcement and an ovation there. My last game was in Los Angeles. It was the last game of the season and my last game. I was behind the plate. They put the salute to me up on the big scoreboard in left field and made the announcement, and then they came out with a half-ton truck filled with presents: sweaters, cigars, a wristwatch, even a knitted suit for my wife. I don't know where it all came from, except I know that O'Malley and Bavasi and Danny Goodman out there have always been nice to me. They gave me a beautiful plaque, too, with pretty much the history of me on it, presented to me by the Dodgers. It said, "We'll miss you."

It was a wonderful send-off. It made me feel great.

And so I retired.

And the next spring I don't think there could have been anybody in the world who felt as depressed as I did, as low, as gloomy, as down in the mouth. I was the lonesomest guy in the world. Giles made me a consultant on umpiring after I retired, to scout young umpires and work with them and advise the league on how they were progressing, and I had done that all through the winter, working with young fellows in the Instructional League in Arizona and again during spring training.

But when spring training ended, and all the clubs went off to

231

start the season, oh, I got lonesome there in Arizona. I didn't have anything to do. I missed the game. Every place I went, people would say, "How does it feel, Jock? Do you miss it?" Every time they asked me, it got worse. I missed it terribly. Because baseball had been everything to me all my life. I appreciated everything that happened to me from it, and now it was over. And I wished it wasn't.

I was surprised at how bad I felt, because I knew what it was going to be like. I'll tell you what I mean. About a year after I retired I was talking to Roy Hamey one day in Arizona. Roy had been general manager of the Phillies and the Yankees before he retired, and he was a real good baseball man.

He said to me, "Has anyone called you about a job?"

"I have a job," I said. "I'm a consultant on umpires."

"I know that," he said. "But I mean, has anybody called you about a job?"

I said, "No."

"They haven't called me, either," he said. Now, Roy wasn't being bitter; and, in fact, he did go back doing some work for the Yankees. But what he meant was: how quickly you can be forgotten, how fast you pass out of the picture. You think you've been an important figure in the game over the years, and all of a sudden you're out of it. You're not important. You're not even a part of it any more.

I knew when I was getting ready to retire that that would happen, and I thought I knew how to take it. Because when I left the White Sox in 1936 to go back down to the minors umpiring, I went through the same thing. During the two years I was with the White Sox, I had everybody calling me up. Come over and talk here. Come over and talk there. I was in the big leagues, and I was in real demand.

When I went down to the minor leagues to umpire and was gone from the majors for five years, the people who were always asking me to talk didn't call me up any more. Five years later I was back in the big leagues again as an umpire. And here came the same people pushing me to talk here, talk there, talk everywhere. I said, "Where have you been the last five years?"

It's just human nature. When you're out in front, they want you. When you're out of the picture, they don't. Not that I was so great, but I was in the major leagues. And that was important.

So, as I say, I knew what was going to happen, and I thought I was ready for it. But I never expected to be as lonesome as I was.

Then a great thing happened. I was out playing golf at the Arizona Country Club, and my wife phoned me.

"Mr. Giles called you long distance from Cincinnati," she said, "and he wants you to call him back."

I phoned him right away, and he said, "How are you? In good shape?"

I said, "I'm in better shape now than I have been in two or three years."

"Great," he said. "I wonder if you could do me a favor. Tom Gorman is sick, and he has to go home and rest for a couple of weeks. Do you think you could fill in for him?"

"Just tell me where you want me to report," I said. "I can be ready to leave in half an hour."

"Fine," he said. "Join the rest of Gorman's team in Los Angeles. You take over and be in charge. I want you to work the St. Louis and Milwaukee series in Los Angeles and then the St. Louis series in San Francisco."

I went off and worked those series and when we finished them I thought I was done, but Giles called me and said, "No. I want you to come east for a few more." I worked the Houston series in Cincinnati and then I went to Milwaukee for a Dodgers series, and by that time Tom Gorman was ready to come back.

It came to a full two weeks of work, and as far as retiring was concerned, it was the best thing that ever happened to me—just to go back and work those two weeks. It took the lonesomeness away, the missing of the game. And while I still miss it today, it doesn't have the same effect it had before. I'm satisfied now.

And another thing. Umpiring those two weeks in 1965 meant

that I could say I umpired in the major leagues in twenty-five seasons, from 1941 to 1965, a quarter of a century. That sounds sort of impressive, doesn't it?

It was really the nicest two weeks I ever had, except for one unfortunate incident, and that incident is why I still get mad even now when I think of what Bobby Bragan said about me one day. He hurt me inside more than I had been hurt in all my years as an umpire.

Bragan was managing the Braves then, and they were playing the Dodgers in Los Angeles. I never had much of an opinion of Bragan. To me, he was a pop-off, a guy who got his name in the paper a lot. As little as I think of Durocher, there is no question in my mind but that he always was a first-class manager. If only he had behaved better, he would have gone down in baseball history as one of the great managers of all time. Bragan couldn't begin to compare with him.

Now, this incident happened when the Braves were playing the Dodgers in Los Angeles. It was the second series after I came back. I had the plate. It was a tough, close ball game, and it was a hot night. When the Dodgers were coming to bat in the last of the ninth, the score was tied. I ducked over into the Milwaukee dugout to get a swallow of water, and then I started back onto the field. As I went past the players, pretty near every one of them said, "Hello, Jock. It's nice to see you back." And I said, "I'm glad to be back. But, boy, is it hot. I hope somebody gets a run."

That's all I said. It's something anybody says in a long, tense game, like this one had been. Fans say it, players say it. *Somebody* score. *Somebody* get a run. It doesn't mean anything. It didn't mean anything to the Braves when I said it.

In the last of the ninth the Dodgers got the bases loaded, and Al Ferrara was up. Denny LeMaster was pitching for the Braves. The count went to two balls and two strikes, and LeMaster threw a pitch that to me was inside, and I called it ball three. It was a close pitch, but there was no doubt in my mind that it was a ball.

There was a kick. The Braves argued. Joe Torre, the catcher, said he thought it was a good strike. I said, "The ball was inside. Let's go."

Now the count was three and two. LeMaster's next pitch was way high, and it was ball four and forced in the winning run.

After the game, in the clubhouse, Bragan was talking to the sportswriters and he said, "Conlan said he hoped somebody would score. He just wanted to get the game over with." What did he mean? That I had deliberately called the pitches bad to give Ferrara a walk and force in the run to end the game?

The writers came in and asked me about it. I said, "I called that pitch a ball because it was a ball. Sure I said I hoped somebody would get a run. I didn't say who. I didn't care who. And it didn't mean anything in the first place. You know that, and so does Bragan. Go ask Bragan which pitch it was they argued about. It was ball three. Ball four was over the batter's head. Why doesn't Bragan ask LeMaster how come he didn't get that pitch over the plate?"

I was furious, and I was disgusted. A guy like Bragan implying that an umpire would call a play wrong just to get a game over with. All right, he probably didn't mean what he said. He was just popping off as usual. But what a thing to say. I had been called a lot of nasty names in my career—rotten things that angry ballplayers said in a fit of temper—but this was the worst insult I ever got. Ballplayers had yelled at me that I was wrong, that I made a bad call, that I was mistaken, but none of them, not even Durocher, ever questioned my integrity. Bragan was the only one.

An umpire doesn't have to be liked, and he doesn't have to run around looking for phony compliments. But he must have respect. His position has to be respected. The players and the manager have to respect his judgment and his motives and his authority.

When an umpire has that respect, he is in control of the game. I have always tried to preach that to young umpires. I get a great deal of pleasure and satisfaction out of working with young umpires. I did when I was still in the league and young umpires were assigned to my crew, and I do now with young fellows down in the minors who are just starting out.

Right after I retired, Giles sent me over to take a look at a young fellow named Harry Wendelstedt, whose contract the league owned. I watched him work in the Instructional League during the winter, and advised him on a few things, and he went up to the International League and then to the National. He was assigned to Shag Crawford. Another umpire in Shag's crew was Doug Harvey, who broke in under me. After Wendelstedt joined them, I had a nice letter from Harvey:

"Hi, Jock:

"Just sitting here thinking of you and thought I'd write. That young fellow Wendelstedt is doing just fine. I'm sure it will interest you because he's told us how nicely you treated him. A very nice kid, and we're getting along great. We ran across Joe Divens last night here in Pittsburgh, and I haven't had such a great time in years. Before it was over we must have had 15 guys there. There was a little fellow named Moe who could talk of nobody but his great pal, Jocko Conlan. We didn't stop laughing all night.

"Looks like it will be another wild race in the National League. All the teams have enough to look good, but I don't think any one of them will be great. We all feel very fortunate in having been put on a strong team of umpires. That's it for now. Give Ruth my best. God keep you well.

> Your pal,
> Doug."

See, umpires have friends.

I liked what Harvey said about Wendelstedt, because I really felt he would turn out to be a big-league umpire. I was talking with Warren Giles on the phone one day and he said, "Your boy is doing a good job for us." I met some baseball people in Toots Shor's in New York and they said, "Hey, Jock. That kid you instructed, that Wendelstedt. He's a hell of a fine umpire. You did a great job on him."

236

It makes you feel good to know that maybe you helped a young fellow a little, showed him a few things that made him a better umpire. Understand, he does it himself; you're not umpiring for him. I can make any young fellow into a good mechanical umpire if he has anything at all. I can teach him balls and strikes, safe or out, just working with him for one week. But I can't teach him the other, the important part. If he hasn't got it himself to begin with, he'll never have it.

But if he does have it, like Wendelstedt, maybe you can correct a few things, show him a few things that you learned from long years of experience that he can't possibly know about yet. It's a good feeling. And it's a better feeling when the young fellow appreciates what you're trying to do.

Here's a letter from Wendelstedt:

"Dear Jocko,

"It's obvious from the tone of your note in St. Louis that you did not receive the letter I wrote to you from St. Petersburg. The moment Mr. Giles told me he was putting me on his staff I wrote you a four-page letter of thanks. I realize that if it weren't for you I would not be here. You are the best friend I've had in baseball, and I'm not such an ungrateful slob that I'd forget to thank the man that made me.

"So far, everything is going very well. I've had the plate four times and had real good games. The crew has been great to me, and we get along fine. Shag Crawford is great to work for. I met your buddy, Joe Divens, in Pittsburgh. What a guy. He and his brothers took Shag, Doug and myself out for the evening, and I never laughed so hard in all my life. What a good-time fellow Joe is.

"How is your wife, Jocko? I hope she is feeling well and that everything is going fine for you and yours. Well, buddy, once again I'll attempt to thank you for all you've done for me. Believe me, I know I owe it all to you and I'll never forget it. I'm proud so say that Jocko Conlan taught me how to umpire. You're the greatest, Jocko. I hope you'll write soon and let me hear how everything is in Scottsdale. All of the crew and what must be 50 friends of yours told me to be sure and say hello when I wrote. I never knew any man who had as many friends as you do.

"Take care of yourself and know I'll be thankful the rest of my life for all you have done for me.

> Your friend,
> Harry."

Now, isn't that nice? I get such a kick out of a letter like that. I suppose I still am lonesome for baseball, at that. Augie Donatelli wrote me—I worked with him eight years—and he said, "Every place we go they ask, 'How's Jocko?' The league isn't the same without you." Augie used to say, "Jock made me an umpire." Ken Burkhart wrote me and he said, "Jock, whatever I know about umpiring, you taught me." I know that this sounds like blowing my own horn, but I don't care. These men are umpires. It means a lot to me to have them say things like that.

I think that's why I enjoy working with the young fellows so much. I want them to become good umpires. A few of the ones I worked with have gone up higher and, of course, Harry Wendelstedt went to the National League. There was a kid in the Texas League I noticed, a young fellow named Bruce Froemming. I was there to scout two other prospects, and I recommended that both be advanced to the International League. But while I was working with them, I found myself watching this boy, Froemming. He was only about my size, maybe a little taller. One day I saw him call a man out on a close play. The fellow argued and then went back to the bench. This was in El Paso. After he got back to the bench he turned and made an obscene gesture at Froemming. Whoom! Froemming threw him right out of the game.

The guy came charging off the bench at Froemming, and they stood there, belly to belly. This kid umpire didn't give an inch, and that player was out of there.

It's great to see a young umpire like that. He's a nice boy, conscientious, hardworking, a million-dollar heart. And guts. They told me that he put an announcer out of the ball park one night in Tulsa. The announcer made some remark or other over the public address system about the umpire. Froemming stopped the game, turned to the announcer and said, "Get out." When I heard about that, I said, "This is something. I'd like to see that, making an announcer leave the ball park."

I talked to some fellows about Froemming. Andy Cohen, the old ballplayer, was coaching there, and I asked him, "What kind of an umpire is he, Andy? This kid Froemming?"

"He reminds me of you, Jock," Andy said. "He has guts."

"Maybe he has too much, huh?" I said, because some young umpires look for trouble.

"No," Cohen said. "He's a nice boy. But he's tough."

I really enjoyed watching Froemming because he was so dedicated. He was only in his twenties and I think he had three or four kids. He told me he drove a breadwagon in Milwaukee in the winter, and he made a good salary there.

I said, "What in the world do you want to umpire for?"

"I like it," he said. "I had to do it."

I have to go for that.

He wrote me a letter:

"Dear Jocko,

"Just a line to let you know everything is going well. I have a good partner who is young and a real good hustler. He takes charge and we get along real well. My trips this year will be longer because of the addition of Little Rock to the league. There are two trips over 900 miles. I talked to Frank Walsh, and he gave me some tips to help me—temper, etc. So many people have told me this, Jocko, that they have made a believer out of me. I just hope I won't become a weaker umpire because of it.

"Jocko, take care of yourself. I hope to see you this summer.

Sincerely yours,
Bruce Froemming."

Isn't that something? He praises his partner. The average guy wouldn't tell you about the other fellow, but he likes him because he takes charge. And about his temper. He wants to control his temper, but he doesn't want that to weaken him as a strong umpire. That's great.

You see, this is my profession, umpiring. I think it's one of the most important jobs in baseball. Maybe it's the most important. The game couldn't exist without good umpires. And to come across young fellows like Wendelstedt, who made it to the majors, and Froemming, who understands what the job is, that's a great thing for an old umpire like me.

I tell these young fellows that they have to be firm to be a good umpire, firm and fair, but strong in their decisions. Make the ballplayers respect you. All of these young fellows can umpire—make the calls. But that's not worth anything without the respect of the players.

You have to be in charge of the game. You have to take command. An umpire should never be afraid to chase a player out of a game, but he has to remember that just chasing a fellow doesn't get respect. Chase them when you have to, but not just to be doing something. If you are firm and fair, and they abuse you, then they don't belong in the game. Chase them then. You are the authority. You run the game. If you can't run it, if you let the players climb all over you, the game falls apart. There is nothing so sad as a weak umpire.

I was a strong umpire. And I was a good umpire. I always respected the ground that a ballplayer walked on, and I respected the player himself. But, in turn, I demanded respect from every player that I came across.

And I got it.

AFTERWORD TO THE BISON BOOKS EDITION
Robert W. Creamer

Jocko Conlan was sixty-seven when this book was published. He had finished his long and distinguished career as a National League umpire two years earlier. His life in a way had ended then because he was out of baseball. No more umpiring. No more crowds. No more spotlight.

And then his autobiography was finished—*his* book, summing up his life, presenting his strong and vigorous ideas (and opinions) about, oh, a lot of things, but mostly about umpiring, which, he let you know clearly, was a noble, admirable, and vitally important profession. Baseball without umpires is nothing, he liked to say.

He had finished his job, and now the show was over. He was almost seventy—sunset and twilight time. A lesser man might have let things slide then, gone off to sit in a corner and let time drift over him. But that wouldn't have been Jocko Conlan. He kept moving, popping up each spring at baseball training camps in Arizona (where he made his home for the last third of his life). He'd take a gander at the new rookies, check to see how young umpires he had recommended were doing, cut up touches with people he knew who were still in the game. He'd go to baseball's All Star game in the summer and to the World Series in the fall. In the winter he'd appear at baseball dinners where he'd meet old friends and make new ones, tell the familiar stories and sometimes fresh ones that he'd never told before. The stories would continue after the dinners, with people gathering around to listen, strangers as well as friends. He had a million stories, and he told all of them well.

Life was still lively for Jocko Conlan. He and his wife Ruth, whom he married when they were both twenty-one, were city kids from Chicago but they fell in love with the Southwest. He was very proud of his daughter, Nona, and his son, John (a graduate of Northwestern and

241

Harvard Law School who later became a U.S. Congressman from Arizona), and his seven grandchildren and seven great-grandchildren. Jocko had a good life in retirement.

The best moment came in 1974, less than a decade after he retired from umpiring, when he was named to baseball's Hall of Fame in Cooperstown. There are several umpires in the Hall now, but before Jocko was elected there had been only two: the almost legendary Bill Klem and little Tommy Connolly, both pioneer arbiters whose umpiring careers had begun seventy years earlier and who for many years after their retirement from the field were the chief or supervising umpires in the National League (Klem) and the American League (Connolly). The two old-timers had been named to the Hall in 1953 as a gesture to the past, a sort of matched set, one for this league, one for that one (although Conlan would tell you almost fiercely that Klem, his hero and mentor, was twice the umpire and ten times the man that Connolly, whom Jocko did not like, was).

Klem was indeed a great umpire, probably the best of all time, but in a sense Jocko Conlan was the first of the breed to be elected to the Hall of Fame purely as an umpire, rather than as an institution. He paved the way for the others who followed him. The honor of being named to Cooperstown pleased him enormously, not only because of what it meant to him personally, but also because he felt that his election was a public salute to the importance of umpires and umpiring.

Conlan liked that, liked being the beau ideal, so to speak, of his profession. He was a curious mixture of vanity and modesty—or perhaps pride and honesty are the more accurate words to describe his blunt and open way. As his son John said, "He'd never win a prize for evasiveness." Near the end of this book, after reading into the text some compliments and admiring letters he had received from younger umpires he had helped, Conlan says, "I know that this sounds like blowing my own horn, but I don't care. It means a lot for me to have them say things like that." He revered good umpires, and those he quoted—Augie Donatelli, Ken Burkhart, Harry Wendelstedt, Bruce Froemming—proved to be among the best in his profession. He was proud of what they said about him, and honest enough to say so out loud.

He said a lot of things out loud. He was never afraid of his own opinion. Everyone who knew him knew that he loathed the volatile manager Leo Durocher, with whom he had many a run-in on the ballfield. Less well known was the outspoken dislike Conlan had for Jackie Robinson, whom he admired as a player but despised personally for the obscene language and antagonistic attitude he said Robinson directed toward him as an umpire. It is an understatement to say that Jackie and Jocko did not get along.

Conlan's antipathy for Robinson put me off a little when we were doing this book because I admired Jackie without qualification for what he had accomplished. It took me a while to reconcile Conlan's negative opinion of Robinson with his admiration and respect for catcher Elston Howard, the first black to play for the New York Yankees, and with his glowing praise for the superb ballplayers in the old Negro Leagues whom he had watched and sometimes played against in semipro games just after the first World War when Conlan, barely out of his teens, was breaking into baseball.

I came to understand that he didn't have any preconceived ideas about all this. He took people as they came, one at a time. He didn't like Robinson; he did like Howard. And his tribute to the old black players was made long before it became fashionable for white baseball fans and the baseball establishment to recall and recognize the remarkable skills of the African-American players who had been kept out of the major leagues because of their color, and, belatedly, to salute them with Hall of Fame induction. In short, praising black ballplayers was not a dutiful, politically correct gesture on Conlan's part. In recalling those days he described not just famous stars like Oscar Charleston, Rube Foster, and Bullet Joe Rogan but also black players I had never heard of: Torriente, a Cuban, "What a hitter he was!"; Heavy Johnson, "who could hit a ball out of any park"; DeMoss, a second baseman who "could drop a bunt on a dime"; Francis, a little third baseman; Beckwith, "a terrific hitter." He remembered them because he had seen them play, and he remembered and admired their skills.

"They had marvelous players, those colored teams," Conlan said. "Oh, they had great ballplayers." This feisty, apolitical man, born before 1900, went on without prompting to say, "All these colored ballplayers I mention would have been stars in the big leagues today.

They would have been stars *then* if they had been given the chance."

As always, Conlan was only telling you what he saw and what he thought of it. He looked at things through his own eyes, always trying to see what was there, always finding things out, always learning. For example: Nowadays the expression "on the black" is common baseball usage, meaning a pitched ball that passes over the extreme edge of the plate. I thought I knew a lot about baseball, but when I began writing this book with Jocko I had never heard the expression. And neither had Conlan, he told me, until one day when he called an outside pitch a strike and the batter said, not arguing, that the pitch "must have been on the black." Conlan didn't know what he meant, and the batter scraped the dirt away from the plate to show the black beveled edge of it. Conlan said to me with wonder that he had been in baseball for something like thirty-five years at the time and had never heard of that before. I liked his admission. Jocko knew a lot and he was never afraid to let people know that he knew a lot, and he inevitably gave some the impression that he was a know-it-all. But a know-it-all has a closed mind, and Jocko's was always open, always receptive. When he discovered something new, especially something new about the game he loved, he was delighted.

He was a learner and thus a compendium of knowledge in areas he was interested in. He didn't depend on the opinion of others to form his own. When we were in New York in the spring of 1966 working on *Jocko* we went one night to a middleweight championship bout in Madison Square Garden between two excellent fighters, Dick Tiger and Emile Griffith. We were sitting thirty or forty feet from the ring. I was rooting for Tiger, who came from Nigeria in West Africa and was a hardworking, crowd-pleasing fighter. Griffith, his opponent, a New Yorker who had come from the Virgin Islands, was more flamboyant and somewhat feminine in appearance despite his great boxing skills. He was not terribly popular. Conlan expressed no choice before the bout began and said little through the first couple of rounds. Most of the crowd, including a couple of loudmouthed fans next to us, were cheering loudly for Tiger and roaring exultantly at every punch Tiger threw. The general opinion, loudly expressed by the fans next to us, was that Tiger was taking Griffith apart.

244

After about the third round Conlan began talking to the loudmouthed fans. "I don't know," he said pleasantly, "I think the other guy is winning." They pooh-poohed his remark and repeated, "Tiger's killing him!"

"I don't know," Jock said, "I don't think so."

I felt the same way the loudmouths did—I thought Tiger was winning big. He was forcing the fight, throwing a lot of punches. I said so to Jocko, but he shook his head. "He's missing with them," he said. "The other guy's slipping those punches and landing his own. He's fighting a much better fight."

"How do you know?" I asked in wonder. "How can you see that?"

"I used to do a little boxing," he said, "and when I was in the minors I refereed fights. You look and you see things."

And, of course, by the seventh or eighth round it was obvious even to me that Griffith was in control of the ring, and he won handily in a unanimous decision.

That was Jocko. Saw things with his own eyes. Didn't let preconceptions affect his judgment. Wasn't afraid to give his opinion, based on what he saw.

Hell, he was an umpire, wasn't he?

He saw things clearly and he had the ability to separate the wheat from the chaff. In the 1960s there was a lot of to-do about pitchers supposedly throwing spitballs, which is against the rules. (The furor has since subsided, but you can bet that whenever the rise and fall of offensive baseball leaves pitchers dominant again the spitball controversy will be revived.) Critics insisted that the pitch was dangerous as well as illegal and were forever badgering umpires to clamp down on the practice. Conlan scoffed at all this, claiming that few pitchers threw spitters and fewer threw them well; even if they did, he argued, what was so all-powerful about it? He pointed out that back in baseball's dark ages when the spitball was legal, the pitch was not considered dangerous and it was not all that effective or everyone would have used it. It was a tempest in a teapot, he felt.

What infuriated Conlan, what he thought baseball ought to do something about, was the beanball, the knockdown pitch, the practice of pitchers deliberately throwing at batters. I can remember the fervor with which he spoke. "*That's* the pitch they all say nobody throws, and it's just the pitch they do throw," he said. "It's not only against the rules now, it always has been against the rules." Conlan was a tough little man, familiar with the rough side of life and the rough side of sport, but he hated the prospect of a player being badly hurt by a pitch thrown at him deliberately. Less than a year later, after this book had gone to press, Tony Conigliaro, the brilliant young home run hitter of the Boston Red Sox, was hit with a pitch; his eyesight was damaged, and his promising career and eventually his life were effectively ruined.

In October 1974, three months after his Hall of Fame induction, Conlan went to Los Angeles for the World Series between the Dodgers and the Athletics. At the first game in Dodger Stadium he suffered a coronary occlusion and had to be rushed from the ballpark to a hospital. He was well enough in a day or so to be transferred to a hospital in Phoenix, near his home in Scottsdale, where he underwent open-heart surgery. He was nearly seventy-five, but he made an excellent recovery and despite the inevitable decline of his boundless energy he continued to savor life for another fourteen years. His mind remained clear and his personality chipper until only a few months before his death on April 16, 1989. He and Ruth, who died five years later, had been married for sixty-eight years.